Flowers over the Wall

By Kelli Grim

Copyright © 2008 Kelli Grim

Acknowledgments

A heartfelt thanks to CW Johnson. I couldn't have done it without his hard work, & encouragement. Watch for his novels:
The Son of Man
The Son of Man 2, Elders of Zion
The Son of Man 3, The Helik
At Amazon.com

To my husband Todd (TeeJ) My best friend, for always supporting me.
.

To Beth C Blake for her much appreciated line-editing services.
Contact Beth here: http://literindie.wordpress.com/

Flowers over the Wall cover art by CW Johnson

Other Books by Kelli Grim

Flowers Over the Wall Two, Busting through the Wall.

Custom Cake Decorating on the Cheap

Flowers over the Wall

Flowers over the Wall

I was saved when I was seventeen years old, but decided when I was nineteen that I wanted to have some "fun," so I put God on the shelf for about ten years and lived the "for tomorrow we may die" philosophy.

That was a dreadful ten years, because I bought all the lies of the world. The lies that tell you that unless you look, act, and are a certain way, you aren't worthwhile. I kept trying to live up to the world's standards. I worked forty-eight hours a week managing a jewelry store. I was making good money for a girl my age, and I had my own apartment. I thought if I just had a better body, some jewelry, and a lot of cute clothes that would make me a better person. I got breast implants and used credit cards to buy jewelry and clothes, but no matter what I did or tried, I still felt worthless. I had spent so much money trying to look perfect that I couldn't afford my apartment. I had to quit my job and move back to my hometown with my sister and her family.

Once I moved in with my sister, I started going out to nightclubs with some of my girlfriends. I saw how much attention the cocktail waitresses got and thought it would be fun to be one. I filled out an application. After showing my legs to the manager, I got a job at one of the more popular private clubs in town. At first, it was really fun because in that environment, especially around closing time, the compliments come in fast and furious. I received a lot of positive reinforcement from guys about my new body. I had what I always thought I wanted, but I still felt worthless. I ended up working there for about five years.

When I was twenty-nine and still working at the disco, I finally met and married the man of my dreams. I rededicated my life to Jesus in my second year of marriage. I had just given birth to my first baby. Having her made me realize how much I needed Jesus in my life. Even though I was now walking with Jesus, I still hated myself. Any self-worth that I ever had was in what I looked like, and I had gained weight. The beauty of youth started to fade as it always does. I was completely worthless in my own eyes. I hated myself. The reason I hated myself was because I was fat. Even though my husband let me know he loved me, I was always afraid he would leave me because when we married I was thin. I couldn't understand why my husband didn't leave me. He was and still is so handsome and intelligent. My highest level of education was seventh grade, so I knew I didn't have a leg to stand on there. The sexual abuse I had endured as a child only reinforced how I felt about myself. I was desperate to lose weight.

It had been a particularly rough week for me. I still had an old friend's words ringing in my head. He had introduced me to his buddy. His comment to his friend was, "She used to be real good-looking until she had a kid and packed on sixty pounds." Apparently, he didn't think his comment should hurt a fat girl.

4

I decided I was going to pray and have faith God would do a miracle and make me skinny. I told Him I was going to have the faith to be down to a certain weight in exactly one month. I was familiar with getting on the scale every day. Sometimes I would check three or four times a day, but I decided for that month I would stay off it. I had a hard time waiting, so by the time the day came I was excited; I just knew God had done a miracle. I stepped up on the scale and… it hadn't moved one millimeter. I was bitterly disappointed and furious with God. I was crying and praying.

I opened the Bible and read,

Isaiah 49:23b (NIV) *Those who hope in Me will not be disappointed."*

I remember being enraged. I basically called God a liar. I *was* disappointed. I remember saying to Him, "I *did* hope in you, this is your Word, and You promise we won't be disappointed. You let me down!" I was still mad at God when I went to church that Sunday. I couldn't even get into the worship which is usually the part I loved the most. The pastor started reading the text for the sermon that day, and I was surprised because it was the same text I had been reading when I got so angry with God.

Isaiah 49:23b (NIV) *Those who hope in Me will not be disappointed."*

I was shocked when, in that church with over five-hundred people listening, the pastor said, "Somebody sitting here today read that Scripture this last week and was mad at God. It's not acceptable to talk to God like that. You need to respect Him, but still, He wants you to know He will answer your prayer. Not because of your righteousness, but for His Glory, and you will not be disappointed. He will fulfill the promise in <u>His time</u>." Then he went on with his sermon. It was about trials and the blessings that come from trials.

The pastor related an incident in his life. He said he used to love to look at the fields out his back window. He loved to sit at his kitchen table and watch the wind make the stalks sway. So, he was particularly disappointed when a contractor started building a subdivision directly behind his house. Where lovely swaying grass once grew, the ground was now full of pockmarks as the foundations for new houses were being dug. He tried to give it to God, but the more he thought about it, the angrier he became.

He knew it was silly to be so upset about an earthly thing, but he just couldn't help it. He had enjoyed his view so much. After a time, he became used to the idea that the fields were gone forever. When his new neighbor moved in he thought maybe they could become friends.

Imagine his disappointment when the neighbor started building an ugly, grey, ten-foot, cinder-block wall. He built his wall so tall that my pastor could barely see the roof of this neighbor's house. The pastor was ashamed to admit it, but he felt bitter against his neighbor every time he looked at the wall.

However, something started to happen over time. Little flowers began peeking up over the wall, and then, more flowers of different types and colors started to spill over. Slowly, but surely, the ugly wall became a mass of beautiful flowers. He said the effect was breathtaking and priceless. It was the focal point of his whole yard and was so much better than the wheat grass with which he had been so enamored. He felt grateful to his neighbor for this wonderful gift.

He said that sometimes God works like that. He may not take the problems away immediately, but like flowers over an ugly wall, our problems can bloom, grow, and fill us with joy. At the time, even though I knew God was talking to me, that sermon didn't hit home. I thought, "Okay now I will be healed of my eating addiction because God spoke directly to me…" But no… I was still as addicted as ever.

Many years later when God did heal me, I recalled the sermon and gratitude overwhelmed me for the trial of being overweight. The flowers I have enjoyed through the years while searching for an answer to my problem have filled my life with beauty. I am so grateful that God gave me the gift of being overweight. My weight problem brought me unimaginable joy. It brought me to my knees. It made me seek God. It made me see the beauty that is my soul, the eternal part of me. The reason outer beauty is so important to the world is because Satan makes the least of us the most important part.

So here it is. I offer it to you, just as it is, seventh-grade grammar problems and all. I would have been embarrassed a few years ago to present such a humble offering, but now I know God will use it because, in my weakness, He is strong.

2 Corinthians 12:9 *And He said to me, "My grace is sufficient for you, for My strength is made perfect in weakness." Therefore most gladly I will rather boast in my infirmities, that the power of Christ may rest upon me.*

God Is Not Mad At You

"UNCLEAN, UNCLEAN." That is what the lepers of Jesus' time had to shout when they walked through the streets. "UNCLEAN!" They were the outcast of society. Wherever they went, they were shunned and mocked. People looked at them in disgust, thankful it wasn't them. We, who are overweight, are the lepers of our day. We don't have to yell out unclean; our bodies do that for us. We are shunned and avoided. We are repulsive joke fodder for popular sit-coms.

A news story told of a rapper in concert who said, "All the beautiful ladies in this audience, get up on the stage and dance with me." Some of the girls in the audience moved to the stage and began dancing. Looking around the stage, the rapper laughed and said, "Look ladies, if you weigh 200 pounds get off my stage." It was appalling to see the smiles being wiped off their beautiful young faces as the girls tried to get off the stage as quickly as possible. They were brave in getting up there. They gambled on the risky prospect of human kindness and lost. Any self-respect they might have gained up to that point was shattered... and I know the pain they suffered. You probably do, too. We suffer with them, knowing the world thinks of us as gross, stupid fools devoid of feelings.

Just as it must have felt hopeless to the lepers in Jesus' time, we feel doomed to failure. We have tried and hoped, and hoped and tried. Maybe this diet will work. Maybe this will be the one. How can being overweight be our fault when we try so hard?

I understand your desire to be slim and healthy. I know because, at one time, the desire to be thin consumed me. I was so humiliated about my weight that I hated to leave the house. I dreaded social situations. Even though he never mentioned my weight, I thought my husband was ashamed of me. No matter how hard I tried, I couldn't lose weight. Just like you, I felt doomed to failure. This Bible study will show that the more willpower you use, and the harder you try to lose weight, the heavier you will be. Dieting creates two obsessions. One, you become fixated on food, and two, you become fixated on your weight.

Believe me when I tell you that you are strong! You! Yes, you! You can be the person you want to be; the person God made you to be. It's not about changing the food you eat. It's about understanding and fixing the reasons you overeat. It's about changing your wrong thinking into right thinking. You have a problem with your weight because you eat more than your body uses, so... stop eating more than your body needs. Don't you wish it were that simple?

Diets try to convince us that we need to change the food we eat. They over simplify, *and* over complicate the whole process. Wouldn't it be easy if we could all simply decide which diet was best for us and then do it? If it was that clear-cut, obesity wouldn't be the second highest preventable cause of death in America. I knew all that, but I couldn't stop myself from overeating. I needed to find the reason I was overeating and why I couldn't stop. That's why I started to write this study. I was desperate. Truth is, I felt like I was in trouble with God.

So...*Is* God mad at us?

Before I knew Him, I thought God, in his Heaven, was saying, "FOLLOW THESE RULES BECAUSE I SAID SO, AND I-AM–THE-BOSS!"

After all, God tells us gluttony is a sin (**Proverbs 23:2**), and for good reason. Being overweight is a serious health condition that can lead to early death. If a person is twenty percent heavier than their ideal weight, they are considered obese --[1]determined by standard medical and insurance data. For example, the normal weight for woman who is 5'7" is 143 pounds, but they are considered obese if they weigh 189 pounds or above.

There are many medical problems associated with being overweight including high blood pressure, heart problems, diabetes, sleep apnea, depression, and arthritis. These problems increase as your weight does. The heart of an obese person has to work harder causing congestive heart failure. Cardiovascular problems are common among obese people. High blood pressure can lead to the development of heart disease, kidney failure, and stroke. God designed our bodies to need only so much food. Overeating puts too much sugar and fat in our system, and our bodies can't handle it, increasing the risk of developing type II diabetes.

But… If gluttony is a sin, God *must* be mad at us!

God loves you, and if He didn't love you, your sinning wouldn't bother Him in the least. Your sin doesn't make Him less of a God. It doesn't make Him look bad in front of His peers. He doesn't have any. Your sin hurts God, because He loves you. That is why Satan detests you, because you are precious to God. The only way Satan can hurt God, is to hurt His beloved.

Galatians 5:14 *For all the law is fulfilled in one word, even in this: "You shall love your neighbor as yourself."*

Notice the prerequisite for loving your neighbor is that you love yourself. Writing this study I have come to know more of the character of our loving father, and through studying His word, I found God is not mad at me at all. I found that God has a plan for our lives, and that plan includes being joyful and successful. He understands our weaknesses.

Hebrews 4:15&16 *For we do not have a High Priest who cannot sympathize with our weaknesses, but was in all points tempted as we are, yet without sin. [16] Let us therefore come boldly to the throne of grace, that we may obtain mercy and find grace to help in time of need.*

It's easy to say I should love myself,
but how can I do that when I look like this?

My husband and I participated in a medical study at a University on how marriage affected blood pressure. They sent us to a lab for blood work. The lab was also conducting a

---

[1] http://www.nhlbisupport.com/bmi/

five-year study on the morbidly obese. I had been on a diet and was almost at my goal weight (Naturally, I later gained it all back and more). The technician who was taking our health histories said, "How refreshing. I'm used to patients having so many health issues because of their weight." She told me how much they suffer.

Hearing this was very painful for me. Being overweight was still very fresh in my mind. I remembered how trapped and desperate I felt. I recalled how my ribs had hurt; how my knees and feet had hurt. I was so tired back then, and I hated myself. I just knew the world thought of me as lazy and stupid. I remember how I wanted to defend myself. "I'm trying to lose weight," I would tell myself. "The person inside here isn't the person you see out there… This isn't me! I'm trapped in this body!"

Because I didn't love myself, I felt as though I wasn't considered valuable. I felt unloved. I felt that the world reserved its goodness for thin people. I felt that people either dismissed or patronized me. I felt that the way most people treated me only confirmed and intensified my feelings. There were times I tried to "dress up" my fat and say I didn't care. There were times I simply gave up. I would wear an old holey tee-shirt and comfy bleach stained sweats everywhere. I hated how I looked and felt every moment of every day.

God doesn't see you that way. He sees the person He created in His image (**Genesis 1:27**). He sees the value of your eternal soul (**Psalm 139: 1-18**). You are important to God and He doesn't want to see you live like this. It doesn't make Him less of a God if you sin. If God didn't love you, your pain wouldn't hurt Him in the slightest. It's your self imposed suffering He labels as sin. God doesn't condemn you (**John 3:17**). All of us have sinned (**Romans 3:23**). He still loves you.

The world gives us plenty of excuses for being overweight. They say it's biological or medical. Sometimes that is true, but most of the time it's because we eat more than our bodies need. I know the excuses from the medical world make us feel justified, but it doesn't help our problem. If you think about it and are honest with yourself, those excuses dash all hope of ever being thin and healthy.

You are probably saying to yourself, "I don't need something else to make me feel guilty, I already feel hopeless." However, I am here to declare to you that there is hope! You are going to tap into the power of the almighty God who created Heaven and Earth. The good news is because gluttony is a sin, and not a defect, you decide to participate in the sin. This Bible study will help you understand the difference and apply the principles from the Bible to recognize and overcome Satan's deception.

When I started writing this Bible study I was well on my way to becoming another sad statistic. I weighed over two hundred pounds and had high blood pressure and high cholesterol. I even had a weight related heart murmur. Food was the first thing I thought of when I woke up in the morning and the last thing I thought of when I went to sleep. I desired it beyond reason. The yearning to chew was irresistible, and I couldn't control it. I didn't want to. The more I ate the more I needed. My desire for food was voracious, and no matter how much I ate, the empty longing was never satisfied.

Then one day my beautiful teenaged foster daughter came home upset. With tears streaming down her sweet face, she told me how a group of teenage boys had driven past her when she was walking home from school. They yelled out the window something rude about her being overweight. She was hurt and humiliated. This beautiful, sweet, young girl who had overcome so much in her life was so wounded. She was wounded by the foolish boys who had no idea of who she was as a person. I could feel her hurt, and I wanted so much to help her.

I found a book on using the Bible as a diet guide. We started to read it. Even though I found the diet to be quite sensible, I quickly realized the religious part of it was based on good works, and not God's abounding grace. I found myself trying to explain why so much of it wasn't Biblical, and we finally gave up. I thought, somebody should write a real born-again, Spirit-filled diet Bible study. I decided to write one for my foster daughter and myself.

I pray it will help you to find the truth about the emptiness we try so desperately to fill.

Understanding the Things of the Spirit

You can't understand the things of the Spirit if you haven't been born of the Spirit. So, having a relationship with Christ is a pre-requisite for this study.

I Corinthians 2:14 (NIV) says, *[14]The man without the Spirit does not accept the things that come from the Spirit of God, for they are foolishness to him, and he cannot understand them, because they are spiritually discerned.*

I am not talking about religion; I mean having a relationship with Jesus Christ. God loves you so much, He wants a relationship with you and has a plan for your life. However, you need to be born of the Spirit. How do you become born of the Spirit?

John 3:1-9 *There was a man of the Pharisees named Nicodemus, a ruler of the Jews. [2] This man came to Jesus by night and said to Him, "Rabbi, we know that You are a teacher come from God; for no one can do these signs that You do unless God is with him." [3] Jesus answered and said to him, "Most assuredly, I say to you, unless one is born again, he cannot see the kingdom of God."*

[4] Nicodemus said to Him, "How can a man be born when he is old? Can he enter a second time into his mother's womb and be born?"

*[5] Jesus answered, "Most assuredly, I say to you, unless one is born of water **and** the Spirit, he cannot enter the kingdom of God. [6] That which is born of the flesh is flesh, and that which is born of the Spirit is spirit. [7] Do not marvel that I said to you, 'You must be born again.' [8] The wind blows where it wishes, and you hear the sound of it, but cannot tell where it comes from and where it goes. So is everyone who is born of the Spirit."*

[9] Nicodemus answered and said to Him, "How can these things be?"

[10] Jesus answered and said to him, "Are you the teacher of Israel, and do not know these things? [11] Most assuredly, I say to you, We speak what We know and testify what We have seen, and you do not receive Our witness. [12] If I have told you earthly things and you do not believe, how will you believe if I tell you heavenly things? [13] No one has ascended to Heaven but He who came down from Heaven, that is, the Son of Man who is in Heaven. [14] And as Moses lifted up the serpent in the wilderness, even so must the Son of Man be lifted up, [15] that whoever believes in Him should not perish but have eternal life. [16] For God so loved the world that He gave His only begotten Son, that whoever believes in Him should not perish but have everlasting life. [17] For God did not send His Son into the world to condemn the world, but that the world through Him might be saved.

Let's take a closer look at this passage. Nicodemus came to Jesus with questions, and at first, Jesus' answers confused him. He asked, "How can a person be born again? Go back into his mother's womb?" Jesus' answer was, "Unless one is born of the water (*the womb*) **and** of the Spirit, he cannot enter the kingdom of God." Then, Jesus tells Nicodemus that flesh is temporary and of the world. It cannot enter into the Kingdom, but the Spirit is eternal. When you get born again it is an awakening of the Holy Spirit within us. Verse eight says, "Have faith! You believe in earthly things you cannot see and not understand." You can't see the change on the outside immediately.

Take note of verse nine. Nicodemus says, "How can these things be?" He wanted to know how to be born of the Spirit. Jesus gives him and us all the answer in verse fifteen. "Whoever believes in Him (*Jesus*) should not perish but have eternal life." God tells us in His word that He wants us all to be with Him in Heaven (**II Peter 3:9**). Yet, Heaven is a perfect place. God won't let it be corrupted by sin of any type (**Revelation 21:27**). So, unless you are perfect and without sin, you are not allowed in Heaven. However, we are all sinners and separated from God. So, now what do you do?

Romans 6:23 *For the wages of sin is death, but the gift of God is eternal life in Christ Jesus our Lord.*

The cost of sinning (*wages*) is death (*separation from God*), but the **Gift** is eternal life. You can't be good enough to get to Heaven on your own. It's a gift!

Ephesians 2:8 *For by grace you have been saved through faith, and that not of yourselves; it is the gift of God, [9] not of works, lest anyone should boast. [10] For we are His workmanship, created in Christ Jesus for good works, which God prepared beforehand that we should walk in them.*

Jesus is the perfect Son of God, and He paid the price for your sin. Because you can't afford it, you can't be perfect. It's important you realize your need for Christ and accept Him as your own savior. Receive the gift of God and confess your sin and need for him.

Romans 10: 8 & 9 *But what does it say? "The word is near you, in your mouth and in your heart"(that is, the word of faith which we preach): [9] that if you confess with your mouth the Lord*

Jesus and believe in your heart that God has raised Him from the dead, you will be saved.

It's as simple as acknowledging you are a sinner and believe in your heart Jesus died on the cross for your sin.

II Peter 3:9 *God is not willing that any should perish but that all would come to repentance.*

If you don't have a relationship with Christ, here is how you start. Pray like this to Jesus, in your own words, and mean it with all your heart.

~Lord Jesus, I know I am a sinner. I believe You died for my sins. Right now, I receive You as my Savior and ask You to forgive my sins. I acknowledge You are the Lord of my life, and I turn my life over to you and ask you to help me turn from my sin and turn to You.
Thank you my Lord, in Jesus name, Amen.~

Now that you have prayed this prayer and meant it, God will begin to change you from the inside out. He will change your desires. In fact, your desire will be for the things of God. By Grace you are saved—a gift from ***Your*** Lord!

Week 1 Day 1
The Diet

Day _____ Date _____

Start now:

Romans 7:4-25 *For we know that the law is spiritual, but I am carnal, sold under sin.* [15] *For what I am doing, I do not understand. For what I will to do, that I do not practice; but what I hate, that I do.* [16] *If, then, I do what I will not to do, I agree with the law that it is good.* [17] *But now, it is no longer I who do it, but sin that dwells in me.* [18] *For I know that in me (that is, in my flesh) nothing good dwells; for to will is present with me, but how to perform what is good I do not find.* [19] *For the good that I will to do, I do not do; but the evil I will not to do, that I practice.* [20] *Now if I do what I will not to do, it is no longer I who do it, but sin that dwells in me.*

[21] *I find then a law, that evil is present with me, the one who wills to do good.* [22] *For I delight in the law of God according to the inward man.* [23] *But I see another law in my members, warring against the law of my mind, and bringing me into captivity to the law of sin which is in my members.* [24] *O wretched man that I am! Who will deliver me from this body of death?* [25] *I thank God—through Jesus Christ our Lord!*

So then, with the mind I myself serve the law of God, but with the flesh the law of sin.

Eat what you want:

The previous Scriptures are about how we are weak in our flesh, how we make rules, and how we try to follow them. We have diet and health rules that seem to change daily. With this diet there are no rules. You can eat anything you want; if you want a candy bar for breakfast eat it! If you want another for lunch or dinner, go ahead. I guarantee you won't want another one for your next meal. This diet takes the attention off the food and places it on God. The more you focus on food, the more you want it. It becomes an obsession.

God formed our bodies to know what they need. He created your taste buds. He knows what you like and what you don't. So, don't be afraid to eat what you like. When I first started eating like this, I went crazy and had many small bites of everything I had denied myself for so long, because I was so excited about being able to eat what I liked. You can eat anything you want! Jesus declared all foods clean!

Mark 7: 18 –23 [18] *So He said to them, "Are you thus without understanding also? Do you not perceive that whatever enters a man from outside cannot defile him,* [19] *because it does not enter his heart but his stomach, and is eliminated,* **thus purifying all foods?"** [20] *And He said, "What comes out of a man, that defiles a man.* [21] *For from within, out of the heart of men, proceed evil thoughts, adulteries, fornications, murders,* [22] *thefts, covetousness, wickedness, deceit, lewdness, an evil eye, blasphemy, pride, foolishness.* [23] *All these evil things come from within and defile a man."*

See! Jesus said in the above Scripture, don't focus on the food. Focus on your spiritual health. The following diet is a guideline. Remember that this diet is a suggested diet. Don't make it into "rules." The worst thing you could do is try to make this diet guideline as an instrument with which to beat yourself. However, if you have food allergies, then by all means, don't eat the foods to which you are allergic. The purpose of this study is to learn how keep your focus off of food and direct it to Jesus.

Slow down:

There have been numerous studies done on the correlation between obesity and how fast a person eats. It was determined in a study done by at the Pennington Biomedical Research Center that "suggests a slower rate of eating results in less food intake compared to a faster, steady rate of eating."

If you eat slower, you will be able to recognize God's built-in cues. The cues are easy to recognize if you are paying attention and know what to look for. You start to notice the food doesn't taste as good and you are feeling satisfied. When you say to yourself, "I think I am getting satisfied," STOP EATING! That is God's prompting. It is at this time you have satisfied your body's need for fuel, and it's time to stop eating, <u>now</u>! Don't worry, you'll be hungry again in three to four hours. Back when I would begin to feel this way, I'd start eating faster, making sure to get it all stuffed in before I was too full. That habit was a huge factor in maintaining my plump figure.

Don't worry if you accidentally eat more than you need. God knows your heart. He understands your weakness and loves you. When I would catch my toddlers misbehaving, I would give them a count of three to stop. I would start counting "one", and usually they would begin to pull away from the misdeed and turn towards me. I would never have punished my child if they had already turned and started towards me and then accidentally fell and failed to make it by the count of three. God is so much more merciful than we are. He knows when we are trying to be obedient.

Only Eat What You REALLY Like:

Don't eat anything you don't like, and make sure you eat what you like the most, first. You are probably doing just the opposite and saving the best for last!

I remember one time when my husband and I were first married, we went out to dinner with friends, and they brought some of their friends along. I had started to gain weight and was so miserable and self-conscience. This was especially prevalent since one of the girls was very thin, and, as usual, I was harshly comparing myself to her. My husband asked me if there was something wrong with my main course because I wasn't eating it, and I told him, "No, I was just saving the best for last."

The thin girl said, "I never save the best for last because I never know when I will get too full, and I am afraid I won't be able eat what I really love." She said, "I always eat what I like best, first. Sometimes I even eat my dessert first".

This was an "Aha!" moment for me. Think about it. When you save the best for last, that's setting yourself up to fail. You will need to retrain yourself to do the exact opposite. You will eat the juicy, sweet, most yummy items first and save the dry things you don't like as much for last. Or better yet, don't even eat them. We think it's sinful to waste food, but it's more sinful to worry about food. Give it to God. Now, I usually eat my dessert right along with my meal. That way I don't have to worry about saving room for it.

God designed your unique body to crave what it needs. We were having a health fair at my work. At one of the booths they were selling supplements that contained high concentrations of the vitamins found in vegetables. My friend and I stopped at the booth and started chatting with the woman who was selling the vitamins. My friend said, "I can't get enough veggies, I love them!" I said, "I hardly ever eat vegetables. I just don't really like them." The sales woman suggested that we try a sample of some liquid she had that would determine if we needed to eat more vegetables. She said, "Depending upon how the liquid tasted to each of us, would indicate if we needed to eat more veggies. We all joked about how we knew that I was the one needing to eat more vegetables. After we had each swallowed the concoction, she asked us what we thought it tasted like. My friend said, I don't really taste anything, and I said "I think it taste like soda water or Alka-Seltzer. She said, "That's odd." She looked at her literature again to make sure she had read it correctly. She said, "If it taste like seltzer, that would indicate you eat enough vegetables. If it didn't have a taste, that meant you needed to eat more."

I concluded from this that God created all of our bodies differently, and we actually crave what our own bodies need. That's why most people don't like to eat leftovers. Don't worry so much about wasting food or put the extra food in the freezer right away to save it for another day.

The Bible says in **Romans 14:20a** *Don't destroy the work of God for the sake of food.*

Read what God told an Old Testament king when he was worried about wasting money.

II Chronicles 25:5-9 *Moreover Amaziah gathered Judah together and set over them captains of thousands and captains of hundreds, according to their fathers' houses, throughout all Judah and Benjamin; and he numbered them from twenty years old and above, and found them to be three hundred thousand choice men, able to go to war, who could handle spear and shield. 6 He also hired one hundred thousand mighty men of valor from Israel for one hundred talents of silver. 7 But a man of God came to him, saying, "O king, do not let the army of Israel go with you, for the LORD is not with Israel—not with any of the children of Ephraim. 8 But if you go, be gone! Be strong in battle! Even so, God shall make you fall before the enemy; for God has power to help and to overthrow."*
9 Then Amaziah said to the man of God, "But what shall we do about the hundred talents which I have given to the troops of Israel?" And the man of God answered, "The LORD is able to give you much more than this."

The food isn't more valuable than your body. Look at what happened to the Israelites when they tried to save extra manna. It turned to maggots!

Exodus 16:17-21 *Then the children of Israel did so and gathered, some more, some less. 18 So when they measured it by omers, he who gathered much had nothing left over, and he who gathered little had no lack. Every man had gathered according to each one's need. 19 And Moses said, "Let no one leave any of it till morning." 20 Notwithstanding they did not heed Moses. But some of them left part of it until morning, and it bred worms and stank. And Moses was angry with them. 21 So they gathered it every morning, every man according to his need. And when the sun became hot, it melted.*

Trust God and soon you will learn how much food you should take, so you won't waste as much. Don't worry. God doesn't mind if you waste a little until you learn how much it takes to make you full. I know this, because there are many instances in the Bible where God tells His children to destroy all the booty left after a battle. I am sure it seemed wasteful to them but was necessary to preserve the purity of God's children. It's the same with us. It's more important that we keep ourselves from the destruction of our bodies.

Beverages:

The only thing I would caution you on is sugary drinks. You should be careful about drinking them between meals, because they don't really satisfy your hunger yet are so high in calories. Between meals, you can drink diet soda, black coffee, and tea. If you like your tea and coffee sweetened, you can use one of the artificial sweeteners on the market. Another option is you can drink a nice cold glass of ice water. Feel free to have sugar in your coffee with breakfast. Just don't drink it all day. Sugary drinks should always be considered as part of the meal. Don't drink sugary drinks unless you are hungry. When I used to drink a lot of soda, I would get cravings for the carbonation. If you drink a big glass of water when you crave the carbonation, your craving will disappear. Try it, it's amazing!

It's hard to remember to drink at least eight glasses of water a day, but it's good for you. I have worked at Boy Scout camp for a number of summers, and you must stay hydrated. It is the difference between feeling lousy or feeling energized and good. If you get a headache while doing this study, it's probably because you are not drinking enough water. According to [2]Mayoclinic.com, we get about 20% of our water intake from the food we eat. So, if you are eating less food, you are probably a bit dehydrated and that is giving you a headache. Being dehydrated can also make you feel a bit shaky. Also, I tend to mistake being thirsty or tired for being hungry. However don't overdo it. Drinking too much water can be bad for you as well, do all things in moderation.

Bible Study:

The most important part of this diet is to examine what God says about your relationship to food. This study will examine the Bible to find the answers to our dieting dilemma. It is designed to be done five days a week, for about thirty minutes a day. Don't try to breeze through it quickly. It's meant for study and contemplation. Some of the points used in this study may seem redundant. I have found it easier to understand a concept if I hear it more than once.

At the end of each day's lesson, there are three activities. First there are some Bible passages related to the study. You should use your Bible and study it. Circle anything that touches you. Read the passage aloud, really work the Scripture. The next activity is to answer three questions relating to the day's lesson. These questions are designed to help you relate the lesson to your own life. As you are reading through the study, underline things that touch you. Then go back through it, pray, and ask God to show you one or more statements or Scriptures from the study. He wants you to understand more and put it into practice. This is a personal question and applies only to you. It has no right or wrong answer.

When considering the second question, spend a little time praying. Ask God how He may want you to respond to this question. Then I'll ask you to reword that statement or Scripture into an expression of faith. That simply means you affirm your belief that God will give you the strength and faith to take those steps. These three questions should become a time of prayer and meditation each day as you ask God what He wants you to do in response to each days study. The following is an example of the way I might have responded to today's study.

- In light of today's study, what was the Scripture or statement in today's lesson that most spoke to your heart? *"Are you thus without understanding also? Do you not perceive that whatever enters a man from outside cannot defile him" And don't focus on the food, focus on your spiritual health.*

- What steps of faith does God want you to take towards Him today? *God wants me to stop being consumed with dieting and food and get my mind on growing my spirit.*

- Rephrase the Scripture or statement into an expression of faith: *Lord thank you for showing me that it's not a diet, or food issue but a heart, and spirit issue. I believe you will teach me how to keep my mind off of dieting and food and direct my thoughts.*

---

[2] http://www.mayoclinic.com

The last activity is to memorize one Scripture a week. This is a very important step in your recovery because the Bible is **_THE_** weapon you use to fight Satan. It is the only thing that can break the bonds Satan has on you. I have a difficult time memorizing anything, so every day I'll take out words. Try to fill in the blanks without looking at the Scripture. I have found this is useful for me. If you are one of those blessed individuals who find it easy to memorize then use your own method. Do whatever is easier for you.

You have to surrender your weight problem to God. You will begin to stop frantically dieting and worrying about what you look like. When you stop running to the refrigerator for physical pleasure and comfort, you will start eating normal foods God created for you to enjoy. You will be eating only when you are actually hungry. You'll be eating about half, or even less of what you have been, and you will lose weight.

Trust God. The Bible lets us know we "are fearfully and wonderfully made," (**Psalm 139:14**). Don't make it too hard. There are no set rules. We are individuals, and God will have a separate plan for each of us. God is brilliant, and His Bible is our manual. By following God's Holy Book, we find the answers for life's problems. Remember you are learning, and God knows your heart.

Read Isaiah 55

- In light of today's study, what was the Scripture or statement in today's lesson that most spoke to your heart?

  _____
  _____
  _____
  _____

- What steps of faith does God want you to take towards Him today?

  _____
  _____
  _____
  _____

- Rephrase the Scripture or statement into an expression of faith

  _____
  _____
  _____
  _____

Scripture to memorize this week

Isaiah 55:9 " _For as the Heavens are higher than the earth, So are My ways higher than your ways, And My thoughts than your thoughts._

Week 1 Day 2
Exposing Strange Doctrines

Day _____ Date _____

We have a tendency to rely on the so-called dieting experts, and God is the last place we go for diet advice. We pray and ask God for help in following the diet of the week, but why? When you think about it, God is the one who formed our bodies and spoke the world into existence. Don't you think it's time we discover what the only true authority has to say about it?

Read **Hebrews 13:8-9** *Jesus Christ is the same yesterday, today, and forever.* [9] *Do not be carried about with various and strange doctrines. For it is good that the heart be established by grace, not with foods which have not profited those who have been occupied with them.*
Answer the following questions:

- Who is the same yesterday, today, and always? _____

- What do you think established by grace means? _____
  _____
  _____
  _____

The dictionary defines "establish" as 1: to institute permanently 2: to put upon a firm basis. "Grace" is defined as 1: unmerited help given to people by God (as in overcoming temptation) 2: freedom from sin by divine Grace.

Do you want a real and lasting change?

List all the diets you can remember being on.

_____
_____
_____
_____
_____
_____

(Use more paper if needed)

Do you remember each of these diets and their premise? Were they about counting calories—food exchanges—more fat—less fat— more carbohydrates or less? Were they all about eating a little or eating a lot; eating only certain foods at certain times of the day? Drinking a lot of water with your food, or no water with your food, all protein? No protein? It's exhausting... All "experts'" claim to have the truth and the only truth.

Read the previous Scripture again: **Hebrews 13:8-9** *Jesus Christ is the same yesterday, today, and forever.* [9] *Do not be carried about with various and strange* **doctrines.** *For it is good that the heart be established by grace,* **not with foods** *which have not profited those who have been occupied with them.*

Doctrine simply means something that is taught. When you think about your dieting history, does it seem as if you were being carried away by strange doctrines? _____

The more you try on your own to overcome your addiction, the more focused you become on the addiction. Most of the world's diets focus on the food. This creates a strong love and desire for it because it's the focal point. The Bible says, "We do not profit by being occupied with foods, but it's good for the heart to be established by grace." We need to be established by grace by focusing on God and His love and not what we can and cannot eat.

We have been working on the wrong problem when we diet because we are trying to change the food we normally eat. We go to a lot of trouble making ourselves different meals than our families, weighing it, and counting the calories, etc— all the while focusing on food. We need to recognize the real problem. We don't need to change the food we eat. It is our hearts we need to change.

Let's say, you do lose weight using one of these methods. You will still have the anxiety you have always had about your weight. However, instead of worrying about being overweight, you will be anxious about gaining it back. Your thoughts will still be obsessed with food, fat, calories, etc. Being thin will not make you happy. You will still yearn for and desire food.

Concentrate on your relationship with God rather than on your relationship with food. Pray and ask God to establish you by grace and to keep you focused on Him through the truth of His word. One of the most necessary elements needed to break your obsession with food is to eat slowly. If you are running headlong into sin, there isn't enough time to let God work with you through the temptation. You can't focus on God when you are hurrying to get the food shoved in. You need to pray before and during your meal. You don't have to pray out loud, of course. Just give God time to work.

I Corinthians 10:13 (The Message) *No test or temptation that comes your way is beyond the course of what others have had to face. All you need to remember is that God will never let you down; he'll never let you be pushed past your limit; he'll always be there to help you come through it.*

How can He help you to avoid being pushed past your limit when you are running away from Him as fast as you can?

Colossians 2:8-10 *Beware lest anyone cheat you through philosophy and empty deceit, according to the tradition of men, according to the basic principles of the world, and not according to Christ. ⁹For in Him dwells all the fullness of the Godhead bodily; ¹⁰ and you are complete in Him, who is the head of all principality and power.*

From verse 10, when does it say you will be complete in Christ? _____
_____

He has already given you everything you need to be all He has planned for you to be. You just need to believe it so you can employ it.

II Corinthians 6 (The Message) *¹⁻⁴Companions as we are in this work with you, we beg you, please don't squander one bit of this marvelous life God has given us. God reminds us, I heard your call in the nick of time; The day you needed me, I was there to help. Well, now is the right time to listen, the day to be helped. Don't put it off; don't frustrate God's work by showing up late, throwing a question mark over everything we're doing.*

Do you think God is able to help you lose weight? _____

Why do you feel that way? _____
_____
_____
_____

Read: **Matthew 7:7-12**

In light of today's study, what was the Scripture or statement in today's lesson that most spoke to your heart? _____
_____
_____
_____

What steps of faith does God want you to take towards Him today? _____
_____
_____
_____

Rephrase the Scripture or statement into an expression of faith _____
_____
_____
_____

Isaiah 55:9. *For as the _____ are higher than the _____, so are My _____ higher than your ways, And My thoughts than your thoughts.*

Week 1 Day 3
Do You Want to Be Healed?

Day _____ Date _____

Do you want to be healed? It's a simple question and the one question Jesus asked almost every person He healed. So I am asking you to carefully consider this question: DO—YOU—WANT—TO—BE—HEALED? Yes or No?

If your answer is no, read through this day then I'll ask again. If your answer is yes, you need to make the commitment right now. Not the commitment to go on another diet, but to change the way you have been thinking for years.

I want to tell you a story that may help you understand why you need to make this commitment. It is a true story about a dear friend of mine. I love my friend but at a young age, she started an unhealthy relationship with an abuser. This abuser was a bully and had no mercy; she would put her down at every turn. The bully would say, "You are stupid. You only have a seventh-grade education. You're a loser and you will never lose weight. You have tried dieting so many times and have never been successful. You're fine for two or three weeks, and then you run out of gas. What makes you think this time is different?"

She would make rude comments on the way my friend looked. She would say, "You have huge pores in your nose and a big white, blubbery, pasty, stomach." She would constantly tell her she was ugly every single time she caught sight of her. She would tell her she was repulsive. It was brutal and constant. Every time my friend had a success, the bully would knock her down. Every time my friend was in a social situation, the bully would point out her faults to everybody. She would tell the other people at the party that my friend was fat.

I think the bully in her own sick way was trying to protect my friend, because she would tell my friend, "They won't accept you if you don't show them you know you're not as good as they are. If I build them up by putting you down they might like you." Then when my friend and the bully were alone, she would berate her for all the stupid things she said at the party.

People who were close to my friend would try to tell her the bully was wrong, but my friend didn't believe anything good about herself. She had listened to the bully too long. The bully drove her to the brink of suicide. She tried to kill herself three times, but thank God, she wasn't successful.

Do you think my friend could ever be successful as long as she continued the relationship with the bully? _____ Why or why not? _____

_____

No matter how much self-esteem you have, if you are constantly told you are bad, you start to believe it. What do you think happened to my friend in the end? _____

_____

If you haven't already guessed, **I am my friend** and **I _was_ also the bully**. The way I used to talk to myself was horrifying. You <u>cannot</u> succeed; let me say that again YOU ABSOLUTELY WILL NOT SUCCEED UNTIL YOU GET OUT OF THE HABIT OF VERBAL SELF ABUSE. You may as well quit now if you can't make the commitment to break this habit. Would you talk to your child the way you talk to yourself? It's time to stop this destructive habit. I can't stress how important it is for you to end this!

You're probably thinking, "I can't stop! I have been doing it too long." If you try, God will bless it. This is how you do it: you look at yourself in the mirror and if you're alone say it out loud, and if not, in your mind, "God made me beautiful. I am beautifully and wonderfully made. I am the temple of the Holy Spirit and my steps are ordered by God. God only sees the good in me. I am well able to fulfill the destiny God has planned for my life. The best is yet to come. God is pleased with me. I am a good friend. I am a wonderful Christian, because if not, God would not have chosen me. I try my hardest all the time. God is perfecting me every day. He is well able to give me all I can ask or imagine because He loves me. Everything that God allows in my life is good. Look at me, you good looking thing you…" I mean, you need to go on and on.

Everyone has a conversation going on in his or her head at all times (your internal dialog). Your subconscious mind records everything people say to you and everything you say to yourself.[3] Your subconscious mind takes everything literally, recording it for later use. If you don't get anything else from this study, take this truth. It is so important.

Your bully may not be as ruthless as mine was, but if you are a habitual dieter, most likely you have a bully. What are some of the things your bully says to you that are not productive?

_____
_____
_____
_____
_____

Okay, I hope you got that out of your system, because you need to make a commitment to yourself and God that this will be the last time you will <u>ever, ever, ever,</u> say those things to yourself.

It's dark and sad and no place for a Christian. It's not arrogant to talk to yourself in a nice way.

Is it a sin if you verbally abuse your child? _____

Is it a sin if you verbally abuse your spouse? _____

---

[3] The Power of Positive Thinking, Norman Vincent Peale

You know it's a sin to verbally abuse another person. What makes you think God says it's OKAY to abuse yourself? You listen to your internal dialog more than you listen to anybody else. You take yourself everywhere you go. We are the temple of the Holy Spirit.

I'm not talking about being egotistical. I'm not talking to the person who thinks they are better than others are. That is a whole other issue. I'm not telling you that you are better than others. I am telling you that you are just as wonderful, special, and blessed as anyone.

Read **I Corinthians 3:17** *If anyone* **defiles** *the temple of God,* **God will destroy him**. *For the temple of God is holy, which temple* **you are.**

Some of the definitions of "defile" are: To profane or sully, to demean the pureness or excellence.

What are you doing to the temple God gave you when you abuse yourself? _____
_____
_____

I was demeaning the beautiful gift God made for me with His own hands. I was so ungrateful.

Finish the blanks from the bolded, underlined section of Scripture above **I Corinthians 3:17** *If anyone* _____ *the temple of God,* _____ *For the temple of God is holy, which temple* _____ .

Underline the word "anyone" in the Scripture above. Who is anyone? _____
_____

Could "anyone" include yourself? _____

We are not immune to God's discipline and it is no wonder my body was falling apart. I was treating it with such distain. Look through all the red text in your New Testament; did Jesus ever, ever put Himself down?

You need to be a caregiver to yourself, not a bully. You need to make the commitment to change the way you talk to yourself, and how you treat yourself. Nurture yourself. See yourself the way God sees you. Nurture yourself with God's words of love to you.

Read **Song of Solomon 2: 10-14** *" Rise up, my love, my fair one, And come away.* [11] *For lo, the winter is past, The rain is over and gone.* [12] *The flowers appear on the earth; The time of singing has come, And the voice of the turtledove Is heard in our land.* [13] *The fig tree puts forth her green figs, And the vines with the tender grapes Give a good smell. Rise up, my love, my fair one, And come away!*

[14] *" O my dove, in the clefts of the rock, In the secret places of the cliff, Let me see your face, Let me hear your voice; For your voice is sweet, And your face is lovely."*

When you get a chance, read the Song of Solomon. It's a beautiful love song to us from God. It illustrates how God sees us and how much He loves us, His bride. I had been saved for thirty years before I could read this book, because I just couldn't see myself the way God sees me.

Now I am going to ask you again the question I asked before…
DO— YOU—WANT—TO—BE—HEALED? Yes or No?

If your answer is no, don't give up, please… just try telling yourself that you are wonderful. You may feel like you're lying to yourself, but you're not. You're telling yourself the truth. Pray that God will show you the truth. I admit it was hard to look at myself in the mirror at first. It was even hard to look at myself in the eyes. I felt humiliated and weird. For so long, I believed I was inferior. It was how I fit in the world, and it was my identity. I didn't know it at the time, but it was how I manipulated people into liking me. It was a very unhappy place to be.

Just try it! You will be so surprised at how fast this bad habit goes away. At first, it is uncomfortable, but after you are finished encouraging yourself in the mirror, you feel wonderful, happy, and light. You will be amazed. It only took two or three days for me to stop putting myself down. I had always known it was bad to put myself down. I was always going to stop the self-abuse, but I didn't know how to do it. I always failed because I didn't know I had the power to overcome it, and I didn't realize how destructive it was. I believed Satan's lies, but now I understand that <u>you cannot succeed if you don't stop self-abusing and start encouraging.</u>

If your answer is yes! Hallelujah! Praise God and let's go… Don't be resistant to the mirror exercise and commit yourself to the healing.

Read **Psalm 8**

In light of today's study, what was the Scripture or statement in today's lesson that most spoke to your heart? _____

_____

_____

_____

What steps of faith does God want you to take towards Him today? _____

_____

_____

_____

Rephrase the Scripture or statement into an expression of faith_____

_____

_____

_____

Isaiah 55:9 *For as the _____ are _____ than the _____, so are My _____ higher than _____ ways, And My _____ than your thoughts.*

Week 1 Day 4
Nourished in the Words of Faith

Day _____ Date _____

Now, we have learned that it does not profit us to be occupied by food. We understand the reason that we are overweight is that we have become too focused on the food and condemning ourselves when we can't control how much we eat. We have also learned that dieting has contributed to the problem. We are infatuated with the latest diet fad, and this takes our heart off God who is the one who truly deserves our love and focus.

Read **I Timothy 4:1-8** *Now the Spirit expressly says that in latter times some will depart from the faith, giving heed to deceiving spirits and doctrines of demons, [2] speaking lies in hypocrisy, having their own conscience seared with a hot iron, [3] forbidding to marry, and commanding to abstain from foods which God created to be received with thanksgiving by those who believe and know the truth. [4] For every creature of God is good, and nothing is to be refused if it is received with thanksgiving; [5] for it is sanctified by the word of God and prayer. [6] If you instruct the brethren in these things, you will be a good minister of Jesus Christ, nourished in the words of faith and of the good doctrine which you have carefully followed. [7] But reject profane and old wives' fables, and exercise yourself toward godliness. [8] For bodily exercise profits a little, but godliness is profitable for all things, having promise of the life that now is and of that which is to come.*

Now let's really work this passage.

According to verse 1, when will these things take place? _____
_____

Circle the words, *latter times* in verse 1.

What kind of spirits does the Bible say you are listening to when you try to change the food and not your heart by abstaining from certain foods God gave you to enjoy? (Verse 1)
_____ _____ and _____ of _____

According to verse 3 above, how are we to receive the gift of food God has provided?
_____

Should we abstain from certain foods such as carbohydrates, meat, and fat? _____

Pray about your next answer. Do you think in these latter times, we Christians have become too concerned about what we look like? _____

This is not to say that we should just go "hog wild" and eat and eat until we die. It means you will now get God involved with your diet. God created all foods, and we can eat them with thanksgiving. God is the same yesterday, today, and always.

I have heard all the objections from Christians. Some say these Scriptures were for Jesus' time. I say they should look at **I Timothy 4:1,** (Latter times) and remember the other Scripture we read that concerned being occupied with food, **Hebrews 13:8-9** (Amplified Bible)

*⁸Jesus Christ (the Messiah) is [always] the same, yesterday, today, [yes] and forever (to the ages). ⁹Do not be carried about by different and varied and alien teachings; for it is good for the heart to be established and ennobled and strengthened by means of grace (God's favor and spiritual blessing) and not [to be devoted to] foods [**rules of diet** and ritualistic meals], which bring no [spiritual] benefit or profit to those who observe them.*

Underline the words "the same" in verse 8 above.

When Is Jesus the same"? _____, _____ and
_____.

Why do you suppose God wrote Jesus is the same yesterday, today, and forever? _____
_____
_____

I believe it was to show our generation that these Scriptures apply to us. I have also heard Christians say, "You should be a vegetarian, because Daniel abstained from the king's food and only ate grains and veggies." I have also heard that we should not eat pork or fat, because of the Old Testament dietary laws. We need to understand and get it fixed in our minds that we are under the New Covenant and this passage proves it. The Bible says ALL creatures, which means ALL creatures!

Look at the line that says "nourished in the words of faith." The word "nourished" is defined as: to promote the growth and development of

Has the circumstance of your being overweight and frantic dieting, made you feel nourished?

List some of the reasons you turn to food when you're not hungry.

_____

_____

_____

_____

_____

_____

_____

_____

_____

_____

_____

_____

_____

_____

We run to food because it gives us a feeling of being nurtured and nourished. Sometimes it helps us to avoid an unpleasant task or feeling. We think it gives us comfort and love. How do you feel after going on an eating binge? _____

_____

_____

_____

Does it feel you have promoted the growth and development of your life in any way? _____

It depresses you and makes you feel ashamed, heartbroken, and tired all the time. It makes you feel down on yourself and gives you a reason for self-abuse. You are going to learn that you're not a slave to your sin. You have been listening to the greatest liar ever. Satan is the father of all lies. Once your body stops growing it is surprising how little food we need to sustain it. You've probably been eating at least twice as much as you need, maybe more.

As mentioned earlier, the dictionary defines nourished as: "to promote the growth and development of..." The dictionary leaves it blank so you can fill it in. I always thought nourished had something to do with food. I associated food with comfort. I think we all do.

Review **I Timothy 4:1-8**. The Bible says to promote and develop the growth of the spirit by the words of faith. Think about the previous diets you've been on. Was the focal point what you look like? We have been trying to fix the wrong problem while being preoccupied with how we look. We've put the solution to our weight problem on the back burner. The answer is to develop our spirit before anything else. Then, all else will correct itself.

Luke 11:9-13 says, *Seek first the kingdom of God and His righteousness and all these things will be added unto you.*

Every time Jesus healed someone, He was always more concerned about their spiritual condition. Read the following passage:

Mark 2:1-12 *And again He entered Capernaum after some days, and it was heard that He was in the house. ² Immediately many gathered together, so that there was no longer room to receive them, not even near the door. And He preached the word to them. ³ Then they came to Him, bringing a paralytic who was carried by four men. ⁴ And when they could not come near Him because of the crowd, they uncovered the roof where He was. So when they had broken through, they let down the bed on which the paralytic was lying.*

⁵ When Jesus saw their faith, He said to the paralytic, "Son, your sins are forgiven you."

⁶ And some of the scribes were sitting there and reasoning in their hearts, ⁷ "Why does this Man speak blasphemies like this? Who can forgive sins but God alone?"

⁸ But immediately, when Jesus perceived in His spirit that they reasoned thus within themselves, He said to them, "Why do you reason about these things in your hearts? ⁹ Which is easier, to say to the paralytic, "Your sins are forgiven you,' or to say, "Arise, take up your bed and walk'? ¹⁰ But that you may know that the Son of Man has power on earth to forgive sins"--He said to the paralytic, ¹¹ "I say to you, arise, take up your bed, and go to your house." ¹² Immediately he arose, took up the bed, and went out in the presence of them all, so that all were amazed and glorified God, saying, "We never saw anything like this!"

Jesus took care of the paralyzed man's spiritual need before healing the physical by saying "your sins are forgiven." Physical healing is important to Jesus, but it was secondary to spiritual healing.

Mark 5:34 *And He said to her, "Daughter, your faith has made you well. Go in peace, and be healed of your affliction."*

When we think of the word peace, we think of peace of mind. The word Shalom is the Hebrew word for Peace, but it means much more. It means completeness; it means salvation. It means a restored relationship. Remember we can only nourish our spirit by things of the Spirit. Nourishing our spirit is critical. When our spirit is well nourished, we won't need to try to fill it with food that doesn't satisfy.

I Timothy 4:8 *For bodily exercise profits a little, but godliness is profitable for all things.*

The dictionary defines "godliness" as being devoted to God. God will be taking the pounds off while the spirit is being filled. The weight will naturally decrease. If you don't exercise you will still lose weight. You may come to a point where you choose to, because it will make you feel better. Remember, however, it only profits a little, so don't put exercise over your daily devotion.

According to the Word of God what is more profitable physical exercise or spiritual exercise?

_____

Write, **I Timothy 4:8** _____

_____

_____

In the second part of **I Timothy 4:8**, What does the verse say godliness is profitable for…

_____ _____

Circle the word "all".

Is godliness profitable for your body? _____

Read the following Scriptures, use your own Bible to fill in the blanks.

Mark 7: 14-20 *when He had called all the multitude to Himself, He said to them, "Hear Me, everyone, and understand:* [15] *There is nothing that enters a man from outside which can defile him; but the things which come out of him, those are the things that defile a man.* [16] *If anyone has ears to hear, let him hear!"* [17] *When He had entered a house away from the crowd, His disciples asked Him concerning the parable.* [18] *"Are you thus without understanding also?* [19&20]

_____

_____

_____

_____

_____

_____ [21] *For from within, out of the heart of men, proceed evil thoughts. Adulteries, fornications, murders,* [22] *thefts, covetousness, wickedness, deceit, lewdness, and evil eye, blasphemy, pride, foolishness.* [23] *All these evil things come from within and defile a man."*

The first day of this diet, we were reminded that Jesus is the same yesterday, today, and forever. In the same Scripture it says, "Do not be occupied with foods." Today we found spiritual well-being is more important than our physical well-being. Do you have the confidence in God, the Creator and Ruler of the universe, to know what your body needs? _____

If you believe that godliness is profitable for ALL THINGS, you need to stop doing weird diets that make you count calories or have only certain foods in certain combinations at certain times of the day. Trust Jesus. Think about Him rather than the latest diet.   He declared all foods clean. Your need, or desire, is not generated from the food. We don't need to overeat; it's the desire from within. The problem with being so preoccupied with how we look and being obsessed with the physical is that it creates the obsession for dieting and food.

READ: Psalm 1 and 118:8-9

In light of today's study, what was the Scripture or statement in today's lesson that most spoke to your heart? _____

_____

_____

_____

What steps of faith does God want you to take towards Him today? _____

_____

_____

_____

Rephrase the Scripture or statement into an expression of faith_____

_____

_____

_____

Isaiah 55:9 *For as the* _____ *are* _____ *than the* _____ *, so* _____ *My* _____ _____ _____ _____ *ways,* _____ *My* _____ *than* _____ _____

Week 1 Day 5
A Change of Heart, a New Creation

Day _____ Date _____

Even though I had been a Christian a long time while reading my Bible almost every day, I never thought to go to the Bible to resolve my weight problem. I didn't consider it a diet guide. I would pray, asking God to help me with a particular diet, but I never thought of the Bible as the starting place. The more I read the Bible, the more I realized it is a rich source of knowledge and insight for every known problem. The Word is our guide for living every aspect of our life. This ancient document is just as practical today as it was thousands of years ago when Solomon wrote:

Ecclesiastes 1:9, 10 *That which has been is what will be, That which is done is what will be done, And there is nothing new under the sun. [10] Is there anything of which it may be said, "See, this is new"? It has already been in ancient times before us.*

Read **Psalm 118:8-9**
It is better to trust in the Lord Than to put confidence in man, [9]It is better to trust in the Lord Than to put confidence in princes.

In whom should you put your confidence, to overcome your obsession with food?

_____

Read **Colossians 2: 20-23** [20] *Therefore, if you died with Christ from the basic principles of the world, why, as though living in the world, do you subject yourselves to regulations— [21] "Do not touch, do not taste, do not handle," [22] which all concern things which perish with the using— according to the commandments and doctrines of men? [23] These things indeed have an appearance of wisdom in self-imposed religion, false humility, and neglect of the body, but are of no value against the indulgence of the flesh.*

This Scripture nails it. It's exactly what we have been doing with our frantic dieting. Why are we living as if we don't have all this knowledge and wisdom at our fingertips?

Flowers over the Wall

It's not a food issue. It's a head and heart problem. The trouble starts when we make the act of eating into a forbidden fruit. An addict is someone who can't get enough; they want more and more. How many people do you know who are addicted to water? We are rebellious. I don't have a problem praying for help finding my keys, yet somehow, I always conveniently forget to pray for help resisting the last of my Mucho Grande, Over-Stuffed, Big, Fat Burrito.

In a recent study done in Switzerland, participants were blindfolded while eating. They ate less and felt just as full. It was determined that when they couldn't see what they were eating, they paid more attention to their inner cues.

The desire for forbidden fruit is our real problem. I read a story recently in my little devotional ""Our Daily Bread." The title was forbidden fruit. It was about a resort hotel in Texas. They had a sign in each room saying, "No fishing off the balcony." Yet every day, hotel guests would throw their lines into the water. When the management decided to just give up and remove the signs, the fishing stopped. We are a defiant people and need to have a heart transformation. If we are ever going to be successful at losing weight, the only way is through the power of the most High God.

Let me ask you a question. Have you felt any of the diets you've tried before, with all their rules and regulations, worked on changing your heart?

Do you think your problem could be, you have been trying to change the food and not your mind/heart? _____

In other words none of these diets did anything to help you battle against the indulgences of the flesh. The way to change your mind is easy. You are in the habit of thinking negatively, listening to Satan's lies, and you need to break that habit. You have to get up every morning and say, "I am a beautiful creation of the Almighty God." Look at yourself in the mirror and say, "I'm beautiful. Thank you, God, for giving me such a fine body. Every part of my body works so well."

If you are going to be successful with this or any other part of your life, you have to love yourself. When you don't feel like you are beautiful, DO NOT ALLOW YOURSELF TO THINK THAT! You must, must get rid of all negative thoughts. These thoughts are not of God. Take control of them by your authority in Christ. Start getting in the habit of complimenting yourself. You take yourself everywhere you go. You might as well start enjoying the company!

Read **Philemon 1:6** *That the sharing of your faith may become effective by the acknowledgment of every good thing which is in you in Christ Jesus.*

Rewrite the previous Scripture in your own words._____
_____
_____

---

4 Our Daily Bread, http://rbc.org/odb/odb.shtml

The verse says, "Every good thing in you is in Christ." God does not want you walking around thinking negatively about yourself. You can't share your faith effectively unless you acknowledge God has created you for good things and that you are good in Christ. You can't be effective in sharing your faith if you have not acknowledged how wonderful God has made you!

Read, **II Corinthians: 5:17** *Therefore, if anyone is in Christ, he is a new creation; old things have passed away; behold, all things have become new.*

When you turned your heart over to Jesus and gave him lordship of your life, you died to your will and the world's rules. You became a new creation in Christ.

Read **Galatians 5:22,23** *But the fruit of the Spirit is love, joy, peace, longsuffering, kindness, goodness, faithfulness,* [23] *gentleness, self-control. Against such there is no law.*

I used to read this Scripture and think that I have joy, peace, and longsuffering, but when I came to the self-control fruit I thought that someday God would give me that gift. I believed a deception, and then it dawned on me. I already have all the fruits of the Spirit. I received them when I asked God into my heart. When you are saved, you automatically get the fruits; it's part of the package. I realized I had been listening to that bully Satan. You have to understand that Satan is a liar. He is the accuser of the brethren.

Read **Revelation 12:10** *Then I heard a loud voice saying in Heaven, "Now salvation, and strength, and the kingdom of our God, and the power of His Christ have come, for the accuser of our brethren,* **who accused them before our God day and night, has been cast down.**

Read about what Jesus said about Satan when the Pharisees were trying to trip Him up with lies.

John 8:44 *You are of your father the devil, and the desires of your father you want to do. He was a murderer from the beginning, and does not stand in the truth, because there is no truth in him. When he speaks a lie, he speaks from his own resources, for he is a liar and the father of it.*

Satan lies to you and tries to make you feel condemned. Don't receive the accusations. Say a Scripture like, "I am the righteousness of God" (**II Corinthians 5:21**). You will make mistakes; allow yourself that. Tell God that you are sorry and get back up! Only allow your heart to remember the sin long enough to ask forgiveness, then mentally push it right back out of your heart.

Read **Romans 7:1-3** *Or do you not know, brethren (for I speak to those who know the law), that the law has dominion over a man as long as he lives? [2] For the woman who has a husband is bound by the law to her husband as long as he lives. But if the husband dies, she is released from the law of her husband. [3] So then if, while her husband lives, she marries another man, she will be called an adulteress; but if her husband dies, she is free from that law, so that she is no adulteress, though she has married another man.*

God opened my eyes to this passage one day. I had read it many times in the past and even heard it used in sermon. They were all about condemning the sinful divorce, but that is not what this Scripture is telling us. That is taken out of context. It is using the adulteress and widow as an illustration of our death to the Law. The Law no longer binds us; in fact, the Law is the tool Satan uses to create the desire to sin.

Continue reading **Romans 7** *[4] Therefore, my brethren, you also have become dead to the law through the body of Christ, that you may be married to another—to Him who was raised from the dead, that we should bear fruit to God. [5] <u>For when we were in the flesh,</u> **THE SINFUL PASSIONS WHICH WERE AROUSED BY THE LAW** were at work in our members to bear fruit to death. [6] But now we have been delivered from the law, having died to what we were held by, so that we should serve in the newness of the Spirit and not in the oldness of the letter.*

*[7] What shall we say then? Is the law sin? Certainly not! On the contrary, I would not have known sin except through the law. For I would not have known covetousness unless the law had said, "You shall not covet." [8] **<u>But sin, taking opportunity by the commandment, produced in me all manner of evil desire</u>**. For apart from the law sin was dead. [9] I was alive once without the law, but when the commandment came, sin revived and I died. [10] And the commandment, which was to bring life, I found to bring death. [11] For sin, taking occasion by the commandment, deceived me, and by it killed me. [12] Therefore the law is holy, and the commandment holy and just and good.*

[13] Has then what is good become death to me? Certainly not! But sin, that it might appear sin, was producing death in me through what is good, so that sin through the commandment might become exceedingly sinful. [14] For we know that the law is spiritual, but I am carnal, sold under sin. [15] For what I am doing, I do not understand. For what I will to do, that I do not practice; but what I hate, that I do. [16] If, then, I do what I will not to do, I agree with the law that it is good. [17] But now, it is no longer I who do it, but sin that dwells in me. [18] For I know that in me (that is, in my flesh) nothing good dwells; for to will is present with me, but how to perform what is good I do not find. [19] For the good that I will to do, I do not do; but the evil I will not to do, that I practice. [20] Now if I do what I will not to do, it is no longer I who do it, but sin that dwells in me.

[21] I find then a law, that evil is present with me, the one who wills to do good. [22] For I delight in the law of God according to the inward man. [23] But I see another law in my members, warring against the law of my mind, and bringing me into captivity to the law of sin which is in my members. [24] O wretched man that I am!

It is evident from the Scriptures above that even Paul struggled with sin. We tend to think of him as "Saint Paul," but he was a sinner saved by grace just like you and me. He goes through his list of sins in frustration with himself. Then just as it seems he will be lost to hopelessness of ever recovering, he ask in the last part of verse 24, *Who will deliver me from this body of death?* Ah... then he remembers, *[25]I thank God—through Jesus Christ our Lord! So then, with the mind I myself serve the law of God, but with the flesh the law of sin.*

It's a little hard to understand these verses in the New King James version. I like how the Message interprets it. The Message version was translated from the original ancient Greek in today's English rhythms and idioms.

Romans 7: 1-3(The Message)

*1-3 You shouldn't have any trouble understanding this, friends, for you know all the ins and outs of the law—how it works and how its power touches only the living. **For instance**, a wife is legally tied to her husband while he lives, but if he dies, she's free. If she lives with another man while her husband is living, she's obviously an adulteress. But if he dies, she is quite free to marry another man in good conscience, with no one's disapproval.*

*4-6 So, my friends, this is something like what has taken place with you. **When Christ died he took that entire rule-dominated way of life down with him and left it in the tomb,** leaving you free to "marry" a resurrection life and bear "offspring" of faith for God. For as long as we lived that old way of life, doing whatever we felt we could get away with, sin was calling most of the shots as the old law code hemmed us in. **And this made us all the more rebellious.** In the end, all we had to show for it was miscarriages and stillbirths. But now that we're no longer shackled to that domineering mate of sin, and out from under all those oppressive regulations and fine print, we're free to live a new life in the freedom of God.*

7 But I can hear you say, "If the law code was as bad as all that, it's no better than sin itself." That's certainly not true. The law code had a perfectly legitimate function. Without its clear guidelines for right and wrong, moral behavior would be mostly guesswork. Apart from the succinct, surgical command, "You shall not covet," I could have dressed covetousness up to look like a virtue and ruined my life with it.

*8-12 Don't you remember how it was? I do, perfectly well. The law code started out as an excellent piece of work. What happened, though, was that sin found a way to pervert the command into a temptation, making a piece of "forbidden fruit" out of it. **The law code, instead of being used to guide me, was used to seduce me. WITHOUT ALL THE PARAPHERNALIA OF THE LAW CODE, SIN LOOKED PRETTY DULL AND LIFELESS,** and I went along without paying much attention to it. But once sin got its hands on the law code and decked itself out in all that finery, I was fooled, and fell for it. The very command that was supposed to guide me into life was cleverly used to trip me up, throwing me headlong. So sin was plenty alive, and I was stone dead. But the law code itself is God's good and common sense, each command sane and holy counsel.*

13 I can already hear your next question: "Does that mean I can't even trust what is good [that is, the law]? Is good just as dangerous as evil?" No again! Sin simply did what sin is so famous for doing: using the good as a cover to tempt me to do what would finally destroy me. By hiding within God's good commandment, sin did far more mischief than it could ever have accomplished on its own.

14-16 I can anticipate the response that is coming: "I know that all God's commands are spiritual, but I'm not. Isn't this also your experience?" Yes. I'm full of myself—after all, I've spent a long time in sin's prison. What I don't understand about myself is that I decide one way, but then I act another, doing things I absolutely despise. So if I can't be trusted to figure out what is best for myself and then do it, it becomes obvious that God's command is necessary.

17-20 But I need something more! For if I know the law but still can't keep it, and if the power of sin within me keeps sabotaging my best intentions, I obviously need help! I realize that I don't have what it takes. I can will it, but I can't do it. I decide to do good, but I don't really do it; I decide not to do bad, but then I do it anyway. My decisions, such as they are, don't result in actions. Something has gone wrong deep within me and gets the better of me every time.

21-23 It happens so regularly that it's predictable. The moment I decide to do good, sin is there to trip me up. I truly delight in God's commands, but it's pretty obvious that not all of me joins in that delight. Parts of me covertly rebel, and just when I least expect it, they take charge.

24 I've tried everything and nothing helps. I'm at the end of my rope. Is there no one who can do anything for me? Isn't that the real question?

*25 **The answer**, thank God, is that Jesus Christ can and does. He acted to set things right in this life of contradictions where I want to serve God with all my heart and mind, but am pulled by the influence of sin to do something totally different.*

Note the Scripture I have underlined above. It says, "Without the law, sin looks pretty dull and lifeless." Isn't that the truth. I mean, Satan has taken something that's a function and made it exciting. I had a thin friend. He told me that eating was like an interruption of stuff he really liked to do. It was something he had to do, like going the bathroom. I found this to be the case with many naturally thin people I have asked.

READ: Romans 8, Colossians 3:10-17 and II Corinthians 5:17

In light of today's study, what was the Scripture or statement in today's lesson that most spoke to your heart? _____

_____
_____
_____

What steps of faith does God want you to take towards Him today? _____

_____
_____
_____

Rephrase the Scripture or statement into an expression of faith_____

_____
_____
_____

Isaiah 55:9 _____

_____
_____

Week 2 Day 1
Establish Being Occupied With Food Is Idolatry

Day _____ Date _____

Before God can begin to work on our problem, we have to admit we do have a problem. We read in **Romans 7:7** *But I can hear you say, "If the law code was as bad as all that, it's no better than sin itself." That's certainly not true. The law code had a perfectly legitimate function. Without its clear guidelines for right and wrong, moral behavior would be mostly guesswork. Apart from the succinct, surgical command, "You shall not covet," I could have dressed covetousness up to look like a virtue and ruined my life with it.*

This day's study is a heavy one, and Satan will try to use it to condemn you. Don't let him! Jesus never condemns. He does bring our sins to light so we can work on them. If you start to feel condemned and hopeless, remember, you can only think one thought at a time, so replace those thoughts with a Scripture like:

Romans 8 :1 *There is therefore now no condemnation to those who are in Christ Jesus, who do not walk according to the flesh, but according to the Spirit.*

I know it's hard to think you may be idol-worshipping when you feel like you can't control it, but to begin to heal, you have to be brutally honest with yourself. Pray that God will show you His truth. Read the definitions below, and see if they apply to your situation.

Definitions:
Idol: a false God: an object of passionate, excessive devotion.
Idolize: to make an idol of, greed selfish desire beyond reason.
Idolatry: to put your trust, Love, devotion in anything other than God.

[5]The Nelson Illustrated Bible Dictionary says, "In the New Testament period, the term idolatry began to be used as an intellectual concept. Idolatry became, not the actual bowing down before a statue, but the replacement of God in the mind of the worshiper."

Colossians 3:1-5 (King James) *If ye then be risen with Christ, seek those things which are above, where Christ sitteth on the right hand of God. [2]Set your affection on things above, not on things on the earth. [3]For ye are dead, and your life is hid with Christ in God.*

[4]When Christ, who is our life, shall appear, then shall ye also appear with him in glory.

[5]Mortify therefore your members which are upon the earth; fornication, uncleanness, inordinate affection, evil concupiscence, and covetousness, which is idolatry:

---

[5] Nelson's Illustrated Bible Dictionary, Thomas Nelson publishers

Colossians 3:1-2 (King James) says, *If ye then be risen with Christ, seek those things which are above, where Christ sitteth on the right hand of God.* *²Set your affection on things above, not on things on the earth.*

"Set your affection" in the Greek is *phroneo which* means to "direct one's mind to a thing, to seek, to strive for". <u>It's the idea that it's not something that is obtained all at once, but studied and searched for.</u>

This is the secret to losing weight. Once you replace those obsessive thoughts of dieting, you will eat like a thin person. It will come naturally and easy to you.

Colossians 3:5 (King James) *Mortify therefore your members which are upon the earth; fornication, uncleanness, inordinate affection, evil concupiscence, and covetousness, which is* **_idolatry_**.

The word "mortify," in the Greek is *nekroō*[6], is translated as "to put to death."

The words inordinate affection in the Strong's is *pathos,* It's defined as: A calamity, mishap, evil, affliction, a feeling which the mind suffers, an affliction of the mind, emotion, passion, in the New Testament, in a bad sense, depraved passion, vile passions.

Evil concupiscence, *epithumia*[7], means almost the same as pathos, but where pathos represents a more passive participation and is an ungovernable desire (addiction). The word epithumia (concupiscence) is the more active side of a vice and is more wide-ranging— Our evil desires.

The Word covetousness, *pleonexia*[8], is translated to have a greedy desire to have more.

What does the word greedy mean to you? _____
_____
_____

The dictionary defines it as a selfish desire beyond reason. If your desire to be thin has consumed your thoughts and almost every waking thought is about your weight and what you look like and feel, I think it's pretty clear that you are worshiping at the feet of an idol. If you are overweight, it is most likely because your thoughts are consumed with thoughts of food as it becomes a forbidden fruit.

---

[6] Blueletterbible.org, Strong's, *"nekroō"* G3499
[7] Blueletterbible.org, Strong's *"epithumia"* G1939
[8] Blueletterbible.org, Strong's *"pleonexia"* G4124

The overeater /dieter must understand the vicious nature of idolatry. While we may not make or bow down to a statue, we have to be on guard constantly so we don't let food and the obsession to be thin come between God and us. As soon as it does, it becomes an idol with being overweight as the evidence. Some of the synonyms for greed are: gluttony, voracity, ravenousness, hunger and self-indulgence. Sound familiar? The antonym for greed is moderation.

Idolatry is a dangerous and deceitful sin. No wonder the prophets preached against it so often and strongly. An idol is defined as: a false god, an object of passionate devotion. How many times have you hidden food or waited until you were alone to eat and then been angry when you were interrupted? God showed me how greedy and passionately devoted I was to my *god* in a somewhat humorous but sobering way one day. Before I tell you this story I need to preface it with a confession of a couple of my many weaknesses. I have a little aversion to germs in food and a terrible phobia of mice. I go into hysterics and panic when I see a mouse.

Now, on with my story. My favorite thing to eat in the whole world is warm pecan pie ala mode. I couldn't wait until the kids went outside to play, because I had made a pecan pie and there were only three pieces left and four people in my family! By the time my girls finally went outside, I was lusting for my treat. There I was all alone with my love. Even though I wasn't the slightest bit hungry, I thought I had better steal the chance while I had it.

I lovingly cut a large piece of the delicious treat, put it on a small decorative desert plate, placed it in the microwave, and set the time so it would be the perfect temperature. I got the vanilla ice cream out of the freezer. I was thinking about how wonderful the warm pie taste with the cold ice cream when, right on time, the microwave beeped, signaling my pie was the ideal temperature. I adoringly pulled my sweet prize out and put the frozen ice cream on the pie. I was just getting ready to plop myself in front of the TV so I could really enjoy the whole experience without having to think.

Just then, the front door slammed and interrupted the moment I was having with my lover. I immediately got angry with the person who would break up my stolen moment. I decided they were out to get me, and came in at this moment just to bug me. My darling but willful five-year-old, Tayler, came in and climbed up on the stool in front of me saying, "I want a piece." Although this made me angry, I held my temper in check, as I was still sane enough to appreciate I was being unreasonable.

I passed her my piece of pie and began to cut another from the pie in the refrigerator. She decided the perfect piece of pie I had given her was not good enough and started poking it with her tiny finger saying, "Look it's too hot to eat Mama. You made it too hot!"

My temper was mounting, and my sanity level was plummeting. Looking at her petulant face, watching her little finger poking holes all over the thing of my affection, and gritting my teeth, I said, "Fine!" and slid the cold piece of pie her direction knowing full well this would not satisfy her. Soon, we were nose to nose, mouths wide open, each throwing a doozey of a tantrum, and trying to outshout each other with she howling and crying and me yelling.

Finally, I sent her to her room, because I was the "biggest." I sat down determined to eat my pie still fuming while looking at what had once been my masterpiece and now was a protuberant lump full of holes. My now cold pie was swimming in warm separated white watery "goo" that used to be ice cream, but I was still determined to eat it. All the while, I was muttering at how she had spoiled everything, because now I couldn't even enjoy my pie— because of the guilt—

I cut a piece with my fork, raised it to my mouth... When my nine year old, who had walked in just before the tantrum episode and was a witness to the unholy melee, said calmly, "Mama, did you know Tayler was playing with the neighbors mouse and didn't even wash her hands?"

That was it! I totally lost control. I was about to do something Tayler would have been punished for. I raised my fork behind my ear and was getting ready to fling it when God chose that moment, sweetly speaking to my raging heart, in a still, small, un-condemning, voice," At this moment, you love this pie more than you love anything."

I was so convicted. As I sat there, I realized that for a moment, I had been worshiping, adoring and loving that mess more than my children and, most of all, my Lord. I had completely lavished all my love and affection on this god. It was my golden calf, and I was worshiping at its feet.

God used this incident to bring me to the realization that I really did have a problem, and it was a problem I couldn't handle on my own. We first have to admit that we have a problem that we have not been able to overcome on our own. You have dieted, failed, and gained all the weight back and usually ten or fifteen pounds more.

Read: **Psalm 107:9** *For He satisfies the longing soul, And fills the hungry soul with goodness.*

Do you feel satisfied, or filled with goodness, after you have eaten the forbidden food? By forbidden, I mean something you eat when you're not physically hungry. How does it make you feel? _____

_____

Does it leave you feeling empty and longing for more? You have a hunger for God and are seeking satisfaction elsewhere. Food will never satisfy you. It will always leave you craving more.

Read **I Corinthians 10:14-32** *Therefore, my beloved, flee from idolatry. [15] I speak as to wise men; judge for yourselves what I say. [16] The cup of blessing which we bless, is it not the communion of the blood of Christ? The bread which we break, is it not the communion of the body of Christ? [17] For we, though many, are one bread and one body; for we all partake of that one bread.*

[18] Observe Israel after the flesh: Are not those who eat of the sacrifices partakers of the altar? [19]

What am I saying then? That an idol is anything, or what is offered to idols is anything? [20] *Rather, that the things which the Gentiles sacrifice they sacrifice to demons and not to God, and I do not want you to have fellowship with demons.* [21] **You cannot drink the cup of the Lord and the cup of demons; you cannot partake of the Lord's table and of the table of demons.** [22] *Or do we provoke the Lord to jealousy? Are we stronger than He?*

[23] *All things are lawful for me, but not all things are helpful; all things are lawful for me, but not all things edify.* [24] *Let no one seek his own, but each one the other's well-being.*

[25] *Eat whatever is sold in the meat market, asking no questions for conscience' sake;* [26] *for "the earth is the LORD's, and all its fullness."*

[27] *If any of those who do not believe invites you to dinner, and you desire to go, eat whatever is set before you, asking no question for conscience' sake.* [28] *But if anyone says to you, "This sake; for "the earth is the LORD's, and all its fullness."* [29] *"Conscience," I say, not your own, but that of the other. For why is my liberty judged by another man's conscience?* [30] *But if I partake with thanks, why am I evil spoken of for the food over which I give thanks?*

[31] *Therefore, whether you eat or drink, or whatever you do, do all to the glory of God.* [32] *Give no offense, either to the Jews or to the Greeks or to the church of God,*

Write **I Corinthians 10:21** _____

_____

_____

_____

Contemplate this Scripture; mull it over in your mind. Write how it makes you feel, to think when you overeat you are **communing, Fellowshipping,** with demons? _____

_____

_____

_____

_____

When I read this passage, it made me sick! The sickening part of this is the objects of worship are actually demons. You can make anything a god, but in doing so, you are worshiping or communing with Satan.

Dictionary.com defines communing as,

1. To converse or talk together, usually with profound intensity, intimacy, etc.; interchange thoughts or feelings.
2. To be in intimate communication or rapport.
3. Interchange of ideas or sentiments.

It's a hard thought to think, but let's be honest; when I was in such a rage over the pie, I wasn't worshipping God. The object wasn't a threat; the pie isn't dangerous. The danger is the demons associated with the idol.

What do you think verse twenty-three from the above Scripture, means when it says, *All things are lawful for me, but not all things are helpful; all things are lawful for me, but not all things edify?* _____

_____

_____

_____

We have liberty, yes. We are not under the law; we can do whatever and still go to Heaven. Overeating and the desire to be thin is not a sin in itself (v23 all things are lawful...). What makes a sin a sin is how you feel about it. If you make something an idol, including the desire to be thin, you have placed it above God and are communing with demons.

Read: **Mark 12:30** *And you shall love the LORD your God with all your heart, with all your soul, with all your mind, and with all your strength. This is the first commandment.*

Love the Lord your God with all your heart. It's your soul that's hungry, not your stomach. Feed it with the Word of God. Go to your true God and worship at His feet. He will satisfy your needy soul.

Read: **Psalm 107:1-9**

In light of today's study, what was the Scripture or statement in today's lesson that most spoke to your heart? _____

_____

_____

What steps of faith does God want you to take towards Him today? _____

_____

_____

Rephrase the Scripture or statement into an expression of faith_____

_____

_____

Memorize the following Scripture this week.

I Corinthians 10: 31 _____, *whether you eat or drink, or* _____ *you do, do all to the* _____ *of God.*

Week 2 Day 2
Die to Your Will

Day _____ Date _____

Satan has deceived you into thinking that losing weight is the most important thing in your life. It's not. What is important is your purpose and destiny in Christ. Satan tries to convince you that you are no good to God being overweight. Satan is distracting you and stealing your spiritual identity. You are here for a purpose, and when you get all caught up in calories, carbohydrates, scales, fat grams, etc., it takes all your time.

The real mistake comes when you let Satan confuse, condemn, and keep you down. Ignore him; get busy doing the thing God put you in your generation to do. Get back up, get your mind off yourself. Praise Jesus for this freedom, ask Him for forgiveness, and forget it. Jesus never condemns you. He may show you where you are sinning, like He did with me when I was so in love with my pecan pie. He showed me that. So you can cry out to Him and ask for help, he doesn't condemn.

The dictionary defines the word condemn as, "To pronounce unfit for use."

Read how the King James Version interprets it.

Romans 7:8 (KJV) [8] *But sin, taking occasion by the commandment, wrought in me all manner of concupiscence. ([from dictionary.com]desire, (R.V., "coveting"); Col. 3:5 (R.V., "desire"). The "lust of concupiscence" denotes evil desire, indwelling sin.) For without the law sin was dead.* [11]*For sin, taking occasion by the commandment, deceived me, and by it slew me.*

(Text in brackets are from Dictionary.com)

What causes the compulsion to overeat? _____
_____
_____

The sin is not just overeating; it's also worrying about overeating or about being thin. It's a sin to overeat and it's also a sin to worry so much about your overeating. When we obsess about looking or being a certain way and don't trust God and His timing, we become fixated and distracted with the thing that takes up so much of our thought life. God wants you to be thin, but He also wants you to learn from being overweight and then teach others.

Completely give up dieting for the sole purpose of being thin. Completely give up condemning yourself for overeating. I know this is a scary concept. To just give it up and not be in control, but dieting has created the addiction. The more you try to diet, the fatter you get. Being overweight doesn't mean you are weaker than thin folks. It just means you have tried harder to lose weight. We need to let it go, and here is how you do that. Every time you eat, and even when you are thinking about eating, pray. Ask God to help you recognize when it's time to stop eating and to help you stop when you are satisfied. Then, and this is the hard part, die to your will.

Romans 8:36-39 *As it is written: "For Your sake we are killed all day long; We are accounted as sheep for the slaughter.*

[37] Yet in all these things we are more than conquerors through Him who loved us. [38] For I am persuaded that neither death nor life, nor angels nor principalities nor powers, nor things present nor things to come, [39] nor height nor depth, nor any other created thing, shall be able to separate us from the love of God which is in Christ Jesus our Lord.

What does the phrase "die to your will" mean to you? _____

_____

_____

_____

I Corinthians 6:12, 13 *All things are lawful for me, but all things are not helpful. All things are lawful for me, but I will not be brought under the power of any. [13] Foods for the stomach and the stomach for foods, but God will destroy both it and them. Now the body is not for sexual immorality but for the Lord, and the Lord for the body.*

And

I Corinthians 10:23 *All things are lawful for me, but not all things are helpful; all things are lawful for me, but not all things edify.*

When you get all caught up in dieting and your weight, it takes your focus off of your purpose. Not only that, but it also makes you feel condemned. Satan is getting a two-for-one, and he loves that.

Read **John 3:17** *For God did not send His Son into the world to condemn the world, but that the world through Him might be saved.*

Romans 8:1 *There is therefore now no condemnation to those who are in Christ Jesus, who do not walk according to the flesh, but according to the Spirit.*

Read **Colossians 2: 20-22** again, *Therefore, if you died with Christ from the basic principles of the world, why, as though living in the world, do you subject yourselves to regulations— [21] "Do not touch, do not taste, do not handle," [22] which all concern things which perish with the using— according to the commandments and doctrines of men?*

How many diets have you been on that didn't perish with use? When you first start a diet, you're filled with hope. You have faith knowing this is the one. Then about three weeks into it or so, you give up. You feel guilty, and for a time, you self-abuse and feel condemned and depressed… Then! You find a new diet and hurrah! You have hope again with a measure of success! Then boredom, a small slip…then failure…It's one of Satan's most successful schemes. He has you in the never-ending cycle and distracted from you real purpose.

You need to keep the positive thoughts going. Keep saying to yourself, "I am a new creation; that old person is dead. I am strong in Christ Jesus." Remember, when you were born again, you received the fruit of self-control. You need to have faith that you received it. Say, "I have self-control," and say it to yourself often. Put up little sticky notes to remind you to say it. Instead of being occupied with the diet and what you eat, be occupied with the goodness God has placed in you.

Philemon 1:6 *That the sharing of your faith may become effective by the acknowledgment of every good thing which is in you in Christ Jesus.*

It is so sad that, in the United States, people are more occupied with diets and thinness than ever before and we have never been fatter. As I mentioned earlier, one diet says to eat carbohydrates (sugar) and very little fat, and another diet declares eat only protein (fat) and very little sugar. Another diet says to only eat fat and carbohydrates in certain combinations and certain times a day. Talk about being occupied! All of these diets have doctors and experts who can, and will, substantiate their claims with an appearance of wisdom. God is not the author of confusion!

I Corinthians 14:33 *For God is not the author of confusion but of peace, as in all the churches of the saints.*

Jesus doesn't want us to be burdened by all these rules. That's why Jesus died so we don't need to live by laws and regulations. In reality, all these laws do is make us more engrossed on the forbidden, like the people in the previous study, at the resort who fished off the balcony.

Review **Colossians 2:23,** The last part of this passage holds the real key *²³These things indeed have an appearance of wisdom in self-imposed religion, false humility, and neglect of the body,* **but are of no value against the indulgence of the flesh.**

In your own words, express what the preceding passage mean to you. _____
_____
_____
_____
_____

All of these rules and regulations are of no value against the indulgence of the flesh. Consider the diets you have been on, have any of these "man-made" rules made you desire less food? _____

They all have an appearance of wisdom. It looks like those diets should be right because they are full of rules. These diets with rules and regulations about what you put into your body do little to change your heart. All they do is cover up the problem. They don't heal the wound. For instance, if I tried to clean up a computer virus by changing my monitor or reinstalling the Office programs, it wouldn't cure the virus. A bad computer virus usually means you have to wipe the whole hard drive and start new and clean.

It's hard to let go of all the rules and give control to God. It's hard to let Him wipe our hard drives clean. But when you try to fix your spiritual problem with non-spiritual remedies, you end up replacing one addiction for another. We have tried all the world has to offer; now it's time to turn to Jesus. He is the only one who can transform you and heal your wounded heart.

Read **Matthew 11:28-30** *Come to Me, all you who labor and are heavy laden, and I will give you rest. ²⁹ Take My yoke upon you and learn from Me, for I am gentle and lowly in heart, and you will find rest for your souls. ³⁰ For My yoke is easy and My burden is light."*

We are heavy laden by all the rules and regulation of dieting. In Jesus, we can have rest from the burden. Notice Jesus doesn't say learn *about* me, He says learn ***from*** me. That suggests a relationship.

In your own words, write what the phrase, "learn from me" means to you?

_____
_____
_____

How has your being overweight made you feel punished? _____
_____
_____
_____
_____
_____

We are a new creation in Christ. We no longer have to sin. Our old sin nature has been replaced by a new creation. You can say no to addictions and mean it. Let's see what the Bible has to say about this old sinful nature.

Read **Romans 6:1-23** *¹What shall we say then? Shall we continue in sin that grace may abound? ² Certainly not! How shall we who died to sin live any longer in it? ³ Or do you not know that as many of us as were baptized into Christ Jesus were baptized into His death? ⁴ Therefore we were buried with Him through baptism into death, that just as Christ was raised from the dead by the glory of the Father, even so we also should walk in newness of life. ⁵ For if we have been united together in the likeness of His death, certainly we also shall be in the likeness of His resurrection, ⁶ knowing this, that our old man was crucified with Him, that the body of sin might be done away with, that we should no longer be slaves of sin. ⁷ For he who has died has been freed from sin. ⁸ Now if we died with Christ, we believe that we shall also live with Him, ⁹ knowing that Christ, having been raised from the dead, dies no more. Death no longer has dominion over Him. ¹⁰ For the death that He died, He died to sin once for all; but the life that He lives, He lives to God. ¹¹ Likewise you also, reckon yourselves to be dead indeed to sin, but alive to God in Christ Jesus our Lord.*

¹² Therefore do not let sin reign in your mortal body, that you should obey it in its lusts. ¹³ And do not present your members as instruments of unrighteousness to sin, but present yourselves to God as being alive from the dead, and your members as instruments of righteousness to God. [14] For sin shall not have dominion over you, for you are not under law but under grace.

[15] What then? Shall we sin because we are not under law but under grace? Certainly not! [16] Do you not know that to whom you present yourselves slaves to obey, you are that one's slaves whom you obey, whether of sin leading to death, or of obedience leading to righteousness? [17] But God be thanked that though you were slaves of sin, yet you obeyed from the heart that form of doctrine to which you were delivered. [18] And having been set free from sin, you became slaves of righteousness. [19] I speak in human terms because of the weakness of your flesh. For just as you presented your members as slaves of uncleanness, and of lawlessness leading to more lawlessness, so now present your members as slaves of righteousness for holiness.

[20] For when you were slaves of sin, you were free in regard to righteousness. [21] What fruit did you have then in the things of which you are now ashamed? For the end of those things is death. [22] But now having been set free from sin, and having become slaves of God, you have your fruit to holiness, and the end, everlasting life. [23] For the wages of sin is death, but the gift of God is eternal life in Christ Jesus our Lord

List some of the fruits you gain by being a slave to Satan _____
_____
_____

Do you feel like a slave to overeating and your weight? _____

When I was obsessed with my weight, I didn't want to go any were or do anything. Nothing fit right, and I felt like people were thinking bad things about me. Being a slave to sin brings death, and always leads to bad things. Being a slave to God always leads to good things. Sin equals: fat, self-hate, fights.

List some of the fruits you gain by being a slave to God _____
_____
_____

By contrast righteousness equals: being thin, healthy, self-love, love of others, etc.

When sin has control, it affects your life and the life of your family, you want to stop, but you can't. You are a spiritual slave to it. Those who are without Christ are slaves to sin, but we who are believers in Christ are free from this bondage, because Jesus has set us free. When you are following Christ and doing His will, you feel full of vitality. Everything feels light and clean, and the whole world seems so much better. You have to receive this by faith.

Fill in the following blanks with the words, "me," and "I". **Romans 6:14** For *sin shall not have dominion over _____, for ____ isnot under law but under grace.*

The Bible says you are free from sin. It does not have power over you. The Bible says you are in control. You can decide to say, "I will resist." You have power and authority to say "NO!" Say the preceding Scripture to yourself and Satan whenever you feel helpless to resist his lies.

John 8:36 *Therefore if the Son makes you free, you shall be free indeed.*

This Scripture says we are free, yet we still hold on to the chains that used to bind us. The lock is broken, but we are holding the chains together because Satan has us convinced we are still bound by them. He is a liar, but we are not blameless. We allow him to convince us with a lie, because it gives us great excuses. Jesus makes it clear. We are without an excuse, and He has set us free.

Romans 1:20 *For since the creation of the world God's invisible qualities—his eternal power and divine nature—have been clearly seen, being understood from what has been made, so that men are without excuse.*

When you seek to gratify your own desire, you become a spiritual two-year-old. You want what you want when you want it! You are being prideful. You don't want to submit to God's plan for your life and that leads to death. We fight against this nature all the time, but there is a right and a wrong way to fight. It's only through faith we can be set free from this bondage and become a new creation in Christ. It's not rules, it's power.

Luke 9:23 *Then He said to them all, "If anyone desires to come after Me, let him deny himself, and take up his cross daily, and follow Me.*

When baptized unto Christ, it symbolizes the old man dying to self and arising as a new creation. There are many Scripture references on the new man. Read the ones I have listed, pray, and spend time in quiet meditation with God. Ask what He wants to show you.

READ Matthew 6 and Matthew 5:6

In light of today's study, what was the Scripture or statement in today's lesson that most spoke to your heart? _____

_____

_____

_____

What steps of faith does God want you to take towards Him today? _____

_____

_____

_____

Rephrase the Scripture or statement into an expression of faith_____

_____

_____

_____

Memorize the following Scripture this week.

I Corinthians 10: 31 *Therefore, whether you eat or drink, or whatever you do, do all to the glory of God.*

Week 2 Day 3
Jesus, Satan is Knocking. Will You Please Answer It?

Day _____ Date _____

In the last study, we learned that when we idolize food and obsess about our weight, we are actually communing with demons. I know this is upsetting, especially when you feel you are powerless to stop, but God has the answer. One of the reasons you are overweight is that while you are eating, you are in denial. When you are stuffing, you zone out. You set your rational thought aside, and just do it. Think about the moment you start to overeat. Your eating speeds up, because you zone out and tell yourself lies. You speed up because you want to get it down before rational thought returns.

Ephesians 4: 17-24 *This I say, therefore, and testify in the Lord, that you should no longer walk as the rest of the Gentiles walk, in the futility of their mind,* [18] *having their understanding darkened, being alienated from the life of God, because of the ignorance that is in them, because of the blindness of their heart;* [19] *who, being past feeling, have given themselves over to lewdness, to work all uncleanness with greediness.*

This study is about being present in the moment. In the next few lessons, we will learn, God fights our battles. You will be learning how to employ His power. The first thing you need to learn is how to be present in the moment. That's sounds like a new *"buzz word"* but what does it mean?

There is power in the moment, right now. Your present moment, this moment right now, shapes your future destiny and determines how long you will be your present weight.

I mindlessly gave up so many of my moments. Probably 95% of your excess weight is due to mindless eating. It's called rationalization when you're not in the moment (or reality).

The definition of rationalization is **1:** to make something irrational appear rational or reasonable **2:** to provide a natural explanation to (as a myth) **3:** to justify one's behavior or weakness **especially to oneself** **4:** to find plausible yet untrue reasons for conduct.

I don't know about you, but that hits home. This is how Satan gets you to sin. He supplies great excuses, and because we want the second cupcake, we are all too willing to go along with it.

So how do we stay in the moment? Think about a sin that would be preposterous for you, such as, committing murder, adultery, or shoplifting. Think of something that is not a temptation to you at all. Now think about what would happen if Satan tempted you with it. You would laugh at the temptation. You would pass it off in your mind as being ridiculous. You wouldn't even contemplate it. That's why Satan doesn't tempt you with those things. His method is to try to destroy you a little at a time. One little moment of weakness, one little suggestion, then another moment, and another suggestion. We all have weaknesses, and Satan will try everything until he finds it; then he exploits it.

God is all-powerful, but because He has given you free will, He won't do anything without your invitation and your faith. The battle is God's, but your part isn't a passive one. You're the one who pulls the trigger, and God is the bomb. Pulling the trigger is an emotional battle for you, because you want the stupid cupcake. You want to zone out and be numb, but after you activate God's power, it's easy.

How do you think you set God's power in motion? What is the trigger? _____
_____

You can set God's power in motion through faith, and prayer. Using the Word as your weapon, giving it to God, and thinking positively about God's power. You say, "God, Satan is knocking at the door. Will you please answer it?" If Satan is still nagging you with rationalizations, put your hand on your stomach. Ask yourself "am I hungry?" Be in the moment. If you're not hungry (don't rationalize), pray more. Satan makes it a bigger deal than it is.

Proverbs 14:16 A *wise man fears and departs from evil, But a fool rages and is self-confident.*

When Satan was tempting Jesus in the wilderness, he tried three times. He won't just go away after the first try. Stay in each moment, moment by moment. Thinking confidently about God's power, Satan will give up eventually.

James 4: 7-10 *Therefore submit to God. Resist the devil and he will flee from you.*

Bombard sin with prayer. Use the "shock and awe" war campaign against the enemy with bombs that are relentless. A typical scenario will be that you're going along great, you're following Jesus, and staying focused on Him. You're feeling wonderful, then you pop a mint in your mouth, which would be okay, other than you start to think it might be bad.

I Corinthians 6:12 All *things are lawful for me, but all things are not helpful. All things are lawful for me, but I will not be brought under the power of any.*

God wants you to understand this concept. He says almost the same thing again.

I Corinthians 10:23 *All things are lawful for me, but not all things are helpful; all things are lawful for me, but not all things edify.*

So now, Satan has a foothold and begins his sinister attack. Then you pop another mint and another. You say to yourself, "It's only a small candy, it won't hurt." Then you start to focus on the food, and love it because it becomes a forbidden fruit. Next comes an extra meal your stomach didn't ask for but you might be hungry!!! It's been an hour or two since your last meal, or your daughter brings home pizza after getting off work at the local pizza joint ,and you have already eaten dinner. How many times do you get the unexpected pleasure of pizza? You tell yourself, "I'll just have a sliver of a piece," and before you know it, you have eaten half a pizza one sliver at a time. You're right back where you started. Satan is saying "You've blown it now, anyway, I guess God can't help you after all." Then your positive thoughts start to become more and more negative, one little thought at a time.

Does this sound familiar? The moment the little suggestion is first made is the best time to take action, but you can take control at any time. A time a scenario like this takes place, you can take control with prayer and positive thoughts of God's power. Pray and ask God to forgive you. Think positive thoughts and just start fresh and new with that. Don't let it become the forbidden fruit. Honestly, the best way for me to do that has been to simply say/pray, "Jesus, Satan is knocking …"

You have a completely fresh moment to begin anew. Satan will come back, no doubt starting with something small and moving up. He will say that you've already blown it and might as well give up.

Job 7:17-18 *"What is man, that You should exalt him, That You should set Your heart on him, [18] That You should visit him every morning, And test him every moment?*

The secret formula is prayer using Scripture and faith (positive thinking) knowing that God will give you the power to resist. Just say no and ask God for help. Say, "God help me," and believe He will protect you from the pizza. Be present in the moment, and then walk away now! Just say no. If you can't get away, pray the whole time. On the other hand, if you don't want God's help because you want the pizza too much, ask God to help you ask for help. Say, "God right now I want this pizza. I don't want your help. Please help me to want your help." IT WORKS! IT WORKS! IT WORKS! Any temptation can be handled this way. God will not forsake you. All the fighting we do is so unnecessary if we could only get a sense of the power we possess through Jesus.

Wrong thinking goes like this. You see a tempting treat. You fight with yourself for a millisecond, but the way you fight is, "I have no self-control. I can't do it", and before you can ask God for strength (because you really want the treat) you stuff it in your mouth. You zone out with vague feelings of self-contempt.

Guess what! I have fabulous news! You do have self-control!

Read **Galatians 5:22-25** *But the fruit of the Spirit is love, joy, peace, longsuffering, kindness, goodness, faithfulness, [23] gentleness, self-control. Against such there is no law. [24] And those who are Christ's have crucified the flesh with its passions and desires. [25] If we live in the Spirit, let us also walk in the Spirit.*

One of the attributes of being saved is you get all the fruits of the Spirit automatically. You don't have to grow into them. They are yours. God won't make you take them, but they are yours if you will have them. You employ them by using your faith.

Read **Isaiah 40: 28-31** *Have you not known? Have you not heard? The everlasting God, the LORD, The Creator of the ends of the earth, Neither faints nor is weary. His understanding is unsearchable. [29] He gives power to the weak, And to those who have no might He increases strength. [30] Even the youths shall faint and be weary, And the young men shall utterly fall, [31] But those who wait on the LORD Shall renew their strength; They shall mount up with wings like eagles, They shall run and not be weary, They shall walk and not faint.*

Copy **Isaiah 40: 31** _____
_____
_____
_____
_____

What does it mean to wait on the Lord? In the Hebrew *"Wait"* is [1]*qavah,* which is translated as, *to wait, look for, hope, expect*

We try so hard to fix things when we are uncomfortable. We are like baby eaglets flapping our wings, working hard to fix our situation. Crying and wondering why God would do this to us. Temptation, like all trials, is a test. God made tests to help you expand your faith and identify areas you need help. Don't try to fight the temptation by flapping your wings and working hard. Rise above it wait for God. He will lift you up and rescue you.

When you are tempted, rise above it like an eagle. Eagles know when a storm is approaching before it breaks, and will fly high above the storm and wait for wind. When the storm hits, he sets his wings so the wind will pick him up and lift him above the storm. While the storm is raging below, he is soaring above the tempest in peace. He doesn't get away from the storm; he uses it to fly higher. He doesn't flap his wings straining to fly higher, he barely moves his wings at all.

It's hard to understand sometimes why God allows us to be tempted. We feel so weak. Just like a baby eagle who doesn't understand when the mom messes up his soft nest. She rips it to pieces until all the soft feather stuff is gone and all that's left is stickers and hard stuff. If that's not bad enough, the momma eagle pushes the baby out of the nest! The baby flaps furiously trying hard to fly, and when all seems lost, the momma swoops down and catches the baby on her back. She does this again and again until the baby eaglet learns to stop flapping and relax into the current. They glide side by side, effortlessly, rising higher and higher.

Read **Deuteronomy 32:11,12** *As an eagle stirs up its nest, Hovers over its young, Spreading out its wings, taking them up, Carrying them on its wings, [12] So the LORD alone led him, And there was no foreign god with him.*

Trying to fight Satan will exhaust you. Just say, "Jesus, Satan is knocking will you answer it?" Then glide away, knowing God has taken care of it. You will soar.

Deuteronomy 32: 13-17 *"He made him ride in the heights of the earth,*
That he might eat the produce of the fields;
He made him draw honey from the rock,
And oil from the flinty rock;

[14] Curds from the cattle, and milk of the flock,
With fat of lambs;
And rams of the breed of Bashan, and goats,
With the choicest wheat;
And you drank wine, the blood of the grapes.

[15] "But Jeshurun grew fat and kicked;
You grew fat, you grew thick,
You are obese!
Then he forsook God who made him,
And scornfully esteemed the Rock of his salvation.
[16] They provoked Him to jealousy with foreign gods;
With abominations they provoked Him to anger.

[17] They sacrificed to demons, not to God,
To gods they did not know,
To new gods, new arrivals
That your fathers did not fear.

When you were saved, you received the Holy Spirit, and one of the fruits, or attributes, of having the Holy Spirit is self-control. You see, Satan is a liar; he is the master of illusion, nothing more. That's what he does, and you have been listening to his lies for so long you believe them. It is time to counter those lies.

Your goal is to be thin, but you have to reach many little goals before you can accomplish your main goal. You are not going to wake up one day at your goal weight. Just as an eaglet learns a moment at a time, it will take many little battles and many little victories, one by one, moment by moment.

Isaiah 28:9, 10 *"Whom will he teach knowledge?*
And whom will he make to understand the message?
Those just weaned from milk?
Those just drawn from the breasts?

[10] For precept must be upon precept, precept upon precept,
Line upon line, line upon line,
Here a little, there a little."

Remember Satan will flee if you resist him, but he tried tempting Jesus three times before he gave up, and he didn't give up for good. The Bible says he went away, waiting for a more opportune moment.

Luke 4:12 13 *Now when the devil had ended every temptation, he departed from Him until an opportune time.*

God gave you a beautiful gift, and it is time to start treating your body, soul, and mind as such. Just as you wouldn't verbally attack your loved ones, you will not allow your inner talk to ridicule, put down, or in any way abuse you. It is time to stop now. The Holy Bible says you have self-control. When you're having a hard time pulling away from that last bite, say to yourself, "I have self-control because I have the Holy Spirit."

II Chronicles 20:14-17 *Then the Spirit of the LORD came upon Jahaziel the son of Zechariah, the son of Benaiah, the son of Jeiel, the son of Mattaniah, a Levite of the sons of Asaph, in the midst of the assembly. [15] And he said, "Listen, all you of Judah and you inhabitants of Jerusalem, and you, King Jehoshaphat! <u>Thus says the LORD to you: 'Do not be afraid nor dismayed because of this great multitude,</u> **for the battle is not yours, but God's**. [16] Tomorrow go down against them. They will surely come up by the Ascent of Ziz, and you will find them at the end of the brook before the Wilderness of Jeruel. [17] You will not need to fight in this battle. Position yourselves,* **<u>stand still and see the salvation of the LORD</u>**.

Say, "Lord, Satan is knocking. Will you please answer it?" Let's see how God answers the door.

II Kings 6: 8-18 *Now the king of Syria was making war against Israel; and he consulted with his servants, saying, "My camp will be in such and such a place." [9] And the man of God sent to the king of Israel, saying, "Beware that you do not pass this place, for the Syrians are coming down there." [10] Then the king of Israel sent someone to the place of which the man of God had told him. Thus he warned him, and he was watchful there, not just once or twice.*
[11] Therefore the heart of the king of Syria was greatly troubled by this thing; and he called his servants and said to them, "Will you not show me which of us is for the king of Israel?"

[12] And one of his servants said, "None, my lord, O king; but Elisha, the prophet who is in Israel, tells the king of Israel the words that you speak in your bedroom."

[13] So he said, "Go and see where he is, that I may send and get him."
And it was told him, saying, "Surely he is in Dothan."

[14] Therefore he sent horses and chariots and a great army there, and they came by night and surrounded the city. [15] And when the servant of the man of God arose early and went out, there was an army, surrounding the city with horses and chariots. And his servant said to him, "Alas, my master! What shall we do?"

[16] So he answered, "Do not fear, for those who are with us are more than those who are with them." [17] And Elisha prayed, and said, "LORD, I pray, open his eyes that he may see." Then the

LORD opened the eyes of the young man, and he saw. And behold, the mountain was full of horses and chariots of fire all around Elisha. [18] So when the Syrians came down to him, Elisha prayed to the LORD, and said, "Strike this people, I pray, with blindness." And He struck them with blindness according to the word of Elisha.

You are God's child, just as Elisha was. He never changes and He is still fighting the enemy with chariots of fire. He answers the door with strength and power.

Genesis 14:11-16 *Now the Valley of Siddim was full of asphalt pits; and the kings of Sodom and Gomorrah fled; some fell there, and the remainder fled to the mountains. [11] Then they took all the goods of Sodom and Gomorrah, and all their provisions, and went their way. [12] They also took Lot, Abram's brother's son who dwelt in Sodom, and his goods, and departed.*

[13] Then one who had escaped came and told Abram the Hebrew, for he dwelt by the terebinth trees of Mamre the Amorite, brother of Eshcol and brother of Aner; and they were allies with Abram. [14] Now when Abram heard that his brother was taken captive, he armed his three hundred and eighteen trained servants who were born in his own house, and went in pursuit as far as Dan. [15] He divided his forces against them by night, and he and his servants attacked them and pursued them as far as Hobah, which is north of Damascus. [16] So he brought back all the goods, and also brought back his brother Lot and his goods, as well as the women and the people.

[17] And the king of Sodom went out to meet him at the Valley of Shaveh (that is, the King's Valley), after his return from the defeat of Chedorlaomer and the kings who were with him.

What do all the Scriptures above have in common with each other? _____

_____

They were all small armies defended by God through faith.

When I would hear the phrase "leave it at the cross," I thought it meant to stop sinning, give the sin to God, and don't pick it back up. I used to get so upset with myself because I couldn't leave the sin at the cross and not pick it back up. I was addicted. Then I realized I had the phrase wrong. The phrase means to accept any answer from God. If God answers your prayer and stops you from overeating, praise Him. If He doesn't, and you continue to overeat, praise Him. This is why this is the hard part. It may not be God's will for you to be thin *yet.* He may want to teach you something first. I say "yet," because I don't believe God wants us to die addicted to anything, but you can't do it on your own. Trying just makes you want it more. Surrender it to God's will and be free from self-condemnation. Have faith in God, and know He has your best interest at heart. The good thing is this takes all the pressure off you. You are giving it to God, and therefore not obsessing over the *law.* Eventually food will become a non-issue for you because it loses its magnetism when it's no longer the forbidden fruit.

Read **Matthew 7: 7-10** *"Ask, and it will be given to you; seek, and you will find; knock, and it will be opened to you. [8] For everyone who asks receives, and he who seeks finds, and to him who knocks it will be opened. [9] Or what man is there among you who, if his son asks for bread, will* *give him a stone? [10] Or if he asks for a fish, will he give him a serpent? [11] If you then, being evil, know how to give good gifts to your children, how much more will your Father who is in Heaven give good things to those who ask Him.*

What purpose would it serve your Father in Heaven if He let you down? The only hard part is breaking through the emotional barrier of wanting His help, or sometimes it's hard to believe God wants to help you.

Read **I Corinthians 10**

In light of today's study, what was the Scripture or statement in today's lesson that most spoke to your heart? _____
_____
_____
_____

What steps of faith does God want you to take towards Him today? _____
_____
_____
_____

Rephrase the Scripture or statement into an expression of faith_____
_____
_____
_____

I Corinthians 10: 31 _____, _____ *you* _____ *or* _____, *or* _____ *you do, do* _____ *to the* _____ *of God.*

[1] Strong's H6960 - *qavah*

Week 2 Day 4
Love the Lord with all your heart

Day _____ Date _____

Matthew 12:30 *And you shall **love** the **LORD** your God with all your heart, with all your soul, with all your mind, and with all your strength.' This is the first commandment.*

God doesn't care so much about what your scale says. He is concerned that your weight is a manifestation of the condition of your heart and what you have been running to for comfort and satisfaction. God is not as concerned about the shape of your body as He is the condition of your heart. What we look like is of vital importance to the world, and we Christians have bought into the lie. We have to run to God for affirmation of our worth, not the mirror and food.

Read **II Corinthians 1: 3-4** *Blessed be the God and Father of our Lord Jesus Christ, the Father of mercies and God of all comfort, [4] who comforts us in all our tribulation, that we may be able to comfort those who are in any trouble, with the comfort with which we ourselves are comforted by God.*

II Corinthians 5:9 (NIV) Says, *So we make it our goal to please him, whether we are at home in the body or away from it.*

I love studying different versions of the Bible. It really gives me a clearer picture of what God is saying. Read the above Scripture in the Message version.

II Corinthians 5:9 *But neither exile nor homecoming is the main thing. Cheerfully pleasing God is the main thing, and that's what we aim to do.*

What is your goal? Be honest with yourself. What is your true purpose for losing weight?

_____
_____
_____
_____

Is your desire to be thin because you want to earn the respect of others? Do you think "they" will love you more? Most people, if they are honest with themselves, admit their motivation for dieting is to look better and no wonder! We are under so much pressure to be perfect. We are assaulted twenty-four hours a day from TV and magazines.

The Bible says seek first the kingdom of God and His righteousness and all these things will be added to you.

Read **Matthew 7:7,8** *"Ask, and it will be given to you; seek, and you will find; knock, and it will be opened to you. [8] For everyone who asks receives, and he who seeks finds, and to him who knocks it will be opened.*

Make it a priority to heal spiritually first, and then the physical will follow. Seeking and knocking may take some time. Wait for it.

An apple tree doesn't strain and groan to get the fruit out. It automatically bears fruit if fed, watered, and if it gets plenty of sunshine. To grow in the Lord, you have to spend time reading the Word and getting to know Jesus by going to church and listening to Christian music. Filling your life and mind with the One who loves you isn't an option. It's a requirement.

John 15:5-8 *"I am the vine, you are the branches. He who abides in Me, and I in him, bears much fruit; for without Me you can do nothing. [6] If anyone does not abide in Me, he is cast out as a branch and is withered; and they gather them and throw them into the fire, and they are burned. [7] If you abide in Me, and My words abide in you, you will ask what you desire, and it shall be done for you. [8] By this My Father is glorified, that you bear much fruit; so you will be My disciples.*

And

James 4: 7-10 *Therefore submit to God. Resist the devil and he will flee from you. [8] Draw near to God and He will draw near to you. Cleanse your hands, you sinners; and purify your hearts, you double-minded. [9] Lament and mourn and weep! Let your laughter be turned to mourning and your joy to gloom. [10] Humble yourselves in the sight of the Lord, and He will lift you up.*

Reject dieting for the purpose of weight loss only. Unlike all the other diets I have been on, the bottom line of this diet is moderation. You don't need to worry about what you eat or how you eat it. You can use that time to fall in love with Jesus.

How do you think you fall in love with Him? How *do* you draw near to God?

_____

_____

_____

You draw near to God by getting to know Him! Spending time with Him. Reading His Word.

Use your own Bible, and write down the following passages:

Philippians 2:3, _____

_____

_____

Psalm 37: 4, _____

_____

_____

Use your own Bible, and fill in the blanks **Romans 8:5-9** _____

_____

_____

_____ _For to be carnally minded is death, but to be spiritually minded is life and peace._ [7] _Because the carnal mind is enmity against God; for it is not subject to the law of God, nor indeed can be._ [8] _So then, those who are in the flesh cannot please God._ [9] _But you are not in the flesh but in the Spirit, if indeed the Spirit of God dwells in you. Now if anyone does not have the Spirit of Christ, he is not His._

What do all these passages have in common? _____

_____

_____

They are all in regards to God being first in your life. Seeking Him and getting to know Him. Acknowledging Him as your Master, accepting the fact that He knows what is best for you, and then He will give you the desires of your heart. He knows what you truly desire better than you do.

When you get to know Jesus through reading His word and spending time with Him, the Holy Spirit will breathe new life and truth into your entire being. You will discover amazing strength when you're empowered by the Holy Spirit. Stop trying to change your eating habits in your own strength. We have read that we are the branches and He is the vine. It's not about you; it's about your ministry and what God has planned for your life. We need to stop wasting so much time worrying about our health, and get busy doing what God has purposed for our lives! He is our life source. Do you believe it?

I think many of us who are overweight, think it's our lot in life, our cross to bear. That's a lie from Satan. We all have to fight the tendency to sin, and gluttony is a sin. Some people may have the tendency toward pornography or homosexuality. You wouldn't think it is okay for them to ruin their lives. By the same token, you wouldn't expect a person to be able to fix it on their own power, just switch off their desire. Neither can you. You need to run to Jesus.

Read **Romans 8:1-17**

In light of today's study, what was the Scripture or statement in today's lesson that most spoke to your heart? _____

_____

_____

_____

What steps of faith does God want you to take towards Him today? _____

_____

_____

_____

Rephrase the Scripture or statement into an expression of faith_____

_____

_____

_____

I Corinthians 10: 31 *Therefore, _____ you _____ or _____ , or _____ you do, do _____ to the _____ of _____ .*

Week 2 Day 5
A way out

Day _____ Date _____

God says that when we are tempted, it is danger, a bad thing. However, when we overeat, we call it "treating ourselves." It's such an illustration of how Satan skews things. It's not a treat. It's hazardous, a soul-eating menace, and we need to escape from it. Run from temptation and escape, because it has wrenching, painful consequences.

The definition of escape is: to get free or away; to avoid a threatening evil; flight from, or avoidance of something unpleasant.

Read **I Corinthians 10:13** *No temptation has overtaken you except such as is common to man; but God is faithful, who will not allow you to be tempted beyond what you are able, but with the temptation will also make the way of escape, that you may be able to bear it.*

Now fill in the blanks with your name.

No temptation has overtaken _____ except which is common to man; but God is faithful, who will not allow _____ to be tempted beyond what _____ is able, but with the temptation will also make the way of escape, that _____ may be able to bear it.

This is a promise from God! To _____!

God does make a way of escape. Sometimes these escapes are blatant, and you can see them for what they are if you're looking. Praying before you eat and asking God to reveal those ways of escape will ensure that you recognize them. When you are being tempted, ask Jesus to let you see and understand the way of escape.

My pecan pie episode, for instance, was an escape. Sometimes the way of escape is blatant; you might drop food down the front of your shirt. Other times the escapes are more subtle, such as a small check in your spirit that makes you want to try to justify the next bite. God is faithful in this, but you have to watch for the way out and don't harden your heart to it when it happens. When you harden your heart to God's prompting, it makes it easier to ignore Him the next time. That could lead you to backslide, because it gives Satan a foothold. You could be right back right back where you started, or worse, because now your faith is damaged.

Matthew 12:43-45 *"When an unclean spirit goes out of a man, he goes through dry places, seeking rest, and finds none. [44] Then he says, 'I will return to my house from which I came.' And when he comes, he finds it empty, swept, and put in order. [45] Then he goes and takes with him seven other spirits more wicked than himself, and they enter and dwell there; and the last state of that man is worse than the first. So shall it also be with this wicked generation."*

The Lord will rescue you from these temptations. Remember they are tests. Tests are given to examine what you have learned and so you may build your faith. Sometimes a temptation is like a pop quiz; it will seize you when you're off guard. That's when you should call out to God and tell Him, "I am weak, Lord, and you are so strong. Help me. I want an extra bite of this delicious food, and I can't resist it."

Remind yourself that He is the vine, you are the branch, and you can't do anything without Him **(John 15:5)**. Recite Scripture to yourself and say, "I believe in You **(Hebrews 11:6).** I believe, greater is He that is in me than he that is in the world **(I John 4:4)**. I believe You will make a way out **(I Corinthians 10:13)**. I believe Your weapons are mighty in demolishing strongholds **(II Corinthians 10:3-6)**. I believe I can run and not grow weary **(Isaiah 40:31)**. I believe I am righteous through Him, **(II Corinthians 5:21),** and Jesus will never permit you to be moved **(Psalm 55:22)**."

I have done this countless times in just this same way, and I'll find myself sort of playing with my food and walking to the sink to throw it down the disposal. When I pray like this, I feel a strong rush of God's mighty power surging through me.

You don't have to use my exact words. Just acknowledge you are out of control and can't handle the situation. Use Scripture and He will quickly come to your rescue. I can testify when I have prayed this way in faith, God has never let me down. However, there have been times when I asked God to help me, and He rushed to rescue me, but I still insisted on my way and exercised my will over His. I had hardened my heart and made it easier for Satan to get a foothold the next time.

Read from your own Bible, and then write down the following Scriptures:

Psalm 55:22 _____
_____
_____

Isaiah 40:29 _____
_____
_____

Isaiah 40: 31 _____
_____
_____

How does the Bible tell us to fight the tendency to sin? _____
_____
_____

You fight the tendency to sin by running to God, using His Word with authority and faith, understanding that it's His power at work, not your willpower.

I have started **II Corinthians 3:4-5** finish the Scripture by filling in the blanks, using your own Bible.

And we have such trust through Christ toward God ⁵ _____

_____

_____

_____

In any of the Scriptures above, does it ever say you are required to stand and fight Satan on our own strength or willpower? _____

You can't! It's impossible. Satan is too cunning. You can't defeat him on your own.

Read **Jude** 9-11: *Yet Michael the archangel, in contending with the devil, when he disputed about the body of Moses, dared not bring against him a reviling accusation, but said, "The Lord rebuke you!"* ¹⁰ *but these speak evil of whatever they do not know; and whatever they know naturally, like brute beasts, in these things they corrupt themselves.*

And

II Tim 4:18 says; *And the Lord will deliver me from every evil work and preserve me for His heavenly kingdom. To Him be glory forever and ever. Amen!*

Psalm 61:1- 4 *Hear my cry, O God; Attend to my prayer.* ² *From the end of the earth I will cry to You, When my heart is overwhelmed; Lead me to the rock that is higher than I.* ³ *For You have been a shelter for me, A strong tower from the enemy.* ⁴ *I will abide in Your tabernacle forever; I will trust in the shelter of Your wings. Selah*

According to the passages, you have just read how are we to approach an attack? _____

_____

_____

Run away from the sin and run to your Father. Trust God to shelter you. Your responsibility in the battle is to ask for help and believe in that power. The hard part is to break through the emotional barrier of "I want it" or in other words, your will. Once you submit your will and ask God for help, He is right there. All the previous Scriptures, and there are many more than these, are all promises God made to you.

Fill in the blanks: **Hebrews 4:14-16** _____

_____

_____ *¹⁵ For we do not have a High Priest who cannot sympathize with our Weaknesses, but was in all points tempted as we are, yet without sin. ¹⁶ Let us therefore come boldly to the throne of grace, that we may obtain mercy and find grace to help in time of need.*

Romans 8: 26_____

_____

_____

_____ *²⁷ Now He who searches the hearts knows what the mind of the Spirit is, because He makes intercession for the saints according to the will of God.*

II Corinthians 12:9, 10 _____

_____

_____ *¹⁰ Therefore I take pleasure in infirmities, in reproaches, in needs, in persecutions, in distresses, for Christ's sake. For when I am weak, then I am strong.*

What does God think about our weakness? _____

_____

God doesn't love you any less when you make mistakes. He wants you to know He understands your weaknesses.

I heard a sermon once; The Pastor took a one-hundred dollar bill out of his pocket. He asked his audience "How much is this worth, a hundred dollars right?" We all agreed with him. Then he crumpled it up and said, "How much is it worth now?" Then he threw it on the ground and stomped on it a few times and he asked "How much is it worth now?" Then he kicked it around for a while. Anyway I think you get the idea. We are not worth any less to God if we make a mistake. He loves you, and He will make a way out. You have to train yourself to look for them. If you're eating and you get a phone call, that could be your way out. You may even find something gross like a hair. As long as you are praying and asking God for help, you will be sensitive to these prompts.

Read: **John 10:25-29**

In light of today's study, what was the Scripture or statement in today's lesson that most spoke to your heart? _____

_____

_____

_____

What steps of faith does God want you to take towards Him today? _____

_____

_____

_____

Rephrase the Scripture or statement into an expression of faith_____

_____

_____

_____

I Corinthians 10: 31 _____

_____

_____

Week 3 Day 1
Faith and the Spies of Canaan

Day _____ Date _____

Faith is belief in, or a confident attitude toward, God that requires a commitment to His will in our life. It is taking God at His word and acting upon it.

According to Dictionary.com, the definition of sin is an offense, especially against God; Fault a weakened state of human nature in which the self is estranged from God.

How do you think we become estranged from God? _____
_____
_____
_____

It isn't God who moves away or loves us less. There have been times when I have felt so far from God, and I didn't know why. When I finally examined myself, I found I was harboring sin. I suppose I felt guilty and blamed God for my sin. Sin makes us feel separated from God, and in a way, we are. When you feel this way remember, it's not God who has moved. He is still on the chosen path, and we have strayed away.

Why do we sin? We all know intellectually that God's path is best possible one, so why do we choose to sin?

Let's examine some of the Ten Commandments and try to identify some of the reasons we prefer to become our own gods by choosing our own path.

- Coveting: lack of faith in God, that He won't give us what we desire
- False witness: Afraid if you tell the truth God won't take care of it
- Stealing: lack of faith that God will provide for your needs.
- Adultery: lack of faith that God has given you the best person to share your life with, or that you are missing something.
- Taking God's name in vain: lack of faith in his superiority and lack of respect.
- Idolatry: lack of faith in God as a provider of all your needs

Can most of our sin can be defined as lack of faith? _____

Faith isn't giving God a list of things you want, faith is trusting that God knows what is best for you and will provide it.

Hebrews 11:6 *But without faith it is impossible to please Him, for he who comes to God must believe that He is, and that He is a rewarder of those who diligently seek Him.*

Romans 14: 23 *But he who doubts is condemned if he eats, because he does not eat from faith; **for whatever is not from faith is sin**.*

Philippians 4:19 *And my God shall supply all your need according to His riches in glory by Christ Jesus.*

There were two times Moses sent spies to investigate the Promised Land, Canaan, let's study the differences between the two examples

Read: **Numbers chapters 13 and 14** *And the LORD spoke to Moses, saying,* [2] *"Send men to spy out the land of Canaan, which I am giving to the children of Israel; from each tribe of their fathers you shall send a man, every one a leader among them."*

[3] *So Moses sent them from the Wilderness of Paran according to the command of the LORD, all of them men who were heads of the children of Israel.* [4] *Now these were their names: from the tribe of Reuben, Shammua the son of Zaccur;* [5] *from the tribe of Simeon, Shaphat the son of Hori;* [6] *from the tribe of Judah, Caleb the son of Jephunneh;* [7] *from the tribe of Issachar, Igal the son of Joseph;* [8] *from the tribe of Ephraim, Hoshea the son of Nun;* [9] *from the tribe of Benjamin, Palti the son of Raphu;* [10] *from the tribe of Zebulun, Gaddiel the son of Sodi;* [11] *from the tribe of Joseph, that is, from the tribe of Manasseh, Gaddi the son of Susi;* [12] *from the tribe of Dan, Ammiel the son of Gemalli;* [13] *from the tribe of Asher, Sethur the son of Michael;* [14] *from the tribe of Naphtali, Nahbi the son of Vophsi;* [15] *from the tribe of Gad, Geuel the son of Machi.*

[16] *These are the names of the men whom Moses sent to spy out the land. And Moses called Hoshea the son of Nun, Joshua.*

[17] *Then Moses sent them to spy out the land of Canaan, and said to them, "Go up this way into the South, and go up to the mountains,* [18] *and see what the land is like: whether the people who dwell in it are strong or weak, few or many;* [19] *whether the land they dwell in is good or bad; whether the cities they inhabit are like camps or strongholds;* [20] *whether the land is rich or poor; and whether there are forests there or not. Be of good courage. And bring some of the fruit of the land." Now the time was the season of the first ripe grapes.*

[21] *So they went up and spied out the land from the Wilderness of Zin as far as Rehob, near the entrance of Hamath.* [22] *And they went up through the South and came to Hebron; Ahiman, Sheshai, and Talmai, the descendants of Anak, were there. (Now Hebron was built seven years before Zoan in Egypt.)* [23] *Then they came to the Valley of Eshcol, and there cut down a branch with one cluster of grapes; they carried it between two of them on a pole. They also brought some of the pomegranates and figs.* [24] *The place was called the Valley of Eshcol, because of the cluster which the men of Israel cut down there.* [25] *And they returned from spying out the land after forty days.*

[26] *Now they departed and came back to Moses and Aaron and all the congregation of the children of Israel in the Wilderness of Paran, at Kadesh; they brought back word to them and to all the congregation, and showed them the fruit of the land.* [27] *Then they told him, and said: "We went to the land where you sent us. It truly flows with milk and honey, and this is its fruit.* [28] *Nevertheless the people who dwell in the land are strong; the cities are fortified and very large; moreover we saw the descendants of Anak there.* [29] *The Amalekites dwell in the land of the*

South; the Hittites, the Jebusites, and the Amorites dwell in the mountains; and the Canaanites dwell by the sea and along the banks of the Jordan."

³⁰ Then Caleb quieted the people before Moses, and said, "Let us go up at once and take possession, for we are well able to overcome it."

³¹ But the men who had gone up with him said, "We are not able to go up against the people, for they are stronger than we." ³² And they gave the children of Israel a bad report of the land which they had spied out, saying, "The land through which we have gone as spies is a land that devours its inhabitants, and all the people whom we saw in it are men of great stature. ³³ There we saw the giants (the descendants of Anak came from the giants); and we were like grasshoppers in our own sight, and so we were in their sight."

Numbers Chapter 14 *So all the congregation lifted up their voices and cried, and the people wept that night. ² And all the children of Israel complained against Moses and Aaron, and the whole congregation said to them, "If only we had died in the land of Egypt! Or if only we had died in this wilderness! ³ Why has the LORD brought us to this land to fall by the sword, that our wives and children should become victims? Would it not be better for us to return to Egypt?" ⁴ So they said to one another, "Let us select a leader and return to Egypt."*

⁵ Then Moses and Aaron fell on their faces before all the assembly of the congregation of the children of Israel.

⁶ But Joshua the son of Nun and Caleb the son of Jephunneh, who were among those who had spied out the land, tore their clothes; ⁷ and they spoke to all the congregation of the children of Israel, saying: "The land we passed through to spy out is an exceedingly good land. ⁸ If the LORD delights in us, then He will bring us into this land and give it to us, "a land which flows with milk and honey. ⁹ Only do not rebel against the LORD, nor fear the people of the land, for they are our bread; their protection has departed from them, and the LORD is with us. Do not fear them."

¹⁰ And all the congregation said to stone them with stones. Now the glory of the LORD appeared in the tabernacle of meeting before all the children of Israel.

¹¹ Then the LORD said to Moses: "How long will these people reject Me? And how long will they not believe Me, with all the signs which I have performed among them? ¹² I will strike them with the pestilence and disinherit them, and I will make of you a nation greater and mightier than they."

¹³ And Moses said to the LORD: "Then the Egyptians will hear it, for by Your might You brought these people up from among them, ¹⁴ and they will tell it to the inhabitants of this land. They have heard that You, LORD, are among these people; that You, LORD, are seen face to face and Your cloud stands above them, and You go before them in a pillar of cloud by day and in a pillar of fire by night. ¹⁵ Now if You kill these people as one man, then the nations which have heard of Your fame will speak, saying, ¹⁶ "Because the LORD was not able to bring this people to the land which He swore to give them, therefore He killed them in the wilderness." ¹⁷ And now, I pray, let the power of my Lord be great, just as You have spoken, saying, [18] "The LORD is longsuffering and abundant in mercy, forgiving iniquity and transgression; but He by no means clears the guilty, visiting the iniquity of the fathers on the children to the third and fourth generation. [19] Pardon the iniquity of this people, I pray, according to the greatness of Your mercy, just as You have forgiven this people, from Egypt even until now."

[20] Then the LORD said: "I have pardoned, according to your word; [21] but truly, as I live, all the earth shall be filled with the glory of the LORD-- [22] because all these men who have seen My glory and the signs which I did in Egypt and in the wilderness, and have put Me to the test now these ten times, and have not heeded My voice, [23] they certainly shall not see the land of which I swore to their fathers, nor shall any of those who rejected Me see it. [24] But My servant Caleb, because he has a different spirit in him and has followed Me fully, I will bring into the land where he went, and his descendants shall inherit it. [25] Now the Amalekites and the Canaanites dwell in the valley; tomorrow turn and move out into the wilderness by the Way of the Red Sea."

[26] And the LORD spoke to Moses and Aaron, saying, [27] "How long shall I bear with this evil congregation who complain against Me? I have heard the complaints which the children of Israel make against Me. [28] Say to them, "As I live,' says the LORD, "just as you have spoken in My hearing, so I will do to you: [29] The carcasses of you who have complained against Me shall fall in this wilderness, all of you who were numbered, according to your entire number, from twenty years old and above. [30] Except for Caleb the son of Jephunneh and Joshua the son of Nun, you shall by no means enter the land which I swore I would make you dwell in. [31] But your little ones, whom you said would be victims, I will bring in, and they shall know the land which you have despised. [32] But as for you, your carcasses shall fall in this wilderness. [33] And your sons shall be shepherds in the wilderness forty years, and bear the brunt of your infidelity, until your carcasses are consumed in the wilderness. [34] According to the number of the days in which you spied out the land, forty days, for each day you shall bear your guilt one year, namely forty years, and you shall know My rejection. [35] I the LORD have spoken this. I will surely do so to all this evil congregation who are gathered together against Me. In this wilderness they shall be consumed, and there they shall die."'

[36] Now the men whom Moses sent to spy out the land, who returned and made all the congregation complain against him by bringing a bad report of the land, [37] those very men who brought the evil report about the land, died by the plague before the LORD. [38] But Joshua the son of Nun and Caleb the son of Jephunneh remained alive, of the men who went to spy out the land.

[39] Then Moses told these words to all the children of Israel, and the people mourned greatly. [40] And they rose early in the morning and went up to the top of the mountain, saying, "Here we are, and we will go up to the place which the LORD has promised, for we have sinned!"

[41] And Moses said, "Now why do you transgress the command of the LORD? For this will not succeed. [42] Do not go up, lest you be defeated by your enemies, for the LORD is not among you. [43] For the Amalekites and the Canaanites are there before you, and you shall fall by the sword; because you have turned away from the LORD, the LORD will not be with you."

44 But they presumed to go up to the mountaintop. Nevertheless, neither the ark of the covenant of the LORD nor Moses departed from the camp. 45 Then the Amalekites and the Canaanites who dwelt in that mountain came down and attacked them, and drove them back as far as Hormah.

The children of Israel wandered for forty years, a trip that should have taken about twelve days. The first time Moses sent spies into the Promised Land, they were looking at the future battle through their own strength, and because of their lack of faith in God, and God said they were rejecting Him. Now see what happened after they had been wandering and learning about God for forty years.

40 Years Later:

Joshua Chapter Two; *1Now Joshua the son of Nun sent out two men from Acacia Grove to spy secretly, saying, "Go, view the land, especially Jericho."*
So they went, and came to the house of a harlot named Rahab, and lodged there. 2 And it was told the king of Jericho, saying, "Behold, men have come here tonight from the children of Israel to search out the country."

3 So the king of Jericho sent to Rahab, saying, "Bring out the men who have come to you, who have entered your house, for they have come to search out all the country."

4 Then the woman took the two men and hid them. So she said, "Yes, the men came to me, but I did not know where they were from. 5 And it happened as the gate was being shut, when it was dark, that the men went out. Where the men went I do not know; pursue them quickly, for you may overtake them." 6 (But she had brought them up to the roof and hidden them with the stalks of flax, which she had laid in order on the roof.) 7 Then the men pursued them by the road to the Jordan, to the fords. And as soon as those who pursued them had gone out, they shut the gate.

8 Now before they lay down, she came up to them on the roof, 9 and said to the men: "I know that the LORD has given you the land, that the terror of you has fallen on us, and that all the inhabitants of the land are fainthearted because of you. 10 For we have heard how the LORD dried up the water of the Red Sea for you when you came out of Egypt, and what you did to the two kings of the Amorites who were on the other side of the Jordan, Sihon and Og, whom you utterly destroyed. 11 And as soon as we heard these things, our hearts melted; neither did there remain any more courage in anyone because of you, for the LORD your God, He is God in Heaven above and on earth beneath. 12 Now therefore, I beg you, swear to me by the LORD, since I have shown you kindness, that you also will show kindness to my father's house, and give me a true token, 13 and spare my father, my mother, my brothers, my sisters, and all that they have, and deliver our lives from death."

14 So the men answered her, "Our lives for yours, if none of you tell this business of ours. And it shall be, when the LORD has given us the land, that we will deal kindly and truly with you." 15 Then she let them down by a rope through the window, for her house was on the city wall; she dwelt on the wall. 16 And she said to them, "Get to the mountain, lest the pursuers meet you. Hide there three days, until the pursuers have returned. Afterward you may go your way."

[17] So the men said to her: "We will be blameless of this oath of yours which you have made us swear, [18] unless, when we come into the land, you bind this line of scarlet cord in the window through which you let us down, and unless you bring your father, your mother, your brothers, and all your father's household to your own home. [19] So it shall be that whoever goes outside the doors of your house into the street, his blood shall be on his own head, and we will be guiltless. And whoever is with you in the house, his blood shall be on our head if a hand is laid on him. [20] And if you tell this business of ours, then we will be free from your oath which you made us swear." [21] Then she said, "According to your words, so be it." And she sent them away, and they departed. And she bound the scarlet cord in the window.

[22] They departed and went to the mountain, and stayed there three days until the pursuers returned. The pursuers sought them all along the way, but did not find them. [23] So the two men returned, descended from the mountain, and crossed over; and they came to Joshua the son of Nun, and told him all that had befallen them. [24] And they said to Joshua, "Truly the LORD has delivered all the land into our hands, for indeed all the inhabitants of the country are fainthearted because of us."

You know the rest of the story. The Hebrews marched around the walls seven times and they crumbled. God demolished that stronghold. The only thing His people had to do was praise His holy name.

Read **Numbers 13:33** again. *[33]There we saw the giants (the descendants of Anak came from the giants); and we were like grasshoppers in our own sight, and so we were in their sight."*

Who were the Israelites depending on to win this battle? _____

What did the enemy look like compared to them? _____

Now read **Joshua 2:8** *Now before they lay down, she came up to them on the roof, [9] and said to the men: "I know that the LORD has given you the land, that the terror of you has fallen on us, and that all the inhabitants of the land are fainthearted because of you. [10] For we have heard how the LORD dried up the water of the Red Sea for you when you came out of Egypt, and what you did to the two kings of the Amorites who were on the other side of the Jordan, Sihon and Og, whom you utterly destroyed. [11] And as soon as we heard these things, our hearts melted; neither did there remain any more courage in anyone because of you, for the LORD your God, He is God in Heaven above and on earth beneath.*

And

Joshua 2:24 again; *[24] And they said to Joshua, "Truly the LORD has delivered all the land into our hands, for indeed all the inhabitants of the country are fainthearted because of us."*

Who did the Israelites depend on to win this battle? _____

What did the enemy look like compared to them? _____

_____

In your own words, explain what made the difference in the two times the spies were sent out to scout out the Promised Land. _____

_____

_____

I believe this second generation grew up depending on the Lord for everything. They didn't have the Egypt baggage of "I can't." They had faith in God's power, not their own "God can." In both instances the enemy was the same and had already been defeated by God. The only thing that was left was to go in and possess the land by faith.

Look at **Joshua 6:20**; *So the people shouted when the priests blew the trumpets. And it happened when the people heard the sound of the trumpet, and the people shouted with a great shout, that the wall fell down flat. Then the people went up into the city, every man straight before him, and they took the city.*

Possession of the land fell simply with a shout of the people. The wall was utterly destroyed in a moment. Doesn't this show God's complete supremacy over all His people's enemies? _____

Read **Hebrews 3: 16-19;** and fill in the blanks. *[16] For who, having heard, rebelled? Indeed, was it not all who came out of Egypt, led by Moses? [17] Now with whom was He angry forty years? Was it not with those who sinned, whose corpses fell in the wilderness? [18] And to whom did He swear that they would not enter His rest, but to those who did not obey? [19]* ____

_____

_____

_____

Unbelief is a sin and when we don't believe God will give us the power to walk away from the food when we are not hungry shows a total lack of faith, just like the first set of spies, you limit God's Power with your lack of faith.

Read **Psalm 78:41, 42** *Yes, again and again they tempted God, And limited the Holy One of Israel. [42] They did not remember His power: The day when He redeemed them from the enemy.*

Our battle with the refrigerator, and all the battles we face every day, in a way parallels this battle. None of them is won by us. It's God, in you, who defeats your enemy. If we see our overeating as the enemy and our being thin as the promised land, we should go in and possess the land by faith and mean it!

I heard a story once that illustrates the battle and how our Father fights for us.

A father and his little girl were driving along in the car when suddenly a bee flew in the window. The girl panicked because she was allergic to bees and could die if stung.

Her father grabbed the bee held it in his fist. He held on tight until the bee stung him, and then he let the bee fly out of his fist.

His little girl screamed in terror "Oh no! Daddy, you let the bee go now he is going to sting me!"

"No, don't worry he can't hurt you anymore," he said opening his fist to show her the stinger still stuck in his palm.

Jesus took Satan's stinger on the cross. We don't have to be afraid of him anymore. The only power he has over us is to scare us by telling lies. The voices you hear in your head are telling you, "you can't do it! Start later." "It's not your fault; go ahead and overeat." These voices are all lies of Satan, and we need to recognize them as such. Then, you can use Scripture to overcome him.

One of my favorites is, **Philippians 4:13** *I can do all things through Christ who strengthens me.*

It's quick, easy, and to the point. The only weapons we need are prayer, the Word of God, and faith in them.

Read **Joshua 6**

In light of today's study, what was the Scripture or statement in today's lesson that most spoke to your heart? _____

_____

_____

_____

What steps of faith does God want you to take towards Him today? _____

_____

_____

_____

Rephrase the Scripture or statement into an expression of faith_____

_____

_____

_____

Memorize the following Scripture this week.

Hebrews 11:6 *But without faith it is impossible to please Him, for he who comes to God must believe that He is, and that He is a rewarder of those who diligently seek Him*

Week 3 Day 2
Jesus in Nazareth

Day _____ Date _____

Read **Mark 6:1-6** *Then He went out from there and came to His own country, and His disciples followed Him.* [2] *And when the Sabbath had come, He began to teach in the synagogue. And many hearing Him were astonished, saying, "Where did this Man get these things? And what wisdom is this which is given to Him, that such mighty works are performed by His hands!* [3] *Is this not the carpenter, the Son of Mary, and brother of James, Joses, Judas, and Simon? And are not His sisters here with us?" So they were offended at Him.*

[4] *But Jesus said to them, "A prophet is not without honor except in his own country, among his own relatives, and in his own house."* [5] *Now He could do no mighty work there, except that He laid His hands on a few sick people and healed them.* [6] *And He marveled because of their unbelief. Then He went about the villages in a circuit, teaching.*

Write **Mark 6:5** from the above Scriptures in the space below. _____
_____
_____
_____
_____ [6] *And He marveled because of their unbelief!!!*

Why do you think Jesus was well received as a young man in Nazareth, (His hometown) but He was rejected as Messiah? _____
_____

     Think about this situation for a moment. What were the people of Nazareth feeling? They had seen Jesus grow up in grace and wisdom. The Elders had taught Him in the synagogue, and He was their star pupil. They probably congratulated themselves often for being such wise and masterful instructors. Then this same young man's knowledge and wisdom surpasses their own understanding. He begins teaching them things they know are true, but don't want to recognize as such.

     The Pharisees were looked upon as being the final say in all matters of the law. They loved their positions; they had gone through the proper political channels, and Jesus had not. Because of their arrogance, they wouldn't humble themselves. They were indignant, and wouldn't accept Him as their superior. The religious leaders refused to see Him as their Messiah, and rejected Him.

Read **Luke 4:16-30** [16] *So He came to Nazareth, where He had been brought up. And as His custom was, He went into the synagogue on the Sabbath day, and stood up to read.* [17] *And He was handed the book of the prophet Isaiah. And when He had opened the book, He found the place where it was written:*
[18] *"The Spirit of the LORD is upon Me, Because He has anointed Me To preach the gospel to the poor; He has sent Me to heal the brokenhearted, To proclaim liberty to the captives And recovery of sight to the blind, To set at liberty those who are oppressed;* [19] *To proclaim the*

acceptable year of the LORD.

²⁰ Then He closed the book, and gave it back to the attendant and sat down. And the eyes of all who were in the synagogue were fixed on Him. ²¹ And He began to say to them, "Today this Scripture is fulfilled in your hearing." ²² So all bore witness to Him, and marveled at the gracious words which proceeded out of His mouth. And they said, "Is this not Joseph's son?"

²³ He said to them, "You will surely say this proverb to Me, "Physician, heal yourself! Whatever we have heard done in Capernaum, do also here in Your country. ²⁴ Then He said, "Assuredly, I say to you, no prophet is accepted in his own country. ²⁵But I tell you truly, many widows were in Israel in the days of Elijah, when the Heaven was shut up three years and six months, and there was a great famine throughout all the land; ²⁶ but to none of them was Elijah sent except to Zarephath, in the region of Sidon, to a woman who was a widow. ²⁷ And many lepers were in Israel in the time of Elisha the prophet, and none of them was cleansed except Naaman the Syrian."

²⁸ So all those in the synagogue, when they heard these things, were filled with wrath, ²⁹ and rose up and thrust Him out of the city; and they led Him to the brow of the hill on which their city was built, that they might throw Him down over the cliff. ³⁰ Then passing through the midst of them, He went His way.

Jesus taught these passages on that day.

Isaiah 61:1, 2 *"The Spirit of the Lord GOD is upon Me, Because the LORD has anointed Me to preach good tidings to the poor; He has sent Me to heal the brokenhearted, To proclaim liberty to the captives, and the opening of the prison to those who are bound; ² To proclaim the acceptable year of the LORD, and the day of vengeance of our God; To comfort all who mourn.*

By citing these words from Isaiah, Jesus was claiming His royalty and His prophetic mission. Jesus proclaimed the fulfillment of God's plan and the promise of Himself, the Messiah. Since He was the figure described in the passage, He was telling them that He was the fulfillment of this prophesy.

He did heal brokenhearted people (still does). He proclaims liberty that through Him we are set free from sin. He did and does heal the blind both physically and spiritually.

The congregation was angry because they were arrogant. They felt He was being presumptuous. They were offended because He had the audacity to put Himself above them by claiming His royal status when they considered Him only a carpenter.

Read **Matthew 9:14-29** *¹⁴When they came to the other disciples, they saw a large crowd around them and the teachers of the law arguing with them. ¹⁵As soon as all the people saw Jesus, they were overwhelmed with wonder and ran to greet him.*

¹⁶"What are you arguing with them about?" he asked.

[17]*A man in the crowd answered, "Teacher, I brought you my son, who is possessed by a spirit that has robbed him of speech.* [18]*Whenever it seizes him, it throws him to the ground. He foams at the mouth, gnashes his teeth and becomes rigid. I asked your disciples to drive out the spirit, but they could not."*

[19]*"O unbelieving generation," Jesus replied, "how long shall I stay with you? How long shall I put up with you? Bring the boy to me."*

[20]*So they brought him. When the spirit saw Jesus, it immediately threw the boy into a convulsion. He fell to the ground and rolled around, foaming at the mouth.*

[21]*Jesus asked the boy's father, "How long has he been like this?"*
"From childhood," he answered. [22]*"It has often thrown him into fire or water to kill him.* **But if you can do anything,** *take pity on us and help us."*

[23]*"* ***'If you can'?*** *" said Jesus. "Everything is possible for him who believes."*

[24]*Immediately the boy's father exclaimed, "I do believe; help me overcome my unbelief!"*

[25]*When Jesus saw that a crowd was running to the scene, he rebuked the evil spirit. "You deaf and mute spirit," he said, "I command you, come out of him and never enter him again."*

[26]*The spirit shrieked, convulsed him violently and came out. The boy looked so much like a corpse that many said, "He's dead."* [27]*But Jesus took him by the hand and lifted him to his feet, and he stood up.* [28]*After Jesus had gone indoors, his disciples asked him privately, "Why couldn't we drive it out?"* [29]*He replied, "This kind can come out only by prayer."*

Write **Matthew 9:23** from the Scripture verses above. _____
_____
_____

      The disciples tried to heal a demon possessed boy and couldn't. Then the desperate father went to Jesus, and Jesus said, "O' faithless generation."… The father of the boy said, "If you can." Jesus said, "***If you*** can believe."

      Sometimes believers can be nagged by doubt. Even though this poor father didn't have the faith, he took the correct course by appealing to Jesus for help with his disbelief. The Father of the possessed boy said, "Lord I believe. Help my unbelief." Jesus healed the boy.

      Later the disciples asked why they couldn't heal him. Jesus said this kind could come out only with fasting and prayer. I used to read this passage and I wonder why this demon-possessed person was harder. Why did this one require fasting and prayer? Then God showed me. We find the clue in the conversation between the father and Jesus. This family had been battling this demon for a very long time. It was deeply entrenched in their psyche. Even though the father of the boy had heard and seen all that Jesus was doing, it was still hard for him to believe that Jesus could help him.

Fasting bolsters our faith. God doesn't need us to fast to perform the miracle, but rather, it's for our benefit. The disciples could not exorcize the demon because the father didn't have enough faith. The power was there, but they couldn't apply it. We actually limit God's power with our unbelief.

Read **Mark 6:5-6** again, in case you missed it the first time. *Now He could do no mighty work there, except that He laid His hands on a few sick people and healed them. ⁶ And He marveled because of their unbelief. Then He went about the villages in a circuit, teaching.* Jesus was amazed at the people of His hometown, because they had so little faith.

I was amazed, too, when I first read **Mark 6:5-6,** because I didn't realize that our faith was so essential for performing miracles.

The passage says; *Now **He-could-do no** mighty work there, except that He laid His hands on a few sick people and healed them. ⁶ And He marveled because of **their unbelief**.*

He couldn't do any mighty works because they didn't believe. I was also taken aback when I realized my lack of faith was rejection of God's sovereignty. When we doubt God can keep us from a candy bar or worry, we are actually rejecting God by not believing He is able to give us the strength to resist the temptation.

Read, **Psalm 78:40-42** *How often they provoked Him in the wilderness, And grieved Him in the desert! ⁴¹ Yes, again and again they tempted God, And **limited** the Holy One of Israel. ⁴² They did not remember His power: The day when He redeemed them from the enemy.*

READ Hebrews 14:8-10 *And in Lystra a certain man without strength in his feet was sitting, a cripple from his mother's womb, who had never walked. ⁹ This man heard Paul speaking. Paul, observing him intently and seeing that he had faith to be healed, ¹⁰ said with a loud voice, "Stand up straight on your feet!" And he leaped and walked.*

Before Paul could pray for this man to be healed, he had to determine whether he had enough faith. Faith is a necessary element to the healing process, and has to be present before the healing is set in motion.

Daily reading: **Romans 5:1-5**

In light of today's study, what was the Scripture or statement in today's lesson that most spoke to your heart? _____

_____

_____

_____

What steps of faith does God want you to take towards Him today? _____

_____

_____

_____

Rephrase the Scripture or statement into an expression of faith_____

_____

_____

_____

Memory Verse

Hebrews 11:6 *But _____ faith it is _____ to please Him, for he who comes to God must believe that He is, and that He is a rewarder of those who _____ _____ Him.*

Week 3 Day 3
You Can't Move a Mountain with a Teaspoon

Day _____ Date _____

Think of your addiction to food as a mountain, and you are in it's cold shadow. You want so badly to get out of that shadow, and into the light that you repeatedly try to climb the mountain. Over and over you try, but you can't seem to make it. You try different routes, time after time, but always find something blocks you way. Sometimes you think you are close, only to fall back down again . No matter how hard you try you can't reach the top or your goal. You experience failure and after failure

Have you gotten to the place where you realize the mountain is impossible to climb, and there is no way up or around it.

Write down some of the ways you have tried to climb the mountain of addiction and failed._____

_____

_____

_____

_____

Mark 11:12-14 *Now the next day, when they had come out from Bethany, He was hungry. [13] And seeing from afar a fig tree having leaves, He went to see if perhaps He would find something on it. When He came to it, He found nothing but leaves, for it was not the season for figs. [14] In response Jesus said to it, "Let no one eat fruit from you ever again."*
And His disciples heard it.

Mark 11:20-24 *Now in the morning, as they passed by, they saw the fig tree dried up from the roots. [21] And Peter, remembering, said to Him, "Rabbi, look! The fig tree which You cursed has withered away."*

[22] So Jesus answered and said to them, "Have faith in God. [23] For assuredly, I say to you, whoever says to this mountain, "Be removed and be cast into the sea,' and does not doubt in his heart, but believes that those things he says will be done, he will have whatever he says.

[24] Therefore I say to you, whatever things you ask when you pray, believe that you receive them, and you will have them.

Picture your food addiction as that mountain. How does Jesus tell us to handle the mountain?

_____

_____

_____

I have heard many sermons on the subject of "laying *it* down at the cross" but no one ever told me how to leave "*it*" there. I tried willpower, diet pills, hypnosis. Nothing worked for me. I was at the end of my rope.

Then one morning I remember telling God, "I can't do it. Satan is too strong for me. I can't live my life without overeating. I am addicted to food and I am sorry but I can't do it.".

I tearfully went to my Bible and read these passages about the mountain. The words "Ask anything and believe without wavering and it's yours," jumped out at me. God showed me I didn't need to be strong and have willpower. I only needed to ask God, through faith to take the mountain away.

I wasn't strong enough but I knew He was. To my surprise, that day was easy. I didn't have to resist the food, it just didn't interest me. It was at that point when God started teaching me how to rely on him by faith. Just as you are saved by faith, you grow and faith makes you strong. Every temptation that befalls you strengthens your faith.

You don't say with your fist clenched, "No I won't have another piece of cheese cake!!" You run to your Father and say, "Lord please. I want that cheesecake so much. It smells so good and looks so good. I am powerless to resist it. Your Word tells me Lord, by faith, I can resist Satan. So, I am asking You to get me past this test. In Jesus' name, Amen." Then you walk away and believe that God will take care of Satan for you and leave the consequences to Him.

Luke 22:40 *When He came to the place, He said to them, "Pray that you may not enter into temptation."*

He has already given you the strength you need. You just need to use it. I promise, sincere prayer works for me every single time. I admit the emotional battle with my own will is hard and there are times when I am not being sincere in my prayer, because I am praying as I am chewing. I know in my heart, that if I pray and believe that God will remove my desire for the food, He will. The problem is I don't want help. I want cheesecake. It is easier to ask for forgiveness than to get permission, but that doesn't fix the problem. To overcome my insincerity, I pray for God to help me ask for help. You have to bombard the mountain with prayer, and let God reduce it to rubble.

You don't need to pray this exact prayer. Just bombard the temptation with prayer. Just try it! I even pray sometimes for God to help me ask for help, because I don't want help. I want cheesecake!

Your overeating is like a stronghold, a mountain, and you are using a teaspoon to get rid of it. All the while, you have the awesome power of the One who created the mountain. If you give Him the mountain, He will smash it down and throw it out of your way. Soon the mountain will be nothing more than a pebble in your shoe, a minor annoyance easily removed with prayer.

Re-read **Mark 11:23** *For assuredly, I say to you, whoever says to this mountain, "Be removed and be cast into the sea,' and does not doubt in his heart, but believes that those things he says will be done, he will have whatever he says.*

In your own words, what does "believe," mean to you? _____

_____

_____

The definition of believe, is to have a religious conviction to have belief confidence trust. The Greek word for believe, literally means "to place ones trust in another."

The battle that takes place in your mind is never easy. There is always a test involved and it takes bombarding the temptation with prayer and reading the Bible. Remember this is God's war, but you are not just a passive observer. You must also get in and fight, though, your position is always standing behind Christ.

Read **James 2: 14-24** (The Message)

Faith in Action
[14-17]Dear friends, do you think you'll get anywhere in this if you learn all the right words but never do anything? Does merely talking about faith indicate that a person really has it? For instance, you come upon an old friend dressed in rags and half-starved and say, "Good morning, friend! Be clothed in Christ! Be filled with the Holy Spirit!" and walk off without providing so much as a coat or a cup of soup—where does that get you? Isn't it obvious that God-talk without God-acts is outrageous nonsense?

[18]I can already hear one of you agreeing by saying, "Sounds good. You take care of the faith department, I'll handle the works department." Not so fast. You can no more show me your works apart from your faith than I can show you my faith apart from my works. Faith and works, works and faith, fit together hand in glove.

[19-20]Do I hear you professing to believe in the one and only God, but then observe you complacently sitting back as if you had done something wonderful? That's just great. Demons do that, but what good does it do them? Use your heads! Do you suppose for a minute that you can cut faith and works in two and not end up with a corpse on your hands?

[21-24]Wasn't our ancestor Abraham "made right with God by works" when he placed his son Isaac on the sacrificial altar? Isn't it obvious that faith and works are yoked partners, that faith expresses itself in works? That the works are "works of faith"? The full meaning of "believe" in the Scripture sentence, "Abraham believed God and was set right with God," includes his action. It's that mesh of believing and acting that got Abraham named "God's friend." Is it not evident that a person is made right with God not by a barren faith but by faith fruitful in works?

In the previous Scriptures how was Abraham and Rahab proving their faith by their actions?

_____

_____

_____

_____

_____

They each had to make a life or death decision. Abraham had to trust God, and give his son over to God while Rahab had to trust that the guards who came looking for the Hebrew spies in Canaan would believe her story. If they didn't, it would mean sure death for her and her family.

Pray when you are tempted, and leave the outcome to God. God may want you to sacrifice being thin for a while. The hard part is leaving the outcome to Him. Leaving it up to God is your mountain. You trusting God and giving Him all the aspects of the situation is your faith in action. You can say, "I believe in God," all you want, but if you don't trust Him, your faith is dead. He will heal you in His time. You will be healed when your faith is strong enough to believe you have been healed.

If you walk away from the food when you are not really hungry, God will provide another delicious meal. It's very unlikely you'll never be able to get that meal or food item again. If it's a fast food item or something from a restaurant that you can't cook yourself, you can just get in the car and get it again when you're hungry. You don't have to worry that if you don't eat it now you will never get another chance again. Satan makes it a bigger deal than it is.

John 6:28-40 *Then they said to Him, "What shall we do, that we may work the works of God?"* [29] *Jesus answered and said to them,* **_"This is the work of God, that you believe in Him whom He sent."_**

Wow did you get that. "This is the work of God **that you believe in Him** whom He sent."

You can believe in something without following it. Satan believes in God. There are two different kinds belief. One is head knowledge and one is faith. Faith requires action.

One of my favorite Bible studies is "Experiencing God" by Henry T. Blackaby and Claude B. King. My favorite quote from that study is, "You can't stay here and go with God."

What does the statement "faith requires action" mean to you? _____
_____
_____
_____

Believe that God will give you strength, and put that faith in action by removing yourself from the situation. Put the leftovers in the refrigerator or give them to the dog.

Genesis 12:1-4 *[1] The LORD had said to Abram, "Leave your country, your people and your father's household and go to the land I will show you. [2] "I will make you into a great nation and I will bless you; I will make your name great, and you will be a blessing. [3] I will bless those who bless you, and whoever curses you I will curse; and all peoples on earth will be blessed through you." [4] So Abram left, as the LORD had told him; and Lot went with him. Abram was seventy-five years old when he set out from Haran.*

Abraham had to leave his family and go to a strange land. He didn't sit around saying, "God has made a bunch of promises to me, and I am going to sit here until he carries me there." No he got up and left his father and mother. He took his family and possessions and moved when God said move. You may think passing up a biscuit isn't a test at all compared to some of the other tests you have been through or have seen others go through, but God is concerned with every aspect of your life.

Think back to the verses about the fig tree at the first of this day's study. I didn't understand why the disciples were so astonished. They had seen Jesus perform so many miracles. Why were they surprised at this?

They had seen him heal the blind and feed five thousand with just a few fishes and loaves of bread. The passage in **Matthew 21:20-22** says, *And when the disciples saw it, they marveled, saying, "How did the fig tree wither away so soon?" [21] So Jesus answered and said to them, "Assuredly, I say to you, if you have faith and do not doubt, you will not only do what was done to the fig tree, but also if you say to this mountain, "Be removed and be cast into the sea,' it will be done. [22] And whatever things you ask in prayer, believing, you will receive."*

The disciples marveled?? This line always puzzled me. Why were they amazed? They had seen Jesus perform many miracles by that time. What was there about the small event that was so amazing? Then it dawned on me that maybe the disciples thought this miracle was too inconsequential. It wasn't a life-changing event.

You might think, as I used to, that God isn't concerned about the way I look, and I shouldn't be concerned about it either. In His grand scheme, my weight is insignificant, but the story doesn't end here. We need to face it. Idolatry and gluttony are sins; committing them places you outside of God's will. We also need to have the correct attitude about our looks.

Isaiah 53:1, 2 *Who has believed our report? And to whom has the arm of the LORD been revealed? [2] For He shall grow up before Him as a tender plant, And as a root out of dry ground. He has no form or comeliness; And when we see Him, There is no beauty that we should desire Him.*

The Bible never gives a physical description of Jesus, but the verse above hints that He was rather ordinary looking. It seems Jesus' human form was de-emphasized on purpose. God didn't want people to be drawn to Him because of His looks, but rather, His message and who He was. Your body is the least important thing about "*You*." It's the only part of "*You*" that's not eternal.

James 4:3 *You ask and do not receive, because you ask amiss, that you may spend it on your pleasures.*

God delights in answering our prayers, but it has to be for the right reason. God wants you to know the importance of your soul. Your body is the temple of the Holy of Holies, the Holy Spirit! He wants to address your inside first. He desires that you trust Him. You have to step out, believe God knows best, and He will fulfill His promises.

John 14: 13,14 *And whatever you ask in My name, that I will do, that the Father may be glorified in the Son.* [14] *If you ask anything in My name, I will do it.*

Think about it. Who will you glorify when you reach your goal weight? We also need to balance this Scripture with God's sovereignty. Understand that God knows the future. You being a millionaire may not fit into His plan for your life, but you being thin is God's will or He wouldn't have said gluttony is a sin.

Read **Galatians 2:16-21 and 3:1-9**

In light of today's study, what was the Scripture or statement in today's lesson that most spoke to your heart? _____

_____

_____

_____

What steps of faith does God want you to take towards Him today? _____

_____

_____

_____

Rephrase the Scripture or statement into an expression of faith_____

_____

_____

_____

Fill in the blanks of our weekly memory verse

Hebrews 11:6 *But _____ faith it is _____ to please Him, for he who comes to God must believe that He is, and that He is a rewarder of those who _____ _____ Him.*

Week 3 Day 4
David's faith

Day _____ Date _____

Read the account of the battle of David and Goliath.

I Samuel 17:1-51. *Now the Philistines gathered their armies together to battle, and were gathered at Sochoh, which belongs to Judah; they encamped between Sochoh and Azekah, in Ephes Dammim.* *² And Saul and the men of Israel were gathered together, and they encamped in the Valley of Elah, and drew up in battle array against the Philistines.* *³ The Philistines stood on a mountain on one side, and Israel stood on a mountain on the other side, with a valley between them.*

⁴ And a champion went out from the camp of the Philistines, named Goliath, from Gath, whose height was six cubits and a span. *⁵ He had a bronze helmet on his head, and he was armed with a coat of mail, and the weight of the coat was five thousand shekels of bronze.* *⁶ And he had bronze armor on his legs and a bronze javelin between his shoulders.* *⁷ Now the staff of his spear was like a weaver's beam, and his iron spearhead weighed six hundred shekels; and a shield-bearer went before him.* *⁸ Then he stood and cried out to the armies of Israel, and said to them, "Why have you come out to line up for battle? Am I not a Philistine, and you the servants of Saul? Choose a man for yourselves, and let him come down to me.* *⁹ If he is able to fight with me and kill me, then we will be your servants. But if I prevail against him and kill him, then you shall be our servants and serve us."* *¹⁰ And the Philistine said, "I defy the armies of Israel this day; give me a man, that we may fight together."* *¹¹ When Saul and all Israel heard these words of the Philistine, they were dismayed and greatly afraid.*

¹² Now David was the son of that Ephrathite of Bethlehem Judah, whose name was Jesse, and who had eight sons. And the man was old, advanced in years, in the days of Saul. *¹³ The three oldest sons of Jesse had gone to follow Saul to the battle. The names of his three sons who went to the battle were Eliab the firstborn, next to him Abinadab, and the third Shammah.* *¹⁴ David was the youngest. And the three oldest followed Saul.* *¹⁵ But David occasionally went and returned from Saul to feed his father's sheep at Bethlehem.*

¹⁶ And the Philistine drew near and presented himself forty days, morning and evening.

¹⁷ Then Jesse said to his son David, "Take now for your brothers an ephah of this dried grain and these ten loaves, and run to your brothers at the camp. *¹⁸ And carry these ten cheeses to the captain of their thousand, and see how your brothers fare, and bring back news of them."*

¹⁹ Now Saul and they and all the men of Israel were in the Valley of Elah, fighting with the Philistines.

²⁰ So David rose early in the morning, left the sheep with a keeper, and took the things and went as Jesse had commanded him. And he came to the camp as the army was going out to the fight and shouting for the battle. *²¹ For Israel and the Philistines had drawn up in battle array, army against army.* *²² And David left his supplies in the hand of the supply keeper, ran to the army, and came and greeted his brothers. ²³ Then as he talked with them, there was the champion, the Philistine of Gath, Goliath by name, coming up from the armies of the Philistines; and he spoke according to the same words. So David heard them. ²⁴ And all the men of Israel, when they saw the man, fled from him and were dreadfully afraid. ²⁵ So the men of Israel said, "Have you seen this man who has come up? Surely he has come up to defy Israel; and it shall be that the man who kills him the king will enrich with great riches, will give him his daughter, and give his father's house exemption from taxes in Israel."*

²⁶ Then David spoke to the men who stood by him, saying, "What shall be done for the man who kills this Philistine and takes away the reproach from Israel? For who is this uncircumcised Philistine, that he should defy the armies of the living God?"

²⁷ And the people answered him in this manner, saying, "So shall it be done for the man who kills him."

²⁸ Now Eliab his oldest brother heard when he spoke to the men; and Eliab's anger was aroused against David, and he said, "Why did you come down here? And with whom have you left those few sheep in the wilderness? I know your pride and the insolence of your heart, for you have come down to see the battle."

²⁹ And David said, "What have I done now? Is there not a cause?" ³⁰ Then he turned from him toward another and said the same thing; and these people answered him as the first ones did

³¹ Now when the words which David spoke were heard, they reported them to Saul; and he sent for him. ³² Then David said to Saul, "Let no man's heart fail because of him; your servant will go and fight with this Philistine."

³³ And Saul said to David, "You are not able to go against this Philistine to fight with him; for you are a youth, and he a man of war from his youth."

*³⁴ But David said to Saul, "Your servant used to keep his father's sheep, and when a lion or a bear came and took a lamb out of the flock, ³⁵ I went out after it and struck it, and delivered the lamb from its mouth; and when it arose against me, I caught it by its beard, and struck and killed it. ³⁶ Your servant has killed both lion and bear; and this uncircumcised Philistine will be like one of them, seeing he has defied the armies of the living God." ³⁷ Moreover David said, "**The***

LORD, who delivered me from the paw of the lion and from the paw of the bear, He will deliver me from the hand of this Philistine."

And Saul said to David, "Go, and the LORD be with you!"

[38] *So Saul clothed David with his armor, and he put a bronze helmet on his head; he also clothed him with a coat of mail.* [39] *David fastened his sword to his armor and tried to walk, for he had not tested them. And David said to Saul, "I cannot walk with these, for I have not tested them." So David took them off.*

[40] *Then he took his staff in his hand; and he chose for himself five smooth stones from the brook, and put them in a shepherd's bag, in a pouch which he had, and his sling was in his hand. And he drew near to the Philistine.* [41] *So the Philistine came, and began drawing near to David, and the man who bore the shield went before him.* [42] *And when the Philistine looked about and saw David, he disdained him; for he was only a youth, ruddy and good-looking.* [43] *So the Philistine said to David, "Am I a dog, that you come to me with sticks?" And the Philistine cursed David by his gods.* [44] *And the Philistine said to David, "Come to me, and I will give your flesh to the birds of the air and the beasts of the field!"*

[45] *Then David said to the Philistine, "You come to me with a sword, with a spear, and with a javelin. But I come to you in the name of the LORD of hosts, the God of the armies of Israel, whom you have defied.* [46] *This day the LORD will deliver you into my hand, and I will strike you and take your head from you. And this day I will give the carcasses of the camp of the Philistines to the birds of the air and the wild beasts of the earth, that all the earth may know that there is a God in Israel.* [47] ***Then all this assembly shall know that the LORD does not save with sword and spear; for the battle is the LORD's, and He will give you into our hands."***

[48] *So it was, when the Philistine arose and came and drew near to meet David, that David hurried and ran toward the army to meet the Philistine.* [49] *Then David put his hand in his bag and took out a stone; and he slung it and struck the Philistine in his forehead, so that the stone sank into his forehead, and he fell on his face to the earth.* [50] *So David prevailed over the Philistine with a sling and a stone, and struck the Philistine and killed him. But there was no sword in the hand of David.* [51] *Therefore David ran and stood over the Philistine, took his sword and drew it out of its sheath and killed him, and cut off his head with it. And when the Philistines saw that their champion was dead, they fled.*

This is an amazing story, and David was a remarkable young man. He evaluated the obstacle from God's perspective. Here was an opportunity for God to display His power. You have to think about what David was dealing with to appreciate his situation.

I am always making excuses for God as to why I don't pray for specific problems publicly. For instance, our neighbors' dogs kept getting into our trash and spreading it all over. I understand it's not a big deal, but it was such an annoyance. God kept prompting me to make it a matter of family prayer, but I was afraid if I prayed it aloud around my kids and God decided not to answer this silly prayer, it would make Him look bad and stunt their faith. (I know my mind works in mysterious ways). I finally did pray with my kids about it, and the dogs never touched the trash again. I have been a Christian for many years, and I had so little faith I couldn't pray for my trash. Consider what David was facing.

First, there was opposition from his family, (verse17:28). Eliab, his oldest brother, was probably worried about his little brother. I'm also sure he felt resentful, thinking he should have been the one to be anointed king by Samuel since he was the oldest son and stronger. I'm sure he was ashamed that he, himself, didn't have the kind of courage his little brother David did. He must have felt resentful that "little David" thought he could do something that he, himself, was so afraid to do, and no wonder let's take a second look at Goliath.

He was the biggest, man of either of the two armies. He was a mountain of a man, fierce to behold in his battle scarred armor. He was a giant trained his whole life in the ways of war. He was not only extremely tall, but also, massive. He wore a bronze helmet that must have been tremendously heavy since the regular troops wore leather. His coat of mail alone weighed about one-hundred, twenty-five pounds! That probably just about matched what David weighed at that time. The head of his spear weighed seventeen pounds. He filled the whole Israelite army with dread. At six cubits and a span, Goliath was over nine feet tall. I drew a picture on butcher paper for a Sunday school class I was teaching to illustrate the size of Goliath. I was amazed at how tall he was. It really put David's situation into perspective for me.

David was a young boy, not even old enough to be in the army. He probably weighed just a little over one-hundred pounds. From the world's perspective, David was doomed. However, David's past victories gave him faith to trust God for victory over Goliath. For David, the issue was more of a spiritual crisis (the Israelites' lack of faith) than a military one.

Read **1 Samuel 17:34-37** *But David said to Saul, "Your servant used to keep his father's sheep, and when a lion or a bear came and took a lamb out of the flock, [35] I went out after it and struck it, and delivered the lamb from its mouth; and when it arose against me, I caught it by its beard, and struck and killed it. [36] Your servant has killed both lion and bear; and this uncircumcised Philistine will be like one of them, seeing he has defied the armies of the living God." [37] Moreover David said, **"The LORD, who delivered me from the paw of the lion and from the paw of the bear, He will deliver me from the hand of this Philistine."** And Saul said to David, "Go, and the LORD be with you!"*

Why do you think David's past victories give him the faith to face Goliath? _____
_____

By relying on God to give him strength to battle these wild animals, He proved God's faithfulness. God had always protected him and he knew He would again. David could have sat around worrying about all the reasons he shouldn't fight the giant. Is it the proper thing to do? What will my family say! What if God doesn't really want me to do this! What if I fail and die! David had to step out in faith first. That's the faith with works we talked about yesterday.

Temptation is always hard to fight. Step out in faith, knowing God will see you through it by praying and asking God to give you the strength you need to resist temptation. Just as the past victories gave David faith in God, so your victories will give you faith to turn down that second piece of cheesecake. Just as choosing correctly will help you win the next battle, so will choosing incorrectly help you lose the next battle. Practice does not make perfect. Perfect practice makes perfect, or success builds on success, and failure builds on failure.

Satan's total goal is that you lose faith. One of his best weapons is, "There is always tomorrow," or, "I'll start later." If you choose to worship the refrigerator just one time, it will give Satan a foothold to undermine your faith, and the next time will be harder for you to resist. So rationalizing that just one time won't hurt you is not true. It does do a lot of damage to your faith, and Satan knows it.

Read, **Psalm 46**

In light of today's study, what was the Scripture or statement in today's lesson that most spoke to your heart? _____

_____

_____

_____

What steps of faith does God want you to take towards Him today? _____

_____

_____

_____

Rephrase the Scripture or statement into an expression of faith_____

_____

_____

_____

Memory Verse

Hebrews 11:6 *But* _____ *faith it is* _____ *to please Him, for he* _____ *comes to God* _____ _____ *that He is, and that He is a* _____ *of those who* _____ _____ *Him.*

Week 3 Day 5
My Dream

Day _____ Date _____

Occasionally I have frightening dreams; I call them my devil dreams. One in particular was even more scary than usual, because all the other times, I would say or think the name Jesus, and I would wake up instantly, but this time it was different. In my dream, I was standing in my kitchen and Satan was sitting in a chair. He started to get up, coming towards me. I rebuked him in Jesus' name. He flew back onto the chair and looked as if he had been beaten. He was shaken and weak and I could tell he was hurt, but it scared me because I didn't wake up as I usually do.

He looked at me slyly and started to get up and come towards me again, I said, "I rebuke you Satan in Jesus' name," this time I said it a little louder, he fell back but not as hard and he got up faster.

He came towards me again, and I yelled "I REBUKE YOU SATAN IN JESUS' NAME!" He fell back to the chair but got right back up. This time I screamed the rebuke as loud as I could, and he just stepped back.

I was so scared because I knew I couldn't scream any louder, I could see him crouching and could sense he was about to fly at me when I heard a still small voice in my heart, "If you have faith you can whisper." I remember looking Satan right in the eye as I spoke softly, whispering, "I rebuke you Satan in Jesus name," and I instantly woke up.

I believe God works through dreams, and this one had a profound effect on me. I reflect on it often, and I think that's why I remember it so vividly.

In my dream when I rebuked Satan, I said the same things with each rebuke. What was different about the last time? _____

_____

I didn't just say the words; I used them with the power of the Holy Spirit. Don't be upset if you use the Word with power and it seems Satan is still harassing you. He doesn't usually give up after only one time. He didn't give up after tempting Jesus. Even when Satan wasn't successful, the Bible says, "He went away until a more opportune time."

We have access to God's power and he gives us the authority, but you have to use that authority. **Luke 9:1** *Then he called his twelve disciples together, and gave them power and authority over all devils, and to cure diseases.*
Jesus gave them (us), power. The word Power is the Greek word, *dynamis.* Its meaning is "Power consisting in or resting upon armies, forces, hosts"
The word "Authority" as used in this verse in the Greek is *exousia* **2)** physical and mental power
a) the ability or strength with which one is endowed, which he either possesses or exercises
3) the power of authority (influence) and of right (privilege)
4) the power of rule or government (the power of him whose will and commands must be submitted to by others and obeyed)

—Synonyms **1.** rule, power, sway. Authority, control, and influence, denote a power or right to direct the actions or thoughts of others. Authority is a power or right, usually because of rank or office, to issue commands and to punish for violations: to have authority over subordinates. Control is either power or influence applied to the complete and successful direction or manipulation of persons or things: to be in control of a project. Influence is a personal and unofficial power derived from deference of others to one's character, ability, or station. **3.** sovereign, arbiter.

Jesus gives you authority over all demons. However if you don't use that authority, it means nothing. You have legal authority over your children, but if you don't use that authority, your authority means nothing. It reminds me of a story I heard about at a high security prison, an error in the computer system left a female guard unarmed and locked in an area with no electricity and thirty hardened male prisoners.

Both the guard and convicts knew that if the men decided to get violent there was no one to help her, and no way that anyone would ever know who did what. She knew the gravity of her situation and knew she had only one thing that could keep her from being raped, beaten, or killed by these rough men, and that was her authority.

She knew that if she showed any weakness at all she was a goner. She used her authority with power she didn't feel. She explained later that at first, the prisoners tested her, and she was afraid, but she never let on. After a few tense minutes of testing, the men backed down. The computer problem was fixed after what seemed like an intolerable amount of time, and to her relief, she was back on safer ground.

Just as these men could not read the guards mind, neither can Satan read ours. **He is not omnipotent like God is.** We have the authority in Christ's Name to stop Satan, but we need to remember to use God's power and keep in mind the strength behind His Word. Unless we use our authority with power and strength, Satan will know that you don't have real faith in God's authority and therefore you don't have it. Our lack of faith in God's supremacy gives Satan the power and authority he craves.

After God had healed me of my addiction to food, I tried to manipulate my weight loss by eating just a little bit. Guess what? I didn't lose a pound for over two months. I was probably eating less than a thousand calories a day, yet I didn't lose one pound. I was trying to use my own might instead of following the principals of this study.

Read **Zechariah 4: 6** *So he answered and said to me: "This is the word of the LORD to Zerubbabel: "Not by might nor by power, but by My Spirit,' Says the LORD of hosts.*

Write in your own words what this Scripture means to you _____

_____

_____

_____

_____

List the things that you have tried to fix, manipulate or have gotten upset and worried about the last week or two._____

_____

_____

_____

_____

Begin to pray about the things that bother you. I'll remind you in about two weeks to come back to this section. In two weeks from today write the results in the next lines leave them blank until then.

_____

_____

_____

Read: **II Corinthians 10:3-6**

In light of today's study, what was the Scripture or statement in today's lesson that most spoke to your heart? _____

_____

_____

_____

What steps of faith does God want you to take towards Him today? _____

_____

_____

_____

Rephrase the Scripture or statement into an expression of faith_____

_____

_____

_____

Memory Verse

Hebrews 11:6 _____

_____

_____

Week 4 Day 1
Daniels decision helped later

Day _____ Date _____

Do the decisions you make today play a role in the decisions you make tomorrow? _____

Explain your answer _____

_____

The decisions you make today play a huge role in the decisions you make tomorrow. You may think that when you yield to temptation, it's a small choice, and we claim God's grace, but the choices you make today influence the choices you make later this week. Let me be clear, I am not proposing that God keeps track of your mistakes, but I am saying when you give into small temptation, it gives Satan a foothold in your mind. Once you ask Jesus to forgive your sins, He doesn't see them anymore. He only sees the good things you do (like most loving parents).

Part of this diet is coming to the realization that we are in control of our choices by faith, our attitude about God, and the way we use faith to make those decisions. When you see yourself as making correct decisions by faith, you believe God is at work in those decisions. The same goes for the wrong decisions. One will lead to another, because that is what you see yourself doing. You not believing God will fight for you is evidence of your lack of faith. God's job is to fight our battles for us. Our job is to fight our will. Our job is to pray for faith until our will has been overcome.

We will be examining the Bible to see decision some young men made, and how those decisions affected their future choices

Read **Daniel 1:5-21** *Then the king instructed Ashpenaz, the master of his eunuchs, to bring some of the children of Israel and some of the king's descendants and some of the nobles, [4] young men in whom there was no blemish, but good-looking, gifted in all wisdom, possessing knowledge and quick to understand, who had ability to serve in the king's palace, and whom they might teach the language and literature of the Chaldeans. [5] And the king appointed for them a daily provision of the king's delicacies and of the wine which he drank, and three years of training for them, so that at the end of that time they might serve before the king. [6] Now from among those of the sons of Judah were Daniel, Hananiah, Mishael, and Azariah. [7] To them the chief of the eunuchs gave names: he gave Daniel the name Belteshazzar; to Hananiah, Shadrach; to Mishael, Meshach; and to Azariah, Abed-Nego.*

[8] But Daniel purposed in his heart that he would not defile himself with the portion of the king's delicacies, nor with the wine which he drank; therefore he requested of the chief of the eunuchs that he might not defile himself. [9] Now God had brought Daniel into the favor and goodwill of the chief of the eunuchs. [10] And the chief of the eunuchs said to Daniel, "I fear my lord the king, who has appointed your food and drink. For why should he see your faces looking worse than the young men who are your age? Then you would endanger my head before the king."

¹¹ So Daniel said to the steward whom the chief of the eunuchs had set over Daniel, Hananiah, Mishael, and Azariah, ¹² "Please test your servants for ten days, and let them give us vegetables to eat and water to drink. ¹³ Then let our appearance be examined before you, and the appearance of the young men who eat the portion of the king's delicacies; and as you see fit, so deal with your servants." ¹⁴ So he consented with them in this matter, and tested them ten days. ¹⁵ And at the end of ten days their features appeared better and fatter in flesh than all the young men who ate the portion of the king's delicacies. ¹⁶ Thus the steward took away their portion of delicacies and the wine that they were to drink, and gave them vegetables.

¹⁷ As for these four young men, God gave them knowledge and skill in all literature and wisdom; and Daniel had understanding in all visions and dreams.

¹⁸ Now at the end of the days, when the king had said that they should be brought in, the chief of the eunuchs brought them in before Nebuchadnezzar. ¹⁹ Then the king interviewed them, and among them all none was found like Daniel, Hananiah, Mishael, and Azariah; therefore they served before the king. ²⁰ And in all matters of wisdom and understanding about which the king examined them, he found them ten times better than all the magicians and astrologers who were in all his realm. ²¹ Thus Daniel continued until the first year of King Cyrus.

Would you consider it a small act of faith that Daniel and his friends decided not to defile themselves with the Kings provisions?_____

The decision Daniel and his friends made was a small act of faith. He didn't have much on the line. To us who are addicted to food, it may seem a huge sacrifice, but not a life or death decision.

What happened when Daniel, and his friends made a decision to step out in faith? _____
_____
_____

Daniel and his friends stepped out in faith, and made a decision. God not only completely supplied their need by maintaining their health, He made them stronger and wiser than all the rest of the young men. God blessed them, they witnessed His power, and God was glorified. He wants you to step out in faith so He can show you how much He loves you.

You're not going to lose weight by waking up one morning and "poof" you're thin. It won't be one big decision. Deciding, "Well I'm going to lose weight now," and then lose it. It's going to be a lot of little decisions upon little decisions, little battles upon little battles. Moment by moment, whether you win or lose the last battle, will affect what sort of decision you'll make on the next temptation you face.

We are enslaved or empowered depending upon our last or past decisions. Daniel's decision not to eat the Babylonian food because it was defiled demonstrated his faith in God, and God blessed him and supplied his need. So the next time was easier to make the right decision.

Daniel 1:8 says *'he proposed in his heart.'*

He decided and made the correct choice. Read what happened years later when *Shadrach, Meshach, and Abed-Nego* were older and had to make a decision that was a life or death situation, requiring a lot of faith.

Daniel 3:8-30 especially verse 28. *Therefore at that time certain Chaldeans came forward and accused the Jews. [9] They spoke and said to King Nebuchadnezzar, "O king, live forever! [10] You, O king, have made a decree that everyone who hears the sound of the horn, flute, harp, lyre, and psaltery, in symphony with all kinds of music, shall fall down and worship the gold image; [11] and whoever does not fall down and worship shall be cast into the midst of a burning fiery furnace. [12] There are certain Jews whom you have set over the affairs of the province of Babylon: Shadrach, Meshach, and Abed-Nego; these men, O king, have not paid due regard to you. They do not serve your gods or worship the gold image which you have set up."*

[13] Then Nebuchadnezzar, in rage and fury, gave the command to bring Shadrach, Meshach, and Abed-Nego. So they brought these men before the king. [14] Nebuchadnezzar spoke, saying to them, "Is it true, Shadrach, Meshach, and Abed-Nego, that you do not serve my gods or worship the gold image which I have set up? [15] Now if you are ready at the time you hear the sound of the horn, flute, harp, lyre, and psaltery, in symphony with all kinds of music, and you fall down and worship the image which I have made, good! But if you do not worship, you shall be cast immediately into the midst of a burning fiery furnace. And who is the god who will deliver you from my hands?"

[16] Shadrach, Meshach, and Abed-Nego answered and said to the king, "O Nebuchadnezzar, we have no need to answer you in this matter. [17] If that is the case, our God whom we serve is able to deliver us from the burning fiery furnace, and He will deliver us from your hand, O king. [18] But if not, let it be known to you, O king, that we do not serve your gods, nor will we worship the gold image which you have set up." [19] Then Nebuchadnezzar was full of fury, and the expression on his face changed toward Shadrach, Meshach, and Abed-Nego. He spoke and commanded that they heat the furnace seven times more than it was usually heated. [20] And he commanded certain mighty men of valor who were in his army to bind Shadrach, Meshach, and Abed-Nego, and cast them into the burning fiery furnace. [21] Then these men were bound in their coats, their trousers, their turbans, and their other garments, and were cast into the midst of the burning fiery furnace. [22] Therefore, because the king's command was urgent, and the furnace exceedingly hot, the flame of the fire killed those men who took up Shadrach, Meshach, and Abed-Nego. [23] And these three men, Shadrach, Meshach, and Abed-Nego, fell down bound into the midst of the burning fiery furnace.

[24] Then King Nebuchadnezzar was astonished; and he rose in haste and spoke, saying to his counselors, "Did we not cast three men bound into the midst of the fire?"
They answered and said to the king, "True, O king."

[25] "Look!" he answered, "I see four men loose, walking in the midst of the fire; and they are not hurt, and the form of the fourth is like the Son of God. [26] Then Nebuchadnezzar went near the mouth of the burning fiery furnace and spoke, saying, "Shadrach, Meshach, and Abed-Nego, servants of the Most High God, come out, and come here." Then Shadrach, Meshach, and Abed-Nego came from the midst of the fire. [27] And the satraps, administrators, governors, and the king's counselors gathered together, and they saw these men on whose bodies the fire had no power; the hair of their head was not singed nor were their garments affected, and the smell of fire was not on them.

*[28] **Nebuchadnezzar spoke, saying, "Blessed be the God of Shadrach, Meshach, and Abed-Nego, who sent His Angel and delivered His servants who trusted in Him, and they have frustrated the king's word, and yielded their bodies, that they should not serve nor worship any god except their own God!** [29] Therefore I make a decree that any people, nation, or language which speaks anything amiss against the God of Shadrach, Meshach, and Abed-Nego shall be cut in pieces, and their houses shall be made an ash heap; because there is no other God who can deliver like this."*

[30] Then the king promoted Shadrach, Meshach, and Abed-Nego in the province of Babylon.

God was victorious, and He was given the glory. Because they had an earlier victory, that proved God's faithfulness. They knew they could trust Him.

Do you think if the three young men had failed the earlier test, they could have gone on to this one and been victorious? _____

Maybe, or maybe not, but I know that Satan is only as strong as you will allow. Not only were they saved from certain death, and blessed, but God was glorified. We think, "What a great story!" but this was a scary and dangerous situation.

Read **Daniel 6:1-23** especially verse 10 *It pleased Darius to set over the kingdom one hundred and twenty satraps, to be over the whole kingdom; [2] and over these, three governors, of whom Daniel was one, that the satraps might give account to them, so that the king would suffer no loss. [3] Then this Daniel distinguished himself above the governors and satraps, because an excellent spirit was in him; and the king gave thought to setting him over the whole realm. [4] So the governors and satraps sought to find some charge against Daniel concerning the kingdom; but they could find no charge or fault, because he was faithful; nor was there any error or fault found in him. [5] Then these men said, "We shall not find any charge against this Daniel unless we find it against him concerning the law of his God."*

⁶ So these governors and satraps thronged before the king, and said thus to him: "King Darius, live forever! ⁷ All the governors of the kingdom, the administrators and satraps, the counselors and advisors, have consulted together to establish a royal statute and to make a firm decree, that whoever petitions any god or man for thirty days, except you, O king, shall be cast into the den of lions. ⁸ Now, O king, establish the decree and sign the writing, so that it cannot be changed, according to the law of the Medes and Persians, which does not alter."

⁹ Therefore King Darius signed the written decree.

¹⁰ Now when Daniel knew that the writing was signed, he went home. And in his upper room, with his windows open toward Jerusalem, he knelt down on his knees three times that day, and prayed and gave thanks before his God, as was his custom since early days.

¹¹ Then these men assembled and found Daniel praying and making supplication before his God. ¹² And they went before the king, and spoke concerning the king's decree: "Have you not signed a decree that every man who petitions any god or man within thirty days, except you, O king, shall be cast into the den of lions?"
The king answered and said, "The thing is true, according to the law of the Medes and Persians, which does not alter."

¹³ So they answered and said before the king, "That Daniel, who is one of the captives from Judah, does not show due regard for you, O king, or for the decree that you have signed, but makes his petition three times a day."

¹⁴ And the king, when he heard these words, was greatly displeased with himself, and set his heart on Daniel to deliver him; and he labored till the going down of the sun to deliver him.

¹⁵ Then these men approached the king, and said to the king, "Know, O king, that it is the law of the Medes and Persians that no decree or statute which the king establishes may be changed."

¹⁶ So the king gave the command, and they brought Daniel and cast him into the den of lions. But the king spoke, saying to Daniel, "Your God, whom you serve continually, He will deliver you." ¹⁷ Then a stone was brought and laid on the mouth of the den, and the king sealed it with his own signet ring and with the signets of his lords, that the purpose concerning Daniel might not be changed.

¹⁸ Now the king went to his palace and spent the night fasting; and no musicians were brought before him. Also his sleep went from him. ¹⁹ Then the king arose very early in the morning and went in haste to the den of lions. ²⁰ And when he came to the den, he cried out with a lamenting voice to Daniel. The king spoke, saying to Daniel, "Daniel, servant of the living God, has your God, whom you serve continually, been able to deliver you from the lions?"

²¹ Then Daniel said to the king, "O king, live forever! ²² My God sent His angel and shut the lions' mouths, so that they have not hurt me, because I was found innocent before Him; and also, O king, I have done no wrong before you."

23 Now the king was exceedingly glad for him, and commanded that they should take Daniel up out of the den. So Daniel was taken up out of the den, and no injury whatever was found on him, because he believed in his God.

24 And the king gave the command, and they brought those men who had accused Daniel, and they cast them into the den of lions--them, their children, and their wives; and the lions overpowered them, and broke all their bones in pieces before they ever came to the bottom of the den.

25 Then King Darius wrote:

To all peoples, nations, and languages that dwell in all the earth:Peace be multiplied to you.

26 I make a decree that in every dominion of my kingdom men must tremble and fear before the God of Daniel. For He is the living God, And steadfast forever; His kingdom is the one which shall not be destroyed, And His dominion shall endure to the end. 27 He delivers and rescues, And He works signs and wonders In Heaven and on earth, Who has delivered Daniel from the power of the lions.

28 So this Daniel prospered in the reign of Darius and in the reign of Cyrus the Persian.

Daniel and his friends made the right decisions no matter the cost. The choices they made earlier gave them the strength and faith they needed later when the real test came.

Romans 6:19-23 *I speak in human terms because of the weakness of your flesh. For just as you presented your members as slaves of uncleanness, and of lawlessness leading to more lawlessness, so now present your members as slaves of righteousness for holiness.*

20 For when you were slaves of sin, you were free in regard to righteousness. 21 What fruit did you have then in the things of which you are now ashamed? For the end of those things is death. 22 But now having been set free from sin, and having become slaves of God, you have your fruit to holiness, and the end, everlasting life. 23 For the wages of sin is death, but the gift of God is eternal life in Christ Jesus our Lord.

Read: **Joshua 24: 1-28**

In light of today's study, what was the Scripture or statement in today's lesson that most spoke to your heart? _____

_____

_____

_____

What steps of faith does God want you to take towards Him today? _____

_____

_____

_____

Rephrase the Scripture or statement into an expression of faith_____

_____

_____

_____

Memorize the following Scripture this week (it's a long one!)

Joshua 24:15 *And if it seems evil to you to serve the LORD, choose for yourselves this day whom you will serve, whether the gods which your fathers served that were on the other side of the River, or the gods of the Amorites, in whose land you dwell. But as for me and my house, we will serve the LORD.*

Week 4 Day 2
David's decision helped later

Day _____ Date _____

The story of David and Goliath is an entertaining one. It's like a true Cinderella story, but put yourself in David's shoes. Think about how much faith it took for him to stand against the giant. I have a hard time blessing my food in front of my coworkers. The giant was so frightening. Whole armies of strong men were intimidated by him.

What gave young David so much courage?

Read **I Samuel**

[1] *Now the Philistines gathered their armies together to battle, and were gathered at Sochoh, which belongs to Judah; they encamped between Sochoh and Azekah, in Ephes Dammim.* [2] *And Saul and the men of Israel were gathered together, and they encamped in the Valley of Elah, and drew up in battle array against the Philistines.* [3] *The Philistines stood on a mountain on one side, and Israel stood on a mountain on the other side, with a valley between them.*

[4] *And a champion went out from the camp of the Philistines, named Goliath, from Gath, whose height was six cubits and a span.* [5] *He had a bronze helmet on his head, and he was armed with a coat of mail, and the weight of the coat was five thousand shekels of bronze.* [6] *And he had bronze armor on his legs and a bronze javelin between his shoulders.*

[7] *Now the staff of his spear was like a weaver's beam, and his iron spearhead weighed six hundred shekels; and a shield-bearer went before him.* [8] *Then he stood and cried out to the armies of Israel, and said to them, "Why have you come out to line up for battle? Am I not a Philistine, and you the servants of Saul? Choose a man for yourselves, and let him come down to me.* [9] *If he is able to fight with me and kill me, then we will be your servants. But if I prevail against him and kill him, then you shall be our servants and serve us."* [10] *And the Philistine said, "I defy the armies of Israel this day; give me a man, that we may fight together."* [11] *When Saul and all Israel heard these words of the Philistine, they were dismayed and greatly afraid.*

[12] *Now David was the son of that Ephrathite of Bethlehem Judah, whose name was Jesse, and who had eight sons. And the man was old, advanced in years, in the days of Saul.*

[13] *The three oldest sons of Jesse had gone to follow Saul to the battle. The names of his three sons who went to the battle were Eliab the firstborn, next to him Abinadab, and the third Shammah.* [14] *David was the youngest. And the three oldest followed Saul.* [15] *But David occasionally went and returned from Saul to feed his father's sheep at Bethlehem.*

[16] *And the Philistine drew near and presented himself forty days, morning and evening.*

[17] *Then Jesse said to his son David, "Take now for your brothers an ephah of this dried grain and these ten loaves, and run to your brothers at the camp.* [18] *And carry these ten cheeses to the captain of their thousand, and see how your brothers fare, and bring back news of them."* [19] *Now*

Saul and they and all the men of Israel were in the Valley of Elah, fighting with the Philistines.

²⁰ *So David rose early in the morning, left the sheep with a keeper, and took the things and went as Jesse had commanded him. And he came to the camp as the army was going out to the fight and shouting for the battle.* ²¹ *For Israel and the Philistines had drawn up in battle array, army against army.* ²² *And David left his supplies in the hand of the supply keeper, ran to the army, and came and greeted his brothers.* ²³ *Then as he talked with them, there was the champion, the Philistine of Gath, Goliath by name, coming up from the armies of the Philistines; and he spoke according to the same words. So David heard them.* ²⁴ *And all the men of Israel, when they saw the man, fled from him and were dreadfully afraid.* ²⁵ *So the men of Israel said, "Have you seen this man who has come up? Surely he has come up to defy Israel; and it shall be that the man who kills him the king will enrich with great riches, will give him his daughter, and give his father's house exemption from taxes in Israel."*

²⁶ *Then David spoke to the men who stood by him, saying, "What shall be done for the man who kills this Philistine and takes away the reproach from Israel? For who is this uncircumcised Philistine, that he should defy the armies of the living God?"*

²⁷ *And the people answered him in this manner, saying, "So shall it be done for the man who kills him."*

²⁸ *Now Eliab his oldest brother heard when he spoke to the men; and Eliab's anger was aroused against David, and he said, "Why did you come down here? And with whom have you left those few sheep in the wilderness? I know your pride and the insolence of your heart, for you have come down to see the battle."*

²⁹ *And David said, "What have I done now? Is there not a cause?"* ³⁰ *Then he turned from him toward another and said the same thing; and these people answered him as the first ones did.*

³¹ *Now when the words which David spoke were heard, they reported them to Saul; and he sent for him.* ³² *Then David said to Saul, "Let no man's heart fail because of him; your servant will go and fight with this Philistine."*

³³ *And Saul said to David, "You are not able to go against this Philistine to fight with him; for you are a youth, and he a man of war from his youth."*

³⁴ **But David said to Saul, "Your servant used to keep his father's sheep, and when a lion or a bear came and took a lamb out of the flock,** ³⁵ **I went out after it and struck it, and delivered the lamb from its mouth; and when it arose against me, I caught it by its beard, and struck and killed it.** ³⁶ **Your servant has killed both lion and bear; and this uncircumcised Philistine will be like one of them, seeing he has defied the armies of the living God."** ³⁷ **Moreover David said, "The LORD, who delivered me from the paw of the lion and from the paw of the bear, He will deliver me from the hand of this Philistine."**

And Saul said to David, "Go, and the LORD be with you!"

³⁸ So Saul clothed David with his armor, and he put a bronze helmet on his head; he also clothed him with a coat of mail. ³⁹ David fastened his sword to his armor and tried to walk, for he had not tested them. And David said to Saul, "I cannot walk with these, for I have not tested them." So David took them off.

⁴⁰ Then he took his staff in his hand; and he chose for himself five smooth stones from the brook, and put them in a shepherd's bag, in a pouch which he had, and his sling was in his hand. And he drew near to the Philistine. ⁴¹ So the Philistine came, and began drawing near to David, and the man who bore the shield went before him. ⁴² And when the Philistine looked about and saw David, he disdained him; for he was only a youth, ruddy and good-looking. ⁴³ So the Philistine said to David, "Am I a dog, that you come to me with sticks?" And the Philistine cursed David by his gods. ⁴⁴ And the Philistine said to David, "Come to me, and I will give your flesh to the birds of the air and the beasts of the field!"

⁴⁵ Then David said to the Philistine, "You come to me with a sword, with a spear, and with a javelin. But I come to you in the name of the LORD of hosts, the God of the armies of Israel, whom you have defied. ⁴⁶ This day the LORD will deliver you into my hand, and I will strike you and take your head from you. And this day I will give the carcasses of the camp of the Philistines to the birds of the air and the wild beasts of the earth, that all the earth may know that there is a God in Israel. ⁴⁷ Then all this assembly shall know that the LORD does not save with sword and spear; for the battle is the LORD's, and He will give you into our hands."

⁴⁸ So it was, when the Philistine arose and came and drew near to meet David, that David hurried and ran toward the army to meet the Philistine. ⁴⁹ Then David put his hand in his bag and took out a stone; and he slung it and struck the Philistine in his forehead, so that the stone sank into his forehead, and he fell on his face to the earth. ⁵⁰ So David prevailed over the Philistine with a sling and a stone, and struck the Philistine and killed him. But there was no sword in the hand of David. ⁵¹ Therefore David ran and stood over the Philistine, took his sword and drew it out of its sheath and killed him, and cut off his head with it. And when the Philistines saw that their champion was dead, they fled. ⁵² Now the men of Israel and Judah arose and shouted, and pursued the Philistines as far as the entrance of the valley and to the gates of Ekron. And the wounded of the Philistines fell along the road to Shaaraim, even as far as Gath and Ekron. ⁵³ Then the children of Israel returned from chasing the Philistines, and they plundered their tents. ⁵⁴ And David took the head of the Philistine and brought it to Jerusalem, but he put his armor in his tent.

⁵⁵ When Saul saw David going out against the Philistine, he said to Abner, the commander of the army, "Abner, whose son is this youth?"

And Abner said, "As your soul lives, O king, I do not know."

⁵⁶ So the king said, "Inquire whose son this young man is."

⁵⁷ Then, as David returned from the slaughter of the Philistine, Abner took him and brought him before Saul with the head of the Philistine in his hand. ⁵⁸ And Saul said to him, "Whose son are you, young man?"

So David answered, "I am the son of your servant Jesse the Bethlehemite."
Read **I Samuel 17:34,35** again,

But David said to Saul, "Your servant used to keep his father's sheep, and when a lion or a bear came and took a lamb out of the flock, [35] I went out after it and struck it, and delivered the lamb from its mouth; and when it arose against me, I caught it by its beard, and struck and killed it.

We usually skip over this part, because the rest of the story is so good, and we like the end. However, God put this Scripture here for a reason. Do you think David could have wrestled and killed these wild animals in his own strength? _____

David knew he couldn't prevail on his own, but by faith he killed the lion and bear. These experiences built his faith in God and gave him the courage and knowledge that he could defeat Goliath, not by his own might, but by the power of God.

Goliath was massive. His armor alone probably weighed more than David did. He was over nine feet tall. He completely demoralized the Israeli army. Why do you think David had more faith than the other men that were older than he was? _____
_____

David didn't just suddenly have enough faith to walk up to the huge giant secure in the knowledge that God would deliver him. I am sure David had spent a lot of alone time with God while he was tending to his family's sheep. His lonely solitude as a shepherd, praying to God and singing praises, all contributed to David's faith. God had tested his faith before, with the lion and the bear. David knew the power of God.

In the last two studies we have been reading about men of God. How their faith was steadfast, and strong, because they had been in training to build their faith muscles. We hate it when the times of testing come, but they are the only way to get your workout. If it were easy, you would never have to rely on God.

Think back on all the men and their lives. Did God bless them? _____ Explain how God was glorified by their lives. _____
_____
_____
_____

God wants us to step out in faith so he can show His glory. Not only were they saved and blessed, but also, God was glorified. King Darieus made a decree that no one would speak evil of The God of Daniel, Shadrach, Meshach and Abed-Nego. In addition, the whole Israel nation was glorifying God after David's act of faith.

Read: **Hebrews chapter 11-12:3**

In light of today's study, what was the Scripture or statement in today's lesson that most spoke to your heart? _____

_____
_____
_____

What steps of faith does God want you to take towards Him today? _____

_____
_____
_____

Rephrase the Scripture or statement into an expression of faith_____

_____
_____

Memorize the following Scripture this week.

And if _____ seems evil to you to _____ the LORD, _____for yourselves this day whom _____ will serve, _____ the gods which your _____ served that were on the other side of the River, or the _____ of the Amorites, in whose _____ _____ dwell. But as for me and my _____, we _____ serve _____ LORD."

Week 4 Day 3
Saul's Decisions

Day _____ Date _____

This study is about Saul. He didn't trust God, and it was reflected in the decisions he made. It tells of his life of hardship jealousy, and pain.

God did not want Israel subject to a king. He was their King. He set up a perfect system for rule. He appointed judges over them. Nevertheless, the people wanted what they perceived to be the "right way" to govern, and God gave them what they wanted, so the first King over Israel was Saul.

Read **I Samuel 12: 12-** *And when you saw that Nahash king of the Ammonites came against you, you said to me, 'No, but a king shall reign over us,' when the LORD your God was your king.* [13] *"Now therefore, here is the king whom you have chosen and whom you have desired. And take note, the LORD has set a king over you.*

Saul was not the most humble of servants. After Saul had reigned a few years, he decided to flex his muscle. The Bible does not say that he consulted God on this decision…that is, until they saw the size of the Philistine army. It seems that he sent for Samuel, the Prophet, and Samuel said he would come to him in seven days, but was a little late.

Read **I Samuel 13:5-15** [5] *Then the Philistines gathered together to fight with Israel, thirty thousand chariots and six thousand horsemen, and people as the sand which is on the seashore in multitude. And they came up and encamped in Michmash, to the east of Beth Aven.* [6] *When the men of Israel saw that they were in danger (for the people were distressed), then the people hid in caves, in thickets, in rocks, in holes, and in pits.* [7] *And some of the Hebrews crossed over the Jordan to the land of Gad and Gilead.*

As for Saul, he was still in Gilgal, and all the people followed him trembling. [8] *Then he waited seven days, according to the time set by Samuel. But Samuel did not come to Gilgal; and the people were scattered from him.* [9] *So Saul said, "Bring a burnt offering and peace offerings here to me." And he offered the burnt offering.* [10] *Now it happened, as soon as he had finished presenting the burnt offering, that Samuel came; and Saul went out to meet him, that he might greet him.*

[11] *And Samuel said, "What have you done?" Saul said, "When I saw that the people were scattered from me, and that you did not come within the days appointed, and that the Philistines gathered together at Michmash,* [12] *then I said, "The Philistines will now come down on me at Gilgal, and I have not made supplication to the LORD.' Therefore I felt compelled, and offered a burnt offering."*

[13] *And Samuel said to Saul, "You have done foolishly. You have not kept the commandment of the LORD your God, which He commanded you. For now the LORD would have established your kingdom over Israel forever.* [14] *But now your kingdom shall not continue. The LORD has sought for Himself a man after His own heart, and the LORD has commanded him to be commander*

over His people, because you have not kept what the LORD commanded you."

[15] Then Samuel arose and went up from Gilgal to Gibeah of Benjamin. And Saul numbered the people present with him, about six hundred men.

At first glance, it doesn't seem that Saul did such a terrible thing. He was scared and offered a burnt offering to God. What is so wrong in that?

Saul knew full well that what he did was not acceptable to God, because Saul was not a descendent of Levi. He broke one of God's laws. Why do you think Saul disobeyed the Law of Moses and God's Prophet Samuel? _____

_____

Saul panicked, and he didn't see the situation from God's prospective. He didn't look at it as an opportunity to show the power of God. He didn't go to the Lord for strength. He tried to fix the problem himself, in his own power.

Saul thought God and Samuel were moving too slow, and he was afraid of what his people would do. He wanted what he wanted when he wanted it and for his own reasons. He evidently didn't learn his lesson and repent, because Saul disobeyed God again by taking spoils of battle when God told him, "Utterly destroy everything."

Read: **I Samuel 15:10-29** *Now the word of the LORD came to Samuel, saying, [11] "I greatly regret that I have set up Saul as king, for he has turned back from following Me, and has not performed My commandments." And it grieved Samuel, and he cried out to the LORD all night. [12] So when Samuel rose early in the morning to meet Saul, it was told Samuel, saying, "Saul went to Carmel, and indeed, he set up a monument for himself; and he has gone on around, passed by, and gone down to Gilgal." [13] Then Samuel went to Saul, and Saul said to him, "Blessed are you of the LORD! I have performed the commandment of the LORD."*

[14] But Samuel said, "What then is this bleating of the sheep in my ears, and the lowing of the oxen which I hear?"

[15] And Saul said, "They have brought them from the Amalekites; for the people spared the best of the sheep and the oxen, to sacrifice to the LORD your God; and the rest we have utterly destroyed."

[16] Then Samuel said to Saul, "Be quiet! And I will tell you what the LORD said to me last night." And he said to him, "Speak on."

[17] So Samuel said, "When you were little in your own eyes, were you not head of the tribes of Israel? And did not the LORD anoint you king over Israel? [18] Now the LORD sent you on a mission, and said, "Go, and utterly destroy the sinners, the Amalekites, and fight against them until they are consumed.' [19] Why then did you not obey the voice of the LORD? Why did you swoop down on the spoil, and do evil in the sight of the LORD?"

²⁰ And Saul said to Samuel, "But I have obeyed the voice of the LORD, and gone on the mission on which the LORD sent me, and brought back Agag king of Amalek; I have utterly destroyed the Amalekites. ²¹ But the people took of the plunder, sheep and oxen, the best of the things which should have been utterly destroyed, to sacrifice to the LORD your God in Gilgal." ²² So Samuel said: "Has the LORD as great delight in burnt offerings and sacrifices, As in obeying the voice of the LORD? Behold, to obey is better than sacrifice, And to heed than the fat of rams. ²³ For rebellion is as the sin of witchcraft, And stubbornness is as iniquity and idolatry. Because you have rejected the word of the LORD, He also has rejected you from being king. ²⁴ Then Saul said to Samuel, "I have sinned, for I have transgressed the commandment of the LORD and your words, because I feared the people and obeyed their voice.

How did Saul react in verses 20-24 When Samuel confronted by him? _____

_____

Saul excused his disobedience by blaming "the people." He tried to justify that he hadn't eliminated the best of the sheep and oxen by suggesting that he had intended it to be a sacrifice to the Lord.

Saul did confess his sin in chapter 24, but still excused himself by saying he feared the people. He did not trust God to defend him, which showed lack of faith.

Saul was very jealous of David after David defeated Goliath. Contrast Saul with David. When he was confronted with his transgressions, David didn't try to rationalize or make excuses for himself. Full expressions of David's confessions are found in **Psalm 51:2; Samuel 12:13.**

Sin for sin, David and Saul are about neck and neck; the difference is David's response to God. When you read the entire book of **I Samuel**, you find out how many times Saul decided not to trust God. He always tried to fix his problems on his own. He didn't trust God to defend him, and it demonstrated his lack of faith when didn't step forward as Israel's champion against Goliath. David, though young and small, stood against the nine-foot giant in the name of the Lord, because he had made correct decisions to trust God earlier and knew God would deliver him. Saul never trusted God to defend him, and it had a tragic effect on his life. At the end of his life he was a bitter, jealous man.

I heard about a giant redwood tree. It stood for years and years. It had been through many disasters, including being hit by lighting twice. It went through countless storms, but still stood tall and strong. Then, suddenly, one day, one sunny day, it just toppled over. The rangers were mystified as it seemed so sturdy, but on closer examination, they found small beetles had infested the tree. Small bugs that could hardly be seen with the naked eye had finally eaten clean through the enormous tree.

Sin is like that. A little compromise here, a little there. Satan doesn't stand up and yell, "Hey I am going to tempt you now!" If he did it would be a lot easier to defend against the attack. No, he is subtle. He starts with small sins and graduates from there.

You may think the right decision is too hard sometimes. Ask God to show you His perspective. Compare David's struggle with Saul's after Samuel had anointed him. They had both already received the promise from God. Saul chose to fear and take matters into his own hands; David chose to trust.

When David was anointed as King of Israel, he was still a young man. Growing into manhood, his strength and ability increased to the point that it looked as if he could take the throne by force if he wanted to. To everyone else but David and God, he had every right to make himself King. Fearing David and not trusting God, Saul tried killing David on many occasions. Nevertheless, David trusted God and waited on Him and the fulfillment of that promise that God would make him King. David had to wait many years, many of them hiding from Saul, but God was faithful.

We need to understand that it is never just a small bite; that small decision gives Satan a foothold, and he will take every advantage of it. C.S. Lewis put it this way, "Every time you make a choice you are turning the central part of you, the part of you that chooses, into something a little different from what it was before."

Read I Samuel Chapters 24 and 26

In light of today's study, what was the Scripture or statement in today's lesson that most spoke to your heart? _____

_____

_____

_____

What steps of faith does God want you to take towards Him today? _____

_____

_____

_____

Rephrase the Scripture or statement into an expression of faith_____

_____

_____

_____

Memorize the following Scripture this week.

Joshua 24:15 *And if _____ seems _____ to you to _____ the LORD, _____ for _____ this day whom _____ will serve, _____ the _____ which your _____ served that _____ on the other side of _____ River, or the _____ of the _____ , in whose _____ _____ dwell. But as for me _____ _____ _____ , we _____ serve _____ LORD."*

Week 4 Day 4
Punished by our sins not for them

Day _____ Date _____

When you accepted Christ as your Savior, you became a new creation and received a wonderful gift beyond imagination. You received the gift of righteousness; your sins are erased, and you will not pay the penalty for them. So does that mean you can just sin all you want, and God will not punish you for it? I went through a season where I thought, "I can't do this diet thing; it is just going to be up to God, and I'm going to stop trying. If God wants me to change, He will change me." I ate anything and everything I wanted and got fatter and fatter.

You do have to fight Satan, but you fight him with prayer. It's the emotional battle of turning from your desire to overeat, asking God to deliver you. Once that's done, God takes over. He will not take away your will.

When I was going through the season I spoke of earlier, I thought when the Bible says, "It's not by my strength," God was going to do it all for me. He does fight for me, but I have to ask for the help. I have to keep in close contact with Him, and I have to give Him my will. I pray and ask God for help, and if I need to, I pray again and again. He always rescues me, but He will not save me from my own will.

I can't give my will to Him one time and expect it is enough. Each time I am tempted, I need to ask Him for help. When you are born-again, it's true that you're not punished *for* your sins *eternally*, but you are punished *by* your sins. In this world, there are consequences for all our choices.

Galatians 6:7-9 *Do not be deceived, God is not mocked; for whatever a man sows, that he will also reap. [8] For he who sows to his flesh will of the flesh reap corruption, but he who sows to the Spirit will of the Spirit reap everlasting life. [9] And let us not grow weary while doing good, for in due season we shall reap if we do not lose heart.*

Think about it. If we steal, we are constantly looking over our shoulder waiting to get caught. The stolen item becomes a thing of shame rather than enjoyment. Every time you look at it or use it, you have the feeling of fear and regret. Same with adulterer, lying constantly on their guard, hoping they don't get caught.

When we overeat, we become overweight. It's that straightforward. When we go against what God has planned for us, we face the consequences of that action.

Proverbs 13:21 *Evil pursues sinners but the righteous good shall be repaid.*

Proverbs11:27 *He who earnestly seeks good finds favor, But trouble will come to him who seeks evil.*

While writing this days study, I knew God had given me the phrase, "We (Christians) are punished by our sins, not for them." But I couldn't think of a Scripture that would support it. I prayed, and asked God to show me, and He reminded me of the following story that perfectly illustrates this idea.

Read: **Luke 15:11-31** *Then He said: "A certain man had two sons. ¹² And the younger of them said to his father, "Father, give me the portion of goods that falls to me.' So he divided to them his livelihood. ¹³ And not many days after, the younger son gathered all together, journeyed to a far country, and there wasted his possessions with prodigal living. ¹⁴ But when he had spent all, there arose a severe famine in that land, and he began to be in want.*

¹⁵ Then he went and joined himself to a citizen of that country, and he sent him into his fields to feed swine. ¹⁶ And he would gladly have filled his stomach with the pods that the swine ate, and no one gave him anything.

¹⁷ "But when he came to himself, he said, "How many of my father's hired servants have bread enough and to spare, and I perish with hunger! ¹⁸ I will arise and go to my father, and will say to him, "Father, I have sinned against Heaven and before you, ¹⁹ and I am no longer worthy to be called your son. Make me like one of your hired servants."'

²⁰ "And he arose and came to his father. But when he was still a great way off, his father saw him and had compassion, and ran and fell on his neck and kissed him. ²¹ And the son said to him, "Father, I have sinned against Heaven and in your sight, and am no longer worthy to be called your son.'

²² "But the father said to his servants, "Bring out the best robe and put it on him, and put a ring on his hand and sandals on his feet. ²³ And bring the fatted calf here and kill it, and let us eat and be merry; ²⁴ for this my son was dead and is alive again; he was lost and is found.' And they began to be merry.

²⁵ "Now his older son was in the field. And as he came and drew near to the house, he heard music and dancing. ²⁶ So he called one of the servants and asked what these things meant. ²⁷ And he said to him, "Your brother has come, and because he has received him safe and sound, your father has killed the fatted calf.'

²⁸ "But he was angry and would not go in. Therefore his father came out and pleaded with him. ²⁹ So he answered and said to his father, "Lo, these many years I have been serving you; I never transgressed your commandment at any time; and yet you never gave me a young goat, that I might make merry with my friends. ³⁰ But as soon as this son of yours came, who has devoured your livelihood with harlots, you killed the fatted calf for him.'

³¹ "And he said to him, "Son, you are always with me, and all that I have is yours. ³² It was right that we should make merry and be glad, for your brother was dead and is alive again, and was lost and is found."

The younger son asked his father for his share of his inheritance. Why do you think he wanted his inheritance early? _____

_____

_____

Just like us, he thought it was too hard to be obedient to his father and do what his father asked. He wanted what he wanted when he wanted it. What happened when the young man received his inheritance? _____

_____

_____

He promptly spent it, and just like us, found out that gorging on pie isn't worth the cost. He found himself worse off than his own father's servants were.

Deciding to swallow his pride and go back to his father was the smartest thing he could have done, and the son's confession of sin brought full restoration, but his inheritance was still gone. He was blessed and still loved by his father just as much as he ever was, but he was still punished by his sin.

Do you think he was having fun while he was away from his father? _____ Why?

_____

_____

_____

At first, the prodigal was having a wonderful time just like eating pecan pie alamode. It tastes so good while you are eating, but then the consequences. Eventually we all have to pay a price for our decisions. As I said earlier, the biggest reason for failure is substituting something you really want for something you want right now.

His money was spent, and his fair-weather friends deserted him. He was hungry, cold and lonely. He was completely dishonored and living with the pigs. In the Jewish culture, that is the worst thing that could possibly happen. Just to feed them was disgraceful enough, but to have to live with them, would be the ultimate humiliation. He was punished by sin, not for them.

Why do you think the older son was upset? _____

_____

_____

When the older son found out what his father was planning, he didn't want to go to the party. He felt it was unfair because he had always served his father while the younger son had been gone. Which son do you think was more satisfied with his life? _____

Why do you think that? _____

_____

The older son thought it wasn't fair but read what the father says in verse thirty-one, *"And he said to him, 'Son, you are always with me, and all that I have is yours.'"* He told his son, "You have always had my blessings, and you didn't have to live with the pigs and go hungry." Furthermore, not only was he blessed, but he still had his inheritance. All the inheritance now belonged to the older son.

The father explained it perfectly to his older son. He reminded him he hadn't been punished like his brother had. The older brother thought the younger had gone out and squandered all his money having a wonderful time, while he was there working, but that's not the case at all.

While sinning, it may seem fun for a season, but eventually you find yourself humiliated and living with the pigs, and sometimes being called one.

Another example of someone being punished by his sin is David. God called him a man after His own heart. However, that didn't mean David could escape God's loving discipline.

II Samuel 11:1-27 *It happened in the spring of the year, at the time when kings go out to battle, that David sent Joab and his servants with him, and all Israel; and they destroyed the people of Ammon and besieged Rabbah. But David remained at Jerusalem.*

² Then it happened one evening that David arose from his bed and walked on the roof of the king's house. And from the roof he saw a woman bathing, and the woman was very beautiful to behold. ³ So David sent and inquired about the woman. And someone said, "Is this not Bathsheba, the daughter of Eliam, the wife of Uriah the Hittite?" ⁴ Then David sent messengers, and took her; and she came to him, and he lay with her, for she was cleansed from her impurity; and she returned to her house. ⁵ And the woman conceived; so she sent and told David, and said, "I am with child."

David tried to cover his tracks by allowing Uriah, Bathsheba's husband, to come home and sleep with her, but Uriah had too much character and would not sleep with his wife when the Ark of the Lord and his fellow soldiers were still on the battlefield. So, David panicked and ordered Uriah to the forefront of the hottest battle and left him there to fight on his own, *"That he may be struck down and die."*

Read what happened when David was confronted with what he had done to Uriah.

II Samuel 12:1-23 *Then the LORD sent Nathan to David. And he came to him, and said to him: "There were two men in one city, one rich and the other poor. ² The rich man had exceedingly many flocks and herds. ³ But the poor man had nothing, except one little ewe lamb which he had bought and nourished; and it grew up together with him and with his children. It ate of his own food and drank from his own cup and lay in his bosom; and it was like a daughter to him. ⁴ And a traveler came to the rich man, who refused to take from his own flock and from his own herd to prepare one for the wayfaring man who had come to him; but he took the poor man's lamb and prepared it for the man who had come to him."*

⁵ So David's anger was greatly aroused against the man, and he said to Nathan, "As the LORD lives, the man who has done this shall surely die! ⁶ And he shall restore fourfold for the lamb, because he did this thing and because he had no pity."

⁷ Then Nathan said to David, "You are the man! Thus says the LORD God of Israel: "I anointed you king over Israel, and I delivered you from the hand of Saul. ⁸ I gave you your master's house and your master's wives into your keeping, and gave you the house of Israel and Judah. And if that had been too little, I also would have given you much more! ⁹ Why have you despised the commandment of the LORD, to do evil in His sight? You have killed Uriah the Hittite with the sword; you have taken his wife to be your wife, and have killed him with the sword of the people of Ammon. ¹⁰ Now therefore, the sword shall never depart from your house, because you have despised Me, and have taken the wife of Uriah the Hittite to be your wife.' ¹¹ Thus says the LORD: "Behold, I will raise up adversity against you from your own house; and I will take your wives before your eyes and give them to your neighbor, and he shall lie with your wives in the sight of this sun. ¹² For you did it secretly, but I will do this thing before all Israel, before the sun."'

¹³ So David said to Nathan, "I have sinned against the LORD."
And Nathan said to David, "The LORD also has put away your sin; you shall not die. ¹⁴ However, because by this deed you have given great occasion to the enemies of the LORD to blaspheme, the child also who is born to you shall surely die." ¹⁵ Then Nathan departed to his house.

As Nathan told this story, he knew David understood the potential of that lamb, David had been a shepherd. David was so furious at the man behind this act, that at first he wanted him dead. That was stronger than the law called for in this case. He then pronounced judgment from the law of God that stated when a sheep was stolen, it had to be restored four fold, and in so, pronounced judgment on himself and his family, as it was David who was guilty.

Exodus 22: 1 *"If a man steals an ox or a sheep, and slaughters it or sells it, he shall restore five oxen for an ox and four sheep for a sheep.*

David lost three sons and his daughter Tamar's life was destroyed. David wouldn't discipline his son Amnon for raping his half-sister, Tamar (David's daughter), probably because he felt guilty for his own sin. He was embroiled in the mess he had made for himself with Bathsheba. Therefore, his son Absalom took matters in his own hands, as Tamar was his full-blooded sister. He killed his half-brother Amnon for raping Tamar.

You can read about that in **II Samuel 13.**

Even though God forgives us, we still reap the consequences. God is not mocked. By sending Uriah the Hittite to the front line of attack, David killed him just as sure as he would have if he would have held the sword himself and he paid back lamb for lamb, or child for child.

II Samuel 12:9 *Why have you despised the commandment of the LORD, to do evil in His sight?*

The word "despised" means to think lightly of. It is the same word used of Esau, when he despised his birthright.

Genesis 25:34 *And Jacob gave Esau bread and stew of lentils; then he ate and drank, arose, and went his way. Thus Esau despised his birthright.*

That's what we do when we don't trust God and act as if our sin of overeating is not that bad.

Read: **Psalm 103:10-13** *He has not dealt with us according to our sins, Nor punished us according to our iniquities.* [11] *For as the Heavens are high above the earth, So great is His mercy toward those who fear Him;* [12] *As far as the east is from the west, So far has He removed our transgressions from us.* [13] *As a father pities his children, So the LORD pities those who fear Him.* [14] *For He knows our frame; He remembers that we are dust.*

God doesn't give us what we deserve, because we deserve death. He throws our sin as far as east is to west and we will live with him forever. That doesn't mean we don't reap the consequences for our sin, and if we are disobedient to the hunger signals God provided, then we will reap a lot of flesh. There are consequences here on earth for the decisions we make right or wrong, good or bad.

The best way to begin to feel good about you is to keep making good choices. The choices may seem too difficult for you at times but if you can get past the emotional barrier of your will, God will do the fighting.

II Corinthians 6:11, 12 *O Corinthians! We have spoken openly to you, our heart is wide open.* [12] *You are not restricted by us, but you are restricted by your own affections.*

God says he calls Heaven and Earth against us as witnesses, that the choices aren't too hard for us. So, we can CHOOSE LIFE!

Read **Deuteronomy 30:11-20**

In light of today's study, what was the Scripture or statement in today's lesson that most spoke to your heart? _____

_____

_____

_____

What steps of faith does God want you to take towards Him today? _____

_____

_____

_____

Rephrase the Scripture or statement into an expression of faith_____

_____

_____

_____

Memory verse

Joshua 24:15 *And if* _____ _____ _____ *to* _____ *to*
_____ *the LORD,* _____ *for* _____ *this day whom*
_____ *will* _____, _____ *the* _____ *which your*
_____ *served that* _____ *on the* _____ _____ *of*
_____ *River, or the* _____ *of the* _____, *in*
_____ _____ _____ *dwell. But as for me*
_____ _____ _____, *we* _____ *serve*
_____ *LORD."*

Week 4 Day 5
The Fight

Day _____ Date _____

God has already won the battle. The following is one of the accounts of an Old Testament battle. In it, you see how God handles your enemy.

Read II Chronicles 20:1-30 *[1] It happened after this that the people of Moab with the people of Ammon, and others with them besides the Ammonites, came to battle against Jehoshaphat. [2] Then some came and told Jehoshaphat, saying, "A great multitude is coming against you from beyond the sea, from Syria; and they are in Hazazon Tamar" (which is En Gedi). [3] And Jehoshaphat feared, and set himself to seek the LORD, and proclaimed a fast throughout all Judah. [4] So Judah gathered together to ask help from the LORD; and from all the cities of Judah they came to seek the LORD.*

[5] Then Jehoshaphat stood in the assembly of Judah and Jerusalem, in the house of the LORD, before the new court, [6] and said: "O LORD God of our fathers, are You not God in Heaven, and do You not rule over all the kingdoms of the nations, and in Your hand is there not power and might, so that no one is able to withstand You? [7] Are You not our God, who drove out the inhabitants of this land before Your people Israel, and gave it to the descendants of Abraham Your friend forever? [8] And they dwell in it, and have built You a sanctuary in it for Your name, saying, [9] 'If disaster comes upon us—sword, judgment, pestilence, or famine—we will stand before this temple and in Your presence (for Your name is in this temple), and cry out to You in our affliction, and You will hear and save.' [10] And now, here are the people of Ammon, Moab, and Mount Seir—whom You would not let Israel invade when they came out of the land of Egypt, but they turned from them and did not destroy them— [11] here they are, rewarding us by coming to throw us out of Your possession which You have given us to inherit. [12] O our God, will You not judge them? For we have no power against this great multitude that is coming against us; nor do we know what to do, but our eyes are upon You."

[13] Now all Judah, with their little ones, their wives, and their children, stood before the LORD. [14] Then the Spirit of the LORD came upon Jahaziel the son of Zechariah, the son of Benaiah, the son of Jeiel, the son of Mattaniah, a Levite of the sons of Asaph, in the midst of the assembly. [15] And he said, "Listen, all you of Judah and you inhabitants of Jerusalem, and you, King Jehoshaphat! Thus says the LORD to you: 'Do not be afraid nor dismayed because of this great multitude, for the battle is not yours, but God's. [16] Tomorrow go down against them. They will surely come up by the Ascent of Ziz, and you will find them at the end of the brook before the Wilderness of Jeruel. [17] You will not need to fight in this battle. Position yourselves, stand still and see the salvation of the LORD, who is with you, O Judah and Jerusalem!' Do not fear or be dismayed; tomorrow go out against them, for the LORD is with you."

[18] And Jehoshaphat bowed his head with his face to the ground, and all Judah and the inhabitants of Jerusalem bowed before the LORD, worshiping the LORD. [19] Then the Levites of the children of the Kohathites and of the children of the Korahites stood up to praise the LORD God of Israel with voices loud and high.

²⁰ So they rose early in the morning and went out into the Wilderness of Tekoa; and as they went out, Jehoshaphat stood and said, "Hear me, O Judah and you inhabitants of Jerusalem: Believe in the LORD your God, and you shall be established; believe His prophets, and you shall prosper." ²¹ And when he had consulted with the people, he appointed those who should sing to the LORD, and who should praise the beauty of holiness, as they went out before the army and were saying:

" Praise the LORD, For His mercy endures forever."

²² Now when they began to sing and to praise, the LORD set ambushes against the people of Ammon, Moab, and Mount Seir, who had come against Judah; and they were defeated. ²³ For the people of Ammon and Moab stood up against the inhabitants of Mount Seir to utterly kill and destroy them. And when they had made an end of the inhabitants of Seir, they helped to destroy one another.

²⁴ So when Judah came to a place overlooking the wilderness, they looked toward the multitude; and there were their dead bodies, fallen on the earth. No one had escaped.

²⁵ When Jehoshaphat and his people came to take away their spoil, they found among them an abundance of valuables on the dead bodies, and precious jewelry, which they stripped off for themselves, more than they could carry away; and they were three days gathering the spoil because there was so much. ²⁶ And on the fourth day they assembled in the Valley of Berachah, for there they blessed the LORD; therefore the name of that place was called The Valley of Berachah until this day. ²⁷ Then they returned, every man of Judah and Jerusalem, with Jehoshaphat in front of them, to go back to Jerusalem with joy, for the LORD had made them rejoice over their enemies. ²⁸ So they came to Jerusalem, with stringed instruments and harps and trumpets, to the house of the LORD. ²⁹ And the fear of God was on all the kingdoms of those countries when they heard that the LORD had fought against the enemies of Israel. ³⁰ Then the realm of Jehoshaphat was quiet, for his God gave him rest all around.

Which side was victorious in this battle, the army of three nations or the few people of Jerusalem? _____

What part did Jehoshaphat play in the battle? _____
_____

He used Prayer and faith. He used the Word and praised his God, because he knew his God knew best! He trusted Him.

Your part in the battle seems so simple. It is when you practice it, but it's your wavering that makes it so difficult to carry out. It is hard work because of our wavering. Faith is difficult, because you have to lay it all on the line and trust God. Will you ever get a chance to have the delicious food you are being tempted to eat when you are not hungry? Of course you will. God will reward you for passing the test, but that is just it. You have to trust. When David stood before the Giant, when Jehoshaphat led his people out to confront the invading army, even when Peter stepped out of the boat onto the water, all of those instances took incredible faith in God.

These people laid their lives and the lives of others in God's hands. When you are in the middle of being carried away by your desires Satan is a powerful and persuasive liar, and there is only one-way to win the battle.

From the previous Scripture write **II Chronicles 20:15** here _____
_____
_____
_____

When God wins the victory, God is always glorified. People will be asking you how you lost your weight, and you will be able to give God all the credit.

Read **James 1:12-18** *Blessed is the man who endures temptation; for when he has been approved, he will receive the crown of life which the Lord has promised to those who love Him. [13] Let no one say when he is tempted, "I am tempted by God"; for God cannot be tempted by evil, nor does He Himself tempt anyone. [14] But each one is tempted when he is drawn away by his own desires and enticed. [15] Then, when desire has conceived, it gives birth to sin; and sin, when it is full-grown, brings forth death.*

What do you think it means to endure temptation? _____
_____

I'll tell you of my personal experience enduring temptation. I was driving along and saw a Tommie's Donut sign. I was all by myself and I was hungry. It would have been okay to eat a donut, except God had been working on another life-dominating sin in me. I was a "spendaholic," and I knew I wasn't supposed to buy one. But I absolutely love Tommie's Donuts, so I pulled in anyway, only to find to my frustration that it was a new store and wouldn't be open for another two days.

God had made a way out, but my desire was kicking in and starting to carry me away. I desired a donut so much, I decided to go way out of my way to a Tommie's I knew was open, and for my trouble I decided to get two donuts.

I could just picture myself eating them and could almost taste them. When I was so close I could see the sign, I ran into a big traffic jam, which frustrated me and was made worse because I was listening to Christian radio. The preacher was talking about being carried away by your own evil desires. I hated the speaker at that moment, because it started me thinking about all the principles God had taught me through this Bible study. I simply said, "Jesus please help me to ask for help."

And therein lays the answer! Your part of the battle is asking for God's help!! I had to ask God for help in asking, because I didn't want help. I wanted two Tommie's Donuts! That was the very moment God got involved. It was the second I humbled myself, and admitted I couldn't do it.

I started telling God how bad I wanted the donuts, but God began to work to soften my heart. Whispering to me about how bad this was for me. It wasn't just buying donuts; it was exalting myself, becoming my own God. Suddenly there was a break in traffic going the opposite direction of Tommie's and towards home. I took it, but I honestly started crying! I was so disappointed, I had wanted that donut so bad I didn't feel happy at that moment. I was mad and frustrated, but the next day when I was tempted to over spend, that decision and battle experience helped me resist overspending at the grocery store. I resisted the Devil through prayer, and he had to retreat. My job wasn't to take on Satan. My job was to ask my Father for protection.

Matthew 9:21-24 *Jesus asked the boy's father, "How long has he been like this?"*
"From childhood," he answered. [22] "It has often thrown him into fire or water to kill him. But if you can do anything, take pity on us and help us."

[23] "'If you can'?" said Jesus. "Everything is possible for him who believes."

[24] Immediately the boy's father exclaimed, "I do believe; help me overcome my unbelief!"

Read **James 4:7, 8** *Therefore submit to God. Resist the devil and he will flee from you. [8] Draw near to God and He will draw near to you. Cleanse your hands, you sinners; and purify your hearts, you double-minded.*

One of the hardest things about our battle with the bulge is thinking it's never going to end. We feel we will always have this intense desire for food, but here is the good news: resist the devil and he will flee!

I Peter 5:10 *be sober be vigilant; because your adversary the devil walks about like a roaring lion, seeking whom he may devour. Resist him, steadfast in the FAITH, knowing that the same sufferings are experienced by your brotherhood in the world, but may the God of all grace, who called us to His eternal glory by Christ Jesus, after you have suffered a while, perfect, establish, strengthen, and settle you.*

II Corinthians 3:4 *And we have such trust through Christ toward God not that we are sufficient of ourselves. But our sufficiency is from God.*

Read **II Kings 19:8-19** *Then the Rabshakeh returned and found the king of Assyria warring against Libnah, for he heard that he had departed from Lachish. [9] And the king heard concerning Tirhakah king of Ethiopia, "Look, he has come out to make war with you." So he again sent messengers to Hezekiah, saying, [10] "Thus you shall speak to Hezekiah king of Judah, saying: 'Do not let your God in whom you trust deceive you, saying, "Jerusalem shall not be given into the hand of the king of Assyria." [11] Look! You have heard what the kings of Assyria have done to all lands by utterly destroying them; and shall you be delivered? [12] Have the gods of the nations delivered those whom my fathers have destroyed, Gozan and Haran and Rezeph, and the people of Eden who were in Telassar? [13] Where is the king of Hamath, the king of Arpad, and the king of the city of Sepharvaim, Hena, and Ivah?'"*

[14] And Hezekiah received the letter from the hand of the messengers, and read it; and Hezekiah

went up to the house of the LORD, and spread it before the LORD. [15] Then Hezekiah prayed before the LORD, and said: "O LORD God of Israel, the One who dwells between the cherubim, You are God, You alone, of all the kingdoms of the earth. You have made Heaven and earth. [16] Incline Your ear, O LORD, and hear; open Your eyes, O LORD, and see; and hear the words of Sennacherib, which he has sent to reproach the living God. [17] Truly, LORD, the kings of Assyria have laid waste the nations and their lands, [18] and have cast their gods into the fire; for they were not gods, but the work of men's hands—wood and stone. Therefore they destroyed them. [19] Now therefore, O LORD our God, I pray, save us from his hand, that all the kingdoms of the earth may know that You are the LORD God, You alone."

And our mighty God's answer **II Kings 19:35-37** *And it came to pass on a certain night that the angel of the LORD went out, and killed in the camp of the Assyrians one hundred and eighty-five thousand; and when people arose early in the morning, there were the corpses—all dead. [36] So Sennacherib king of Assyria departed and went away, returned home, and remained at Nineveh. [37] Now it came to pass, as he was worshiping in the temple of Nisroch his god, that his sons Adrammelech and Sharezer struck him down with the sword; and they escaped into the land of Ararat.*

Which side was victorious in this battle? Was it the Assyrian army that destroyed the nations of Gozan, Haran, and Rezeph, and the people of Eden, Hamath, the king of Arpad, and the king of the city of Sepharvaim, Hena, and Ivan? All of those civilizations where destroyed by the Assyrian army, and that very large 185,000-man army was coming for Hezekiah's Kingdom.

Who won the battle? _____

What part did *Hezekiah* play in the battle? _____

I John 5:1-5 *Whoever believes that Jesus is the Christ is born of God, and everyone who loves Him who begot also loves him who is begotten of Him. [2] By this we know that we love the children of God, when we love God and keep His commandments. [3] For this is the love of God, that we keep His commandments. And His commandments are not burdensome. [4] For whatever is born of God overcomes the world.* <u>*And this is the victory that has overcome the world—**OUR FAITH**.*</u>

[5] *Who is he who overcomes the world, but he who **believes** that Jesus is the Son of God?*

The first part of this Scripture is somewhat intimidating. Let's face it, we all break commandments every day. Then, He goes on to say we overcome sin by faith and belief in Jesus. We also need to stay focused on the fight. Jesus isn't some fat commander sitting at a desk at headquarters. He is right in the thick of battle leading us. When you're in the battle, you're not focused on TV or the price of gas. No, you are totally focused on the bullets flying, and your essential equipment: Faith, Hope, and Love.

II Corinthians 4:16-18 *Therefore we do not lose heart. Even though our outward man is perishing, yet the inward man is being renewed day by day.* [17] *For our light affliction, which is but for a moment, is working for us a far more exceeding and eternal weight of glory,* [18] *while we do not look at the things which are seen, but at the things which are not seen. For the things which are seen are temporary, but the things which are not seen are eternal.*

II Timothy 2:1:11 [1] *You therefore, my son, be strong in the grace that is in Christ Jesus.* [2] *And the things that you have heard from me among many witnesses, commit these to faithful men who will be able to teach others also.* [3] *You therefore must endure hardship as a good soldier of Jesus Christ.* [4] *No one engaged in warfare entangles himself with the affairs of this life, that he may please him who enlisted him as a soldier.* [5] *And also if anyone competes in athletics, he is not crowned unless he competes according to the rules.* [6] *The hardworking farmer must be first to partake of the crops.*

[7] *Consider what I say, and may the Lord give you understanding in all things.* [8] *Remember that Jesus Christ, of the seed of David, was raised from the dead according to my gospel,* [9] *for which I suffer trouble as an evildoer, even to the point of chains; but the word of God is not chained.*

[10] *Therefore I endure all things for the sake of the elect, that they also may obtain the salvation which is in Christ Jesus with eternal glory.* [11] *This is a faithful saying: For if we died with Him, We shall also live with Him.* [12] *If we endure, We shall also reign with Him. If we deny Him, He also will deny us.* [13] *If we are faithless, He remains faithful; He cannot deny Himself.*

Jude 24,25 *Now to Him who is able to keep you from stumbling, And to present you faultless Before the presence of His glory with exceeding joy,* [25] *To God our Savior, Who alone is wise, Be glory and majesty, Dominion and power, Both **now** and forever. Amen.*

*Reminder: Go to week 3 day 5, titled, "My Dream", and list how prayer has influenced the areas of your life that concern you. Spend time in quiet reflection and thanksgiving.

Read. I Timothy 6:11-16

In light of today's study, what was the Scripture or statement in today's lesson that most spoke to your heart? _____

_____

_____

_____

What steps of faith does God want you to take towards Him today? _____

_____

_____

_____

Rephrase the Scripture or statement into an expression of faith_____

_____

_____

_____

Memory verse:
Joshua 24:15 _____

_____

_____

_____

_____

Week 5 Day 1
It's not your fight.

Day _____ Date _____

We use God's power to defeat the enemy. The actual battle is not our battle. We are involved by means of humbling ourselves, and we do that by praising God, giving up our will, and resisting Satan-- having faith in God. The actual physical fighting is God's.

Our part is easy, but because Satan is a master of deceit. We are fooled into thinking it's up to us. Nothing could be further from the truth. We simply say/pray, "Lord this is your battle. I praise you because every word in your Book is the truth, and you say it's your battle. I believe it." Then walk away. Pray like the Old Testament Kings we read about earlier.

"Lord you who made Heaven and Earth, the Lord over all things, remember your promise to me that you will fight my battles. Oh Lord, Satan, your enemy, is tempting me. Lord defeat him so you will be glorified. Show everybody I know your power by empowering me to resist this temptation so I will be thin and healthy. Show Your power by making food a non-issue in my life and break my habit of overeating."

Don't harbor the sin. If Satan comes back (he always does), then you say/pray/praise it again. Satan will probably come knocking again, and you simply say, "God, Satan is at the door will you please answer it? I praise you because you protect me and will lead me safely into your heavenly kingdom." Then walk away in the knowledge and faith that God has it taken care of. He will take care of it. He ALWAYS does. I am serious. There has never been a time that I have done this that God didn't take care of it for me. I simply lost the desire or forgot that I wanted to overeat.

The problem always lies with me wanting what Satan so eagerly presents. I lust after what he is offering, and I don't want God to answer the door. It is a matter of me turning my will to God's will. He will never force you to do His will, but as soon as you let go of your own, he is right there, battle ready, and Satan runs.

The more we practice this behavior, the better at it we get. You will make mistakes and "blow your diet." It's human nature. The trick is realizing that every second is a new beginning. When you are in Christ Jesus, every moment offers us an opportunity for forgiveness and a fresh start.

Do you remember yesterday's study, when we read in **II Chronicles 20:1-30**, Jehoshaphat led the people of Judah and Jerusalem, in prayer to the Lord after he heard the armies where coming against him? God's answer was. [17] ***You will not need to fight** in this **battle. Position yourselves, <u>stand still</u> and see the salvation of the LORD, who is with you, O Judah and Jerusalem!' Do not fear or be dismayed; tomorrow go out against them, for the*

LORD is with you."

God told His people to sing to praise Him. They had to leave the outcome to Him.

II Chronicles 20: 21*"Praise the LORD, For His mercy endures forever."*
Write verse seventeen from the preceding passage. _____
_____
_____
_____
_____
_____

What were the three things that Jehoshaphat and his people needed to win the battle?
1. _____ 2. _____ 3._____

They needed to: 1. Stand Still, or humble themselves, realize they can't do it on their own (Give it to God), 2. Do not fear (have faith in God) and, 3. Praise God, Give Him the glory. That is the whole of your responsibility.

When you learn to give your will immediately upon being tempted, it is a quiet realization of God's power; a flying above the fray.

I Chronicles 5:19, 20 *They made war with the Hagrites, Jetur, Naphish, and Nodab.* [20] *And they were helped against them, and the Hagrites were delivered into their hand, and all who were with them, for they cried out to God in the battle. He heeded their prayer, because they put their trust in Him.*

There are so many battles in the Bible, just like the preceding ones. They are examples to us on how to fight Satan. Stand Still (Give it to God), Have Faith (know God will fight it), and Praise God. Stand Still, Have Faith, and Praise God. That should be your mantra.

To fight the battle, it is helpful to understand the enemy's game plan. His plan is deception. He is a liar and the father of lies. He twists the truth. Satan cons us, and we fall so easily because of our lust. A good con man knows how to hook his victims, by giving them what they desire. Even the savviest skeptic can be hooked by lust and greed.

I read where one of the most successful sting operations for the police is to lure the hardest to capture criminals by sending them prize notices. The police set an elaborate scene. They pose as prizewinners and employees. They announce the winner and as the whole place is clapping for them and they are so excited to have won, they walk behind a screen where they are arrested and brought to justice. This operation is a success because it taps into people's lust.

Satan is *THE* con artist. He does the same thing, by promising quick pleasure. Then he chains you. He knows how to hook you, and the only way out is to give your will to God.

What is God's truth? **Romans 12:21** *Do not be overcome by evil, but overcome evil with good.*

We are no longer prisoners of our lusts.

II Peter 1:2-11 *Grace and peace be multiplied to you in the knowledge of God and of Jesus our Lord, [3] as His divine power has given to us all things that pertain to life and godliness, through the* **knowledge** *of Him who called us by glory and virtue, [4] by which have been given to us exceedingly great and precious promises, that through these you may be partakers of the divine nature, having escaped the corruption that is in the world through lust. [5] But also for this very reason, giving all diligence, add to your faith virtue, to virtue knowledge, [6] to knowledge self-control, to self-control perseverance, to perseverance godliness, [7] to godliness brotherly kindness, and to brotherly kindness love. [8] For if these things are yours and abound, you will be neither barren nor unfruitful in the knowledge of our Lord Jesus Christ. [9] For he who lacks these things is shortsighted, even to blindness, and has forgotten that he was cleansed from his old sins.*

[10] Therefore, brethren, be even more diligent to make your call and election sure, for if you do these things you will never stumble; [11] for so an entrance will be supplied to you abundantly into the everlasting kingdom of our Lord and Savior Jesus Christ.

John 17:19 *And for their sakes I sanctify myself, that they also may be sanctified in truth.*

Sanctify means to make holy, to set apart for holiness. We are chosen by God and given to Jesus. He thanked God for giving us to Him. He loves us, and we are so precious to Him. He laid down His life for us. Jesus prayed for us right before He was crucified. This precious prayer is so full of wonderful insight.

John 17:6-26 *I have manifested Your name to the men whom You have given Me out of the world. They were Yours, You gave them to Me, and they have kept Your word. [7] Now they have known that all things which You have given Me are from You. [8] For I have given to them the words which You have given Me; and they have received them, and have known surely that I came forth from You; and they have believed that You sent Me.*

[9] "I pray for them. I do not pray for the world but for those whom You have given Me, for they are Yours. [10] And all Mine are Yours, and Yours are Mine, and I am glorified in them. [11] Now I am no longer in the world, but these are in the world, and I come to You. Holy Father, keep through Your name those whom You have given Me, that they may be one as We are. [12] While I was with them in the world, I kept them in Your name. Those whom You gave Me I have kept; and none of them is lost except the son of perdition, that the Scripture might be fulfilled. [13] But now I come to You, and these things I speak in the world, that they may have My joy fulfilled in themselves. [14] I have given them Your word; and the world has hated them because they are not of the world, just as I am not of the world. [15] I do not pray that You should take them out of the world, but that You should keep them from the evil one. [16] They are not of the world, just as I am not of the world. [17] Sanctify them by Your truth. Your word is truth. [18] As You sent Me into the

world, I also have sent them into the world. ¹⁹ *And for their sakes I sanctify Myself, that they also may be sanctified by the truth.* ²⁰ *"I do not pray for these alone, but also for those who will believe in Me through their word;* ²¹ *that they all may be one, as You, Father, are in Me, and I in You; that they also may be one in Us, that the world may believe that You sent Me.* ²² *And the glory which You gave Me I have given them, that they may be one just as We are one:* ²³ *I in them, and You in Me; that they may be made perfect in one, and that the world may know that You have sent Me, and have loved them as You have loved Me.*

²⁴ *"Father, I desire that they also whom You gave Me may be with Me where I am, that they may behold My glory which You have given Me; for You loved Me before the foundation of the world.* ²⁵ *O righteous Father! The world has not known You, but I have known You; and these have known that You sent Me.* ²⁶ *And I have declared to them Your name, and will declare it, that the love with which You loved Me may be in them, and I in them."*

Look at verse seventeen "Sanctify them by your truth <u>YOUR WORD IS TRUTH</u>." The truth will set you free.

John 8:31-36 *Then Jesus said to those Jews who believed Him, "If you abide in My word, you are My disciples indeed.* ³² *And you shall know the truth, and the truth shall make you free."*

³³ *They answered Him, "We are Abraham's descendants, and have never been in bondage to anyone. How can You say, "You will be made free'?"*

³⁴ *Jesus answered them, "Most assuredly, I say to you, whoever commits sin is a slave of sin.*

³⁵ *And a slave does not abide in the house forever, but a son abides forever.*

³⁶ *Therefore if the Son makes you free, you shall be free indeed."*

No matter how Satan tries to deceive, we need to run to the truth, because the only weapon Satan has is deceit, but he is powerful in it.

I have mentioned before, I have a terrible phobia of mice. It's getting better, but at one time, it was so bad that I moved out of my sister's house at 2:00 A.M. because *she* saw a mouse! I didn't even see it! It was so comical, and my sister was so sweet, she gathered some of my things, then she helped me move a chair from behind met to the front of me. I would step on that chair, then she moved the one behind me, in front of me, and I would step on that one. I continued doing that until I reached the front door.

I could tell you so many stupid stories like that one. I have allowed this minute creature so much power over me. I could step on it, and smash it flat. What is the worst thing that could happen to me? Eeeww! It could touch me! Just thinking about it gives me the creeps.

You're probably thinking, "Okay, this woman is ridiculous, and you're right!" Yet, look at what you do. What kind of power do you give Satan? Compared to God, Satan has even less muscle over God than a mouse has over me, and God has given us access to that power and authority, in Jesus Christ. Satan has no power over you that you don't allow him to have.

You choose to allow Satan the power. You don't need to eat that brownie, but Satan can convince you to eat it when you're not hungry because he is so good at the con. He knows exactly what your weakness is, and plays on it. STOMP HIM WITH THE POWER OF THE ALMIGHTY GOD.

By the way, I would appreciate some prayer for my phobia.

Read: **Isaiah 40:25-31**

In light of today's study, what was the Scripture or statement in today's lesson that most spoke to your heart? _____

_____
_____
_____

What steps of faith does God want you to take towards Him today? _____

_____
_____
_____

Rephrase the Scripture or statement into an expression of faith_____

_____
_____
_____

Memory verse:

Romans 8:31 *What then shall we say to these things? If God is for us, who can be against us?*

Week 5 Day 2
Walking in the Spirit

Day _____ Date _____

Read the following Scriptures and determine who was walking in the Spirit and who was not, and place a check in the correct column.

Bible Verses	Walking	Not Walking
Moses, Exodus 4:1-14		
Moses, Hebrews 11: 23-29		
Abraham, Hebrews 11: 17-20		
Abraham, Genesis 12:10-13		
David, I Samuel17:42-47		
David, II Samuel 11: 1-4		
Elijah, I Kings 18: 20-39		
Elijah, I Kings 19:1-4		
Peter, Mark 8: 31-33		
Peter, Act 2: 14-38		

What did each of these men have in common when they weren't walking in the spirit?

_____

_____

They were all dwelling on the problems, and trusting in their own strength to get them through the battle.   Looking to their own strength, not God's.

What did each of these men have in common when they were walking in the Spirit?

_____

_____

They were strong and secure in their faith. They had all come to the realization that the outcome did not depend on them or their strength, but the power of the Almighty God. They knew their God, and they knew He would never let them down, and that is the only thing you need when you fight the battle.

It's an important concept, and I missed it for so many years. It doesn't take a strong will or a particular character trait. It takes faith to fight the emotional battle of temptation, fighting minute to minute, and resisting one suggestion from Satan at a time. Walking in the Spirit is to die to our desires, replacing them with what God wants us to do.

Matthew 16:24 *Then Jesus said to His disciples, "If anyone desires to come after Me, let him deny himself, and take up his cross, and follow Me.*

You won't wake up one morning and suddenly be thin. The fight is one battle on top of another battle, one little decision on top of another little decision, taking one-step at a time. We are to take up our cross and walk behind Jesus, following Him to the goal. When you think or do something negative, you are not walking in the Spirit. However, it's easy to get right back in step with Jesus. Just tell Him you are sorry. Start thinking positive thoughts of His power again, and you are right back on the path, walking with Jesus.

Read **Galatians 5: 16- 25** *I say then: Walk in the Spirit, and you shall not fulfill the lust of the flesh. [17] For the flesh lusts against the Spirit, and the Spirit against the flesh; and these are contrary to one another, so that you do not do the things that you wish. [18] But if you are led by the Spirit, you are not under the law. [19] Now the works of the flesh are evident, which are: adultery, fornication, uncleanness, lewdness, [20] idolatry, sorcery, hatred, contentions, jealousies, outbursts of wrath, selfish ambitions, dissensions, heresies, [21] envy, murders, drunkenness, revelries, and the like; of which I tell you beforehand, just as I also told you in time past, that those who practice such things will not inherit the kingdom of God.*

[22] But the fruit of the Spirit is love, joy, peace, longsuffering, kindness, goodness, faithfulness,

[23] gentleness, self-control. Against such there is no law. [24] And those who are Christ's have crucified the flesh with its passions and desires. [25] If we live in the Spirit, let us also walk in the Spirit.

It's hard to think about being totally in control at all times. When you look at it like that, it seems impossible, and you are looking at it the wrong way. We need to take one little step at a time.

How would you explain the action of walking? _____
_____
_____
_____

The dictionary defines walk as to 1,.to advance or travel on foot at a moderate speed or pace; proceed by steps; move by advancing the feet alternately so that there is always one foot on the ground self-propelled movement.

Walking is slow and methodical, with a goal in mind. It's not running, and it's not meandering. When you walk, you are going forward at a slow steady pace.

When you take a walk, you advance, move forward, taking one-step at a time. You take a step in a moment, then another step in another moment, and so on. Walking in the Spirit involves the same moment-by-moment action. Each action you take examined from the perspective of the Holy Spirit. When you examine something, I don't mean tear it apart and spend a lot of time studying the situation. You don't do that when you walk. You take a step looking ahead avoiding obstacles by sidestepping them. When a situation or temptation arises, put it away in your mind and sidestep it. It only takes a second to say, "No, in Jesus name, I'll live in this moment and use the power of the Holy Spirit." Just like when you first learned to walk, you had to learn one step at a time. The more you practice the easier it gets.

You must be in the Word, and have time with God daily.

John 15:5 *"I am the vine, you are the branches. He who abides in Me, and I in him, bears much fruit; for without Me you can do nothing.*

Warren Wiersbe said it this way:

> Unless we meet Christ personally and privately each day, we will soon end
> up like Martha: busy but not blessed. Often in my pastoral ministry, I have
> asked people with serious problems, "Tell me about your devotional life."
> The usual response has been an embarrassed look, a bowed head, and the
> quiet confession, "I stopped reading my Bible and praying a long time ago."
> And they wondered why they had problems!

Luke 10:41-42 *"Martha, Martha, " the Lord answered, "you are worried and upset about many things, but only one thing is needed* [42] *But one thing is needed, and Mary has chosen that good part, which will not be taken away from her."*

Luke 4:8 *Worship the Lord your God and serve Him only*

Abide means to walk with or, in this case, walk in. When you live moment by moment, taking one-step at a time, you live this way, and it is much more peaceful. There is no stress! You do what is best in every situation. There is great peace walking in the Spirit.

II Corinthians 5:7, 8 *For we walk by faith, not by sight.* [8] *We are confident, yes, well pleased rather to be absent from the body and to be present with the Lord.*

When you walk, it is for a purpose. You have a goal in mind. You walk to get somewhere. You don't take a step, and "poof" you are where you want to be. You have to take a step then another, and each step gets you closer to the goal. With each step, you have met a baby goal.

Romans 13:12-14 *The night is far spent, the day is at hand. Therefore let us cast off the works of darkness, and let us put on the armor of light.* [13] *Let us walk properly, as in the day, not in revelry and drunkenness, not in lewdness and lust, not in strife and envy.* [14] *But put on the Lord Jesus Christ, and make no provision for the flesh, to fulfill its lusts.*

Read **Romans 8: 1-11** *There is therefore now no condemnation to those who are in Christ Jesus, who do not walk according to the flesh, but according to the Spirit.*

Just as Jesus walked step-by-step to the cross to save us all from our sins, and fulfill His mighty purpose, so must we walk step-by-step through our lives to fulfill our purpose. One step at a time, moment by moment.

John 13: 1-10 *Now before the Feast of the Passover, when Jesus knew that His hour had come that He should depart from this world to the Father, having loved His own who were in the world, He loved them to the end.*

2 And supper being ended, the devil having already put it into the heart of Judas Iscariot, Simon's son, to betray Him, 3 Jesus, knowing that the Father had given all things into His hands, and that He had come from God and was going to God, 4 rose from supper and laid aside His garments, took a towel and girded Himself. 5 After that, He poured water into a basin and began to wash the disciples' feet, and to wipe them with the towel with which He was girded. 6 Then He came to Simon Peter. And Peter said to Him, "Lord, are You washing my feet?"

7 Jesus answered and said to him, "What I am doing you do not understand now, but you will know after this."

8 Peter said to Him, "You shall never wash my feet!"

Jesus answered him, "If I do not wash you, you have no part with Me."

9 Simon Peter said to Him, "Lord, not my feet only, but also my hands and my head!"

10 Jesus said to him, "He who is bathed needs only to wash his feet, but is completely clean; and you are clean

Peter said, "Lord, You shouldn't wash my feet." Peter wanted to do it himself. That's how so many people feel. "God doesn't want to bother with my problems." However, Jesus says, if you don't accept my cleansing, you don't have any part of me. Then, Peter says, "Okay, then wash all of me." Then Jesus says, "You have already been washed clean." That happened when Peter accepted Jesus as his Messiah. Now all Peter needs is the daily wash from the dirt (sin) that has accumulated from walking wrong paths.

Read: **Luke 22:39-71 & Luke 23**

In light of today's study, what was the Scripture or statement in today's lesson that most spoke to your heart? _____

_____

_____

_____

What steps of faith does God want you to take towards Him today? _____

_____

_____

_____

Rephrase the Scripture or statement into an expression of faith_____

_____

_____

_____

Memory verse:
Romans 8:31 *What _____ shall we _____ to these things? If God is _____ us, who can be against us?*

Week 5 Day 3
Fearfully and Wonderfully Made

Day _____ Date _____

If you have ever "suffered through" a study on crucifixion, you begin to understand the depth of Jesus' love for you. He doesn't just tolerate you. He adores you, just as you treasure your own children and are jealous for them. You want them to have the best clothes, the best teacher, the best college, etc. God is jealous for you too. He wants what is best for you, and He knows what is best.

Read **Psalm 56:8, 9** *You number my wanderings; Put my tears into Your bottle; Are they not in Your book?* [9] *When I cry out to You, Then my enemies will turn back; This I know, because God is for me.*

Now fill in the blanks with your name.

You number _____'s wanderings; Put _____'s tears into Your bottle; Are they not in your book? When _____ cries out to You, Then _____'s enemies will turn back; This I know, because God is for _____

We can be confident that God knows and cares about our every pain and unhappiness. He saves our tears. They don't just dry up and go away. He saves them, and writes them in a book.

Write **Psalm 56:8** from the passages above, _____
_____
_____

God is in love with you. He desires so much to have that personal relationship with you!
Read **Psalm 139** *O LORD, You have searched me and known me.* [2] *You know my sitting down and my rising up; You understand my thought afar off.* [3] *You comprehend my path and my lying down, And are acquainted with all my ways.* [4] *For there is not a word on my tongue, But behold, O LORD, You know it altogether.* [5] *You have hedged me behind and before, And laid Your hand upon me.* [6] *Such knowledge is too wonderful for me; It is high, I cannot attain it.* [7] *Where can I go from Your Spirit? Or where can I flee from Your presence?* [8] *If I ascend into Heaven, You are there; If I make my bed in hell, behold, You are there.* [9] *If I take the wings of the morning, And dwell in the uttermost parts of the sea,* [10] *Even there Your hand shall lead me, And Your right hand shall hold me.* [11] *If I say, "Surely the darkness shall fall on me," Even the night shall be light about me;* [12] *Indeed, the darkness shall not hide from You, But the night shines as the day; The darkness and the light are both alike to You.* [13] *For You formed my inward parts; You covered me in my mother's womb.* [14] *I will praise You, for I am fearfully and wonderfully made; Marvelous are Your works, And that my soul knows very well.* [15] *My frame was not hidden from You,* **When I was made in secret, And skillfully wrought** *in the lowest parts of the earth.* [16] *Your eyes saw my substance, being yet unformed. And in Your book they all were written, The days fashioned for me, when as yet there were none of them.* [17] *How precious also are Your thoughts to me, O God! How great is the sum of them!* [18] *If I should count them, they would be more in*

number than the sand; When I awake, I am still with You. ¹⁹ *Oh, that You would slay the wicked, O God! Depart from me, therefore, you bloodthirsty men.* ²⁰ *For they speak against You wickedly; Your enemies take Your name in vain.* ²¹ *Do I not hate them, O LORD, who hate You? And do I not loathe those who rise up against You?* ²² *I hate them with perfect hatred; I count them my enemies.*

²³ *Search me, O God, and know my heart; Try me, and know my anxieties;* ²⁴ *And see if there is any wicked way in me, And lead me in the way everlasting.*

Write down your thoughts and feelings after reading this passage. _____
_____
_____
_____

This beautiful passage is of a cherished relationship of a loving and devoted Father to His children. God used His skill to make you. I feel incredibly humbled by the idea that God chose me. I seemed so broken, and He fixed me.

He not only chose us, but also died a horrific death to prove it. He could have come to Earth when they had a more humane way to execute, but He chose the most horrifying death to show us His love for us. He must have thought we were worth it. We need to remember our cost and our worth.

Write down **James 1:18** _____
_____
_____

James 1:18 *Of His own will He brought us forth by the word of truth, that we might be a kind of firstfruits of His creatures.*

Our bodies are incredible! We are majestic beings created in God's image. Universities have whole courses teaching one characteristic of the brain, because it's so complicated. Simple tasks we do every day would cost billions and billions of dollars to replicate, and the world's clumsy attempt to do so, fall far short of the incredible complexity of the smallest movement of the human body, and we haven't even started talking about our spirit.

We are complex creatures, and God loves each one of us. Especially we who have the Spirit of God, we are His first fruits.

Numbers 18:12 explains what it means by firstfruits. It says, *"All the best of the oil, all the best of the new wine and the grain, their firstfruits which they offer to the LORD, I have given them to you.*

It means we are the best of all His creation. When you look at a soaring mountain range, with its layers of rock, beautiful in its majesty. When we stand by the ocean feeling and hearing the tremendous pounding, when you see a breathtaking sunset with all the incredibly beautiful colors fading into each other across the expanse of the sky, we revere God's creation, and can't believe the power of it.

Look at pictures of our universe; the stars and planets are stunning in their brilliance. Try to grasp the concept that just one of us is a more complex creation than all of those are.

God creates us with bated breath. We are **<u>fearfully</u>** and **<u>wonderfully</u>** made. We are awesome creatures, absolutely awe-inspiring to think of "you" as the most excellent creation of the Almighty, Awesome Father. He made you in His Image, and He treasures you.

I love Steven Curtis Chapman song, "The Finger Prints of God." The chorus of the song says:

> I can see the fingerprints of God
> When I look at you
> I can see the fingerprints of God
> And I know it's true
> You're a masterpiece that all creation
> Quietly applauds
> And you're covered with
> The fingerprints of God.

The Bible says the same thing in **Isaiah 55: 12** *"For you shall go out with joy, And be led out with peace; The mountains and the hills Shall break forth into singing before you, And all the trees of the field shall clap their hands.*

Out of all the millions and millions of humans God has created, there has never been another "you." The things you have experienced in your life is unique to you. There never has been, and never will be another "you."

Read **Psalm 49:6-9** *Why should I fear in the days of evil, When the iniquity at my heels surrounds me? [6] Those who trust in their wealth And boast in the multitude of their riches, [7] None of them can by any means redeem his brother, Nor give to God a ransom for him-- [8] For the redemption of their souls is costly, And it shall cease forever-- [9] That he should continue to live eternally, And not see the Pit.*

The redemption of our souls is costly.

Read **Ephesians 1:4-14** *just as He chose us in Him before the foundation of the world, that we should be holy and without blame before Him in love, [5] having predestined us to adoption as sons by Jesus Christ to Himself, according to the good pleasure of His will, [6] to the praise of the glory of His grace, by which He made us accepted in the Beloved.*

[7] In Him we have redemption through His blood, the forgiveness of sins, according to the riches of His grace [8] which He made to abound toward us in all wisdom and prudence, [9] having made known to us the mystery of His will, according to His good pleasure which He purposed in Himself, [10] that in the dispensation of the fullness of the times He might gather together in one all things in Christ, both which are in Heaven and which are on earth--in Him. [11] In Him also we have obtained an inheritance, being predestined according to the purpose of Him who works all things according to the counsel of His will, [12] that we who first trusted in Christ should be to the praise of His glory.

[13] In Him you also trusted, after you heard the word of truth, the gospel of your salvation; in whom also, having believed, you were sealed with the Holy Spirit of promise, [14] who is the guarantee of our inheritance until the redemption of the purchased possession, to the praise of His glory.

In your own words sum up your thoughts and feelings about this passage of Scripture:

_____
_____
_____

It's remarkable; the blueprint God used to create us was love. He lovingly and thoughtfully planned our lives.

My husband was a computer programmer. He was explaining to me that when you create a program, you have to create little programs inside of programs, because depending on what the user may decide, various things might happen. Let's say the program was written for a fast food restaurant. The program may ask the user if they want extra sauce, depending on the answer any number of things could happen. If the customer says yes, the program might change his total. The program may also need to take something out of inventory, add something to a shopping list, and tally how many are left. It could track the item to see if it were a good seller. It could also track how many customers preferred extra sauce. If the program was advanced, it may even change the profit and loss statement.

When my husband was explaining this to me, I had the thought that we are somewhat like that: unbelievably complex computer programs. We have a decision set before us. If we make one choice, it will affect our lives one way. If we make another, it will affect it another way, only with billions and billions of different outcomes. Of course, this is just me speculating about how awesome God is.

We need to keep in mind, we are important. God wants you to succeed, and has given you every tool you need to achieve it.

Philippians 4:19 *And my God shall supply all your need according to His riches in glory by Christ Jesus.*

I used to wonder why God made things happen: why I was fat, why did He make me lose my front teeth in an accident, why did I have big pores on my nose. I was already so ashamed of myself and the way I looked, I didn't need any more faults.

My husband still looks as good as the day we were married, and he has never had self-esteem issues. Why did God allow me to get to what I thought was so ugly?

When I used to hear the saying, "You have to like yourself for others to like you," I didn't know what that meant. Now I finally understand; I would have never treated others the way I used to treat myself. I would yell at myself and call myself names in my mind. I hated my body; I would pick out imperfections every time I looked in a mirror. How awful and mean I was to God and myself. Why would God want to bless me when I was so awful about the gift He gave me? Now I am so thankful for my body and spirit. God made me beautiful. Everything on my body works so well, even with all the abuse I have heaped upon it.

Read Romans 8:31-39

In light of today's study, what was the Scripture or statement in today's lesson that most spoke to your heart? _____

_____
_____
_____

What steps of faith does God want you to take towards Him today? _____

_____
_____
_____

Rephrase the Scripture or statement into an expression of faith_____

_____
_____
_____

Memory verse:

Romans 8:31 *What _____ _____ we _____ to _____ things? If God is _____ us, who _____ be against us?*

143

Week 5 Day 4
God Doesn't Choose Losers

Day _____ Date _____

What is the value of a man? There are different ways of calculating our worth. It's been said that if you break down the basic elements of our bodies, they are worth about 98 cents. However, you can turn around and sell one eyeball for $10,000 dollars.

People pay millions of dollars each year for plastic surgery, trying to gain back their youth. The focus of our world is on our outward appearance. Even standing in the checkout line at the grocery store comparing ourselves with the magazine covers can make us feel worthless. Being just a few pounds overweight can cause deep depression, but read what the Bible says about that.

Use your own Bible, and fill in the blanks,

Ephesians 2:10 *For _____ are _____ workmanship; created in _____ Jesus for good works, which _____ prepared beforehand that _____ should walk in them.*

Ephesians 2:10 *For we are His workmanship, created in Christ Jesus for good works, which God prepared beforehand that we should walk in them.*

Revelation 12:10 *Then I heard a loud voice saying in Heaven, "Now salvation, and strength, and the kingdom of our God, and the power of His Christ have come, for the accuser of our brethren, who accused them before our God day and night, has been cast down. [11] And they overcame him by the blood of the Lamb and by the word of their testimony, and they did not love their lives to the death.*

Zechariah 3:1-4 *Then he showed me Joshua the high priest standing before the Angel of the LORD, and Satan standing at his right hand to oppose him. [2] And the LORD said to Satan, "The LORD rebuke you, Satan! The LORD who has chosen Jerusalem rebuke you! Is this not a brand plucked from the fire?" [3] Now Joshua was clothed with filthy garments, and was standing before the Angel. [4] Then He answered and spoke to those who stood before Him, saying, "Take away the filthy garments from him." And to him He said, "See, I have removed your iniquity from you, and I will clothe you with rich robes."*

Satan stands before God night and day accusing you. Read how he accused Job.

Job 1:6-12 *Now there was a day when the sons of God came to present themselves before the LORD, and Satan also came among them. [7] And the LORD said to Satan, "From where do you come?"*

So Satan answered the LORD and said, "From going to and fro on the earth, and from walking back and forth on it."

144

[8] Then the LORD said to Satan, "Have you considered My servant Job, that there is none like him on the earth, a blameless and upright man, one who fears God and shuns evil?"

[9] So Satan answered the LORD and said, "Does Job fear God for nothing? [10] Have You not made a hedge around him, around his household, and around all that he has on every side? You have blessed the work of his hands, and his possessions have increased in the land. [11] But now, stretch out Your hand and touch all that he has, and he will surely curse You to Your face!"

[12] And the LORD said to Satan, "Behold, all that he has is in your power; only do not lay a hand on his person."

So Satan went out from the presence of the LORD.

When Satan accuses you and convinces you to feel condemned, and you start thinking bad thoughts about yourself, remember to capture the negative self-talk. It's one of the vital steps in the healing process. You will not succeed until you learn to encourage yourself. Don't ever put yourself down. If you are still doing that, you need to pray God will heal you. It is devastating, and you will never find it encouraged in the Bible. Jesus never put Himself down, and He is our example.

I admit, over and over again, I have found it hard to ignore Satan. Being overweight made me feel less valuable. I am so glad God cares about my spirit more than my body. The older I get, the easier it becomes to capture my thoughts earlier. I used to dwell on them. Now, as soon as I start to feel negative, I have a song I sing. It's a short chorus from a Don Francisco song. It goes:

> Praise the Lord, hallelue, I don't care what the Devil's going to do.
> A word in faith is my sword and shield, Jesus is Lord of the way I feel.

You can use any song to get you back up. This one is for me! It is peppy, and I start dancing around and being goofy, and in seconds, my negative emotions are under control, and I am back to having the correct perspective.

How can you be a loser, if you're saved? Your soul is not less precious to God because your outward appearance is not up to the world's standards.

Read: **Corinthians 4:16** *Therefore we do not loose heart. Even though our outward man is perishing, yet the inward man is being renewed day by day" [17] For our light affliction, which is but for a moment, is working for us a far more exceeding weight in of glory, [18] while we do not look at the things which are seen, but at the things which are not seen. For the things which are seen are temporary, but the things which are not seen are eternal.*

God places all value of you, in your spirit, not what is seen. The body is temporary. These trials are perfecting you and making your soul more full, because of what your soul has gained in the process. We are being created day by day.

Write **James 1:2, 3** _____

_____

_____

_____

James 1:2, 3 *My brethren, count it all joy when you fall into various trials,* ³ *knowing that the testing of your faith produces patience.* ⁴ *But let patience have its perfect work, that you may be perfect and complete, lacking nothing.* ⁵ *If any of you lacks wisdom, let him ask of God, who gives to all liberally and without reproach, and it will be given to him.* ⁶ *But let him ask in faith, with no doubting, for he who doubts is like a wave of the sea driven and tossed by the wind.*

When you were born, that wasn't the end of you being created. It was only the beginning, and you are a very complex creature. You are valuable to God, because you are unique. There has never been another spirit like yours and never will be, even if you are a twin you would still have different life experiences.

Read in your own Bible **Philippians 1:6** and fill write out the Scripture. _____

_____

_____

Philippians 1:6 *being confident of this very thing, that He who has begun a good work in you will complete it until the day of Jesus Christ.*

It is so hard to have this confidence when you are in the midst of fighting an addiction. You feel like it will never be conquered, but we need to press on. Even Paul felt defeated sometimes.

Read **Romans7:14-25** *For we know that the law is spiritual, but I am carnal, sold under sin.* ¹⁵ *For what I am doing, I do not understand. For what I will to do, that I do not practice; but what I hate, that I do.* ¹⁶ *If, then, I do what I will not to do, I agree with the law that it is good.* ¹⁷ *But now, it is no longer I who do it, but sin that dwells in me.* ¹⁸ *For I know that in me (that is, in my flesh) nothing good dwells; for to will is present with me, but how to perform what is good I do not find.* ¹⁹ *For the good that I will to do, I do not do; but the evil I will not to do, that I practice.* ²⁰ *Now if I do what I will not to do, it is no longer I who do it, but sin that dwells in me.*

²¹ *I find then a law, that evil is present with me, the one who wills to do good.* ²² *For I delight in the law of God according to the inward man.* ²³ *But I see another law in my members, warring against the law of my mind, and bringing me into captivity to the law of sin which is in my members.* ²⁴ *O wretched man that I am! Who will deliver me from this body of death?* ²⁵ *I thank God--through Jesus Christ our Lord!*

So then, with the mind I myself serve the law of God, but with the flesh the law of sin.

This passage is such a wonderful glimpse into Paul's mind, and an illustration of the way our minds wander. He says, "Oh wrenched man that I am, who will save me?" He starts to lose it. You can see the moment he captures his thoughts in verse twenty-five. This passage is a great example of how you capture your thoughts. We must capture our thoughts! The battle is in your thoughts or mind.

Write down **Philippians 3:12** _____

_____

_____

_____

Philippians 3:12-14 *Not that I have already attained, or am already perfected; but I press on, that I may lay hold of that for which Christ Jesus has also laid hold of me. [13] Brethren, I do not count myself to have apprehended; but one thing I do, forgetting those things which are behind and reaching forward to those things which are ahead, [14] I press toward the goal for the prize of the upward call of God in Christ Jesus.*

It is hard not to feel condemned when the master of lies is accusing us.

Read **Romans 8:1** *There is therefore now no condemnation to those who are in Christ Jesus, who do not walk according to the flesh, but according to the Spirit.*

What does the Bible say about Christians being condemned? _____

_____

_____

_____

He has assigned angels to watch over you **Matthew 18:10** *"Take heed that you do not despise one of these little ones, for I say to you that in Heaven their angels always see the face of My Father who is in Heaven.*

And

Hebrews 1:14 *Are they not all ministering spirits sent forth to minister for those who will inherit salvation?*

And

Luke 15:7 *I say to you that likewise there will be more joy in Heaven over one sinner who repents than over ninety-nine just persons who need no repentance.*

George McDonald, who was C.S. Lewis' mentor, wrote:
"I would rather be what God chose to make me, than the most glorious creature that I could think of; for to have been thought about, born in God's thought and then made by God, is the dearest, grandest and most precious thing in all thinking."

Your soul is the grandest thing about you and God doesn't choose losers. God sees your angels every day, and they watch out for you. How will that help you make the correct decisions for your future? _____

_____

_____

_____

We are no longer victims. We can stand and fight. One of the best Bible studies I have ever done was "Experiencing God", by Henry T. Blackaby. I highly recommend it. A phrase in the Bible study that was helpful to me was, "You can't go with God and stay in the same place."

Run the race. It's a process. Keep working on yourself to become what God would have you be. When you fail, don't think that is the end product. Tell yourself that you are a work in progress who is learning from your mistakes.

Hebrews 12:1, 2 *Therefore we also, since we are surrounded by so great a cloud of witnesses, let us lay aside every weight, and the sin which so easily ensnares us, and let us run with endurance the race that is set before us, [2] looking unto Jesus, the author and finisher of our faith, who for the joy that was set before Him endured the cross, despising the shame, and has sat down at the right hand of the throne of God.*

What do you think is the "joy" this Scripture talks about? _____

_____

_____

The joy the Scripture is talking about is **You**!

John 15:16 *You did not choose Me, but I chose you and appointed you that you should go and bear fruit, and that your fruit should remain, that whatever you ask the Father in My name He may give you.*

I Peter 2: 4, 5 *Coming to Him as to a living stone, rejected indeed by men, but **chosen by God and precious**, [5] you also, as living stones, are being built up a spiritual house, a holy priesthood, to offer up spiritual sacrifices acceptable to God through Jesus Christ.*

I Peter 2:9,10 *But you are a chosen generation, a royal priesthood, a holy nation, **His own special people**, that you may proclaim the praises of Him who called you out of darkness into His marvelous light; [10] who once were not a people but are now the people of God, who had not obtained mercy but now have obtained mercy.*

Read **Ephesians 1**

In light of today's study, what was the Scripture or statement in today's lesson that most spoke to your heart? _____

_____
_____
_____

What steps of faith does God want you to take towards Him today? _____

_____
_____
_____

Rephrase the Scripture or statement into an expression of faith_____

_____
_____
_____

Memory verse:

Romans 8:31 *What _____ _____ we _____ to _____ things? If*
_____ is _____ us, _____ _____ be _____ us?

Week 5 Day 5
The Power of Jesus Name

Day _____ Date _____

We will start this study out by taking a short test. Write the answers in the spaces provided.

What is the opposite of:

Good _____
White_____
Sin _____

Up _____
Love_____
Satan _____

If your answer to the last question was Jesus, you couldn't be more wrong. Satan is a created being, and Jesus is God. Satan doesn't come anywhere close to being as powerful as Jesus. The best you could do for the opposite of Satan would be Michael, the archangel. God has no opposites. He is all-powerful, omnipotent, and supreme; there is none like Him. Every breath you take is by the grace of God, and He loves you.

John 14:13-14 *And whatever you ask in My name, that I will do, that the Father may be glorified in the Son.* [14] *If you ask anything in My name, I will do it.*

When you pray in the name of Jesus, you shouldn't be giving Him a list of the things you desire, you should be praying for the will of God.

I John 5:14-15 *Now this is the confidence that we have in Him, that if we ask anything according to His will, He hears us.* [15] *And if we know that He hears us, whatever we ask, we know that we have the petitions that we have asked of Him.*

You can have confidence knowing God does not want you to stay in your affliction. He may have you stay in sickness to accomplish His will. However, it is never His will for you to stay in sin, and we have established that overeating is a sin. However, it may take a while for you to gain the faith you need to understand this.

Ephesians 1:16-23 *I do not cease to give thanks for you, making mention of you in my prayers:* [17] *that the God of our Lord Jesus Christ, the Father of glory, may give to you the spirit of wisdom and revelation in the knowledge of Him,* [18] *the eyes of your understanding being enlightened; that you may know what is the hope of His calling, what are the riches of the glory of His inheritance in the saints,* [19] *and what is the exceeding greatness of His power toward us who believe, according to the working of His mighty power* [20] *which He worked in Christ when He raised Him from the dead and seated Him at His right hand in the heavenly places,* [21] *far above all principality and power and might and dominion, and every name that is named, not only in* *this age but also in that which is to come. ²² And He put all things under His feet, and gave Him to be head over all things to the church, ²³ which is His body, the fullness of Him who fills all in all.*

I heard a story once about a police officer who saved a child in a mall who had started choking on a hard candy. He noticed the child was having problems, and immediately sprang into action. All his training came to the front of his brain, and he did everything correctly. He saved the child from choking, the mother was grateful, and he received accolades from the city and the media.

He was still basking in the light of this attention, when not long after, his own four-year-old son started choking on a marshmallow. All the training that had served him so well with the stranger left his brain. He went into panic mode with his own child that he loved so much, and was powerless to help him. As his child lay, fading in his arms, he couldn't even pray. The only thing that broke through his frantic mind was the name, Jesus. So with all his heart and everything that was in him he said, "Jesus, Jesus, Jesus." He just kept holding that lifeless limp baby, and saying "Jesus," past hope. He just kept saying "Jesus," and suddenly, his son coughed up the marshmallow. It was a miracle, when the only thing the policeman could do was the very best thing he could do, and that was to say the mighty name of his Lord, Jesus.

The Almighty Christ Jesus protects us. You are not only His child, but also a soldier in His army. As long as you are in formation and snapped to attention, the enemy cannot hurt you. He can try, and he will try, but if your focus is on the commander, you will stay in step. When we fall out of formation is when we get in trouble. That's when Satan can get a foothold and start confusing you.

I Timothy 4:1 *Now the Spirit expressly says that in latter times some will depart from the faith, giving heed to deceiving spirits and doctrines of demons.*

The spirits will try to deceive you. Your role in this battle is not a passive one. You have to realize that all these negative thoughts are not your own. There are principalities at work, and you need to arm yourself against them. You have to take authority over them with the power of Jesus' name.

Luke 10:17 *Then the seventy returned with joy, saying, "Lord, even the demons are subject to us in Your name." ¹⁸ And He said to them, "I saw Satan fall like lightning from Heaven. ¹⁹ Behold, I give you the authority to trample on serpents and scorpions, and over all the power of the enemy, and nothing shall by any means hurt you.*

The disciples were amazed at the power of Jesus' name. They said, "In your name." We have that same power available to us. Satan has already been defeated. That's what Jesus was saying when He said, "I saw Satan fall like lightning from Heaven." He wasn't saying Satan was defeated only for the disciples. Satan is defeated for all time, and because he was defeated and we are children of the King. We have authority over him.

We lack understanding of who we are and our position in Christ. We have authority in His name to stop Satan. We are under God's lordship, but we have the authority of an heir. You have that right. Satan is not Jesus' equal. Jesus has all authority in Heaven and Earth.

Matthew 28:18 *And Jesus came and spoke to them, saying, "All authority has been given to Me in Heaven and on earth.*

Satan is under us through Jesus. Once we realize we are not powerless or defenseless, we can start taking the authority through the power of name of Jesus. The power of the word "NO" in Jesus' name is a potent and breathtaking weapon.

I used to love reading the comics when I was a kid, and one of my favorites was Beetle Bailey. He was always messing up and getting creamed (beat up) by the Sarge. Imagine if Beetle Bailey ordered the Sarge to do K.P. duties; the Sarge would have creamed Beetle. Now picture Beetle deceptively putting on the General Halftrack's stars, and convincing the Sarge he had the right to wear the rank. If the Sarge believed him, he would be up to his elbows in potatoes doing K.P., while Beetle and his friends were laughing. That is exactly what happens every time you are deceived into thinking you can't overcome a temptation. If Beetle deceived the Sarge into thinking he has more authority, the Sarge will live as if Beetle Bailey does have the power to order him around.

I John 5:18-21 *We know that whoever is born of God does not sin; but he who has been born of God keeps himself, and the wicked one does not touch him.*

[19] We know that we are of God, and the whole world lies under the sway of the wicked one. [20] And we know that the Son of God has come and has given us an understanding, that we may know Him who is true; and we are in Him who is true, in His Son Jesus Christ. This is the true God and eternal life. [21] Little children, keep yourselves from idols. Amen.

Ephesians 6:10 *Finally, my brethren, be strong in the Lord and in the power of His might.*

Romans 13:14 *But put on the Lord Jesus Christ, and make no provision for the flesh, to fulfill its lusts.*

Satan can and does hurt our bodies through sickness, but he can only access your spirit through your mind, and you have to allow it. Make sure you are capturing your thoughts. Don't provide what is required to fulfill lust.

II Corinthians 11:3 *But I fear, lest somehow, as the serpent deceived Eve by his craftiness, so your minds may be corrupted from the simplicity that is in Christ.*

Satan needs you to allow your thoughts to wander where he is leading them. Satan needs you to believe you don't have any control over your thoughts and giving in to temptation.

Your position in Christ is secure. You are his beloved child. Whenever Satan comes against you, meet him head on through the power of Jesus. Satan cannot, cannot!!! touch your spirit, unless you allow it by giving into his lies.

Romans 8:37-39 *Yet in all these things we are more than conquerors through Him who loved us. [38] For I am persuaded that neither death nor life, nor angels nor principalities nor powers, nor things present nor things to come, [39] nor height nor depth, nor any other created thing, shall be able to separate us from the love of God which is in Christ Jesus our Lord.*

Ephesians 6:12 *For we do not wrestle against flesh and blood, but against principalities, against powers, against the rulers of the darkness of this age, against spiritual hosts of wickedness in the heavenly places.*

II Corinthians 10: 3-6 *For though we walk in the flesh, we do not war according to the flesh. [4] For the weapons of our warfare are not carnal but mighty in God for pulling down **strongholds**, [5] casting down arguments and every high thing that exalts itself against the knowledge of God, bringing every thought into captivity to the obedience of Christ, [6] and being ready to punish all disobedience when your obedience is fulfilled.*

The definition of stronghold is "a fortified place." Fortified: to strengthen by military forces. Stronghold in this Scripture is logismos and refers to strongholds in the mind, wrong ways of thinking. Some of these thoughts have been entrenched in your mind for so many years that they can only be removed by using your mighty weapons.

For so many years, I was afraid of my thoughts. Thinking I couldn't control them, but we have the authority to take them captive. Lock them up immediately; don't even allow the thought to process.

We have the military strength to lock that private up, and throw away the key, even though the private is bigger and smarter than we are. We have the military forces to back us up!

John 8:43,44 *Why do you not understand My speech? Because you are not able to listen to My word. [44] You are of your father the devil, **and the desires of your father you want to do.** He was a murderer from the beginning, and does not stand in the truth, because there is no truth in him. When he speaks a lie, he speaks from his own resources, for he is a liar and the father of it.*

Satan is a liar. All sin begins as a thought, and the Bible says you can capture your thoughts. A general doesn't argue with a private; he expects his orders to be carried out immediately because of his position of authority.

However, don't fool yourself into thinking you have authority over Satan on your own. Don't even think about it. Just as a general couldn't fight a young private who was strong, and just for the sake of this illustration, a black-belt in a martial arts. The older man wouldn't stand a chance, but if he has the military force behind him, that's a different story. Without the authority of Jesus, you have no power against Satan.

Read **Jude 9** *Yet Michael the archangel, in contending with the devil, when he disputed about the body of Moses, dared not bring against him a reviling accusation, but said, "The Lord rebuke you!"*

We need the name of Jesus because the evil one is prince of this world and has access to every deceitful trick.

John 14:30 *I will no longer talk much with you, for the ruler of this world is coming, and he has nothing in Me.*

We have the authority because we have access to our Father's mighty power through the name of Jesus Christ.

Romans 16:20 *And the God of peace will crush Satan under your feet shortly.*

Which part of your body does the battle of temptation take place? _____

The center of spiritual bondage is in your mind; that's where all the battles with Satan are fought.

Romans 7:23-25 *But I see another law in my members, warring against the law of my mind, and bringing me into captivity to the law of sin which is in my members.* [24] *O wretched man that I am! Who will deliver me from this body of death?* [25] *I thank God--through Jesus Christ our Lord! So then, with the mind I myself serve the law of God, but with the flesh the law of sin.*

And **Romans 8:5-7** *For those who live according to the flesh set their minds on the things of the flesh, but those who live according to the Spirit, the things of the Spirit.* [6] *For to be carnally minded is death, but to be spiritually minded is life and peace.* [7] *Because the carnal mind is enmity against God; for it is not subject to the law of God, nor indeed can be.* [8] *So then, those who are in the flesh cannot please God.*

Who is the responsible party when you decide to sin? _____

Read **Romans 6:12-14** *Therefore do not let sin reign in your mortal body, that you should obey it in its lusts.* [13] *And do not present your members as instruments of unrighteousness to sin, but present yourselves to God as being alive from the dead, and your members as instruments of righteousness to God.* [14] *For sin shall not have dominion over you, for you are not under law but under grace.*

How do you present yourself to God? _____

_____

_____

Pray, pray for help to resist temptation. Pray that you will break through the emotional barrier of, "I WANT".

Flip Wilson was a famous comedian in the seventies. He had a bit he'd do, and it was hilarious, because his expression was so comical. He would get an innocent look on his face after being caught by the camera doing something wrong, open his eyes real wide and announce, "The devil made me do it!" Regrettably, though, we use that excuse ourselves way too often, and it's not funny. Satan doesn't have any power that we don't give him.

Satan picks on us, and it's ironic, because he thought he had done a number on Jesus at the cross; it looked as if evil had triumphed over good. Satan played right into God's hands, and we know who won the victory.

Colossians 2:15 *Having disarmed principalities and powers; He made a public spectacle of them, triumphing over them in it.*

How do we overcome sin?

Read **I John 5:4** *For whatever is born of God overcomes the world. And this is the victory that has overcome the world—__our faith__.*

Look at that promise, contemplate it. Write **I John 5:4** _____

_____

_____

By our faith in God, we overcome anything the world (Satan) sends our way. That is an awesome promise from God. By faith, we release the promises of His power in our lives.

Let's look at the rest of **Colossians 2:15-23**

Having disarmed principalities and powers, He made a public spectacle of them, triumphing over them in it.

[16] So let no one judge you in food or in drink, or regarding a festival or a new moon or sabbaths, [17] which are a shadow of things to come, but the substance is of Christ. [18] Let no one cheat you of your reward, taking delight in false humility and worship of angels, intruding into those things which he has not seen, vainly puffed up by his fleshly mind, [19] and not holding fast to the Head, from whom all the body, nourished and knit together by joints and ligaments, grows with the increase that is from God.

[20] Therefore, if you died with Christ from the basic principles of the world, why, as though living in the world, do you subject yourselves to regulations-- [21] "Do not touch, do not taste, do not handle," [22] which all concern things which perish with the using--according to the

commandments and doctrines of men? [23] *These things indeed have an appearance of wisdom in self-imposed religion, false humility, and neglect of the body, but are of no value against the indulgence of the flesh.*

Pray that God will give you the discernment to see Satan's lies and show you the truth.

Ephesians 1:15-23 *Therefore I also, after I heard of your faith in the Lord Jesus and your love for all the saints,* [16] *do not cease to give thanks for* <u>you, making mention of you in my prayers:</u> [17] *that the God of our Lord Jesus Christ, the Father of glory, may give to you the spirit of wisdom and revelation in the knowledge of Him,* [18] *the* <u>eyes of your understanding being enlightened;</u> *that you may know what is the hope of His calling, what are the riches of the glory of His inheritance in the saints,* [19] <u>*and what is the exceeding greatness of His power toward us who believe, according to the working of His mighty power*</u> [20] *which He worked in Christ when He raised Him from the dead and seated Him at His right hand in the heavenly places,* [21] *far above all principality and power and might and dominion, and every name that is named,* **<u>not only in this age but also in that which is to come.</u>**

[22] *And He put all things under His feet, and gave Him to be head over all things to the church,* [23] *which is His body, the fullness of Him who fills all in all.*

To reinforce this amazing passage, fill in the missing words using your own Bible or the text above.

Ephesians 1:15-23 *Therefore I also, after I heard of your faith in the Lord Jesus and your love for all the saints,* [16] *do not cease to give thanks for you, _____*

*_____: * [17] *that the God of our Lord Jesus Christ, the Father of glory, may give to you the spirit of wisdom and revelation in the knowledge of Him,* [18] *the _____*

_____; that you may know what is the hope of His calling, what are the riches of the glory of His inheritance in the saints, [19] *_____*

_____

[20] *which He worked in Christ when He raised Him from the dead and seated Him at His right hand in the heavenly places,* [21] *far above all principality and power and might and dominion, and every name that is named, _____*

_____.

[22] *And He put all things under His feet, and gave Him to be head over all things to the church,* [23] *which is His body, the fullness of Him who fills all in all.*

Read **Ephesians chapter 2.**

In light of today's study, what was the Scripture or statement in today's lesson that most spoke to your heart? _____

_____

_____

_____

What steps of faith does God want you to take towards Him today? _____

_____

_____

_____

Rephrase the Scripture or statement into an expression of faith_____

_____

_____

_____

Romans 8:31 _____

_____

_____

Week 6 Day 1
Taste and See That the Lord is Good

Day _____ Date _____

If you think being thin will make you happy, I am sorry to tell you this, but it won't. There will always be someone thinner, and even if your body were perfect, you still wouldn't be content. Look at the life of Michael Jackson and others like him who strive for perfect bodies and are addicted to plastic surgery. Their every waking moment is focused on what they look like and how others perceive them.

Solomon had every single earthly thing he could wish for. His riches were unsurpassed and he had everything his heart desired. At the end of his search for things and experiences, he found nothing and he felt empty. He said it was vapor grasping for the wind. He ended up hating his life and called his quest for possessions "labor."

Read **Ecclesiastes chapters 1 & 2**
The words of the Preacher, the son of David, king in Jerusalem. ² "Vanity of vanities," says the Preacher; "Vanity of vanities, all is vanity."

³ What profit has a man from all his labor In which he toils under the sun? ⁴ One generation passes away, and another generation comes; But the earth abides forever.

⁵ The sun also rises, and the sun goes down, And hastens to the place where it arose. ⁶ The wind goes toward the south, And turns around to the north; The wind whirls about continually, And comes again on its circuit. ⁷ All the rivers run into the sea, Yet the sea is not full; To the place from which the rivers come, There they return again. ⁸ All things are full of labor; Man cannot express it. The eye is not satisfied with seeing, Nor the ear filled with hearing.

⁹ That which has been is what will be, That which is done is what will be done, And there is nothing new under the sun. ¹⁰ Is there anything of which it may be said, "See, this is new"? It has already been in ancient times before us. ¹¹ There is no remembrance of former things, Nor will there be any remembrance of things that are to come By those who will come after.

¹² I, the Preacher, was king over Israel in Jerusalem. ¹³ And I set my heart to seek and search out by wisdom concerning all that is done under Heaven; this burdensome task God has given to the sons of man, by which they may be exercised. ¹⁴ I have seen all the works that are done under the sun; and indeed, all is vanity and grasping for the wind.

¹⁵ What is crooked cannot be made straight, And what is lacking cannot be numbered.

¹⁶ I communed with my heart, saying, "Look, I have attained greatness, and have gained more wisdom than all who were before me in Jerusalem. My heart has understood great wisdom and knowledge." ¹⁷ And I set my heart to know wisdom and to know madness and folly. I perceived that this also is grasping for the wind.

¹⁸ For in much wisdom is much grief, And he who increases knowledge increases sorrow.

Chapter 2

Pleasure Is Vain

[1] *I said in my heart, "Come now, I will test you with mirth; therefore enjoy pleasure"; but surely, this also was vanity.* [2] *I said of laughter--"Madness!"; and of mirth, "What does it accomplish?"* [3] *I searched in my heart how to gratify my flesh with wine, while guiding my heart with wisdom, and how to lay hold on folly, till I might see what was good for the sons of men to do under Heaven all the days of their lives.* [4] *I made my works great, I built myself houses, and planted myself vineyards.* [5] *I made myself gardens and orchards, and I planted all kinds of fruit trees in them.* [6] *I made myself water pools from which to water the growing trees of the grove.* [7] *I acquired male and female servants, and had servants born in my house. Yes, I had greater possessions of herds and flocks than all who were in Jerusalem before me.* [8] *I also gathered for myself silver and gold and the special treasures of kings and of the provinces. I acquired male and female singers, the delights of the sons of men, and musical instruments of all kinds.* [9] *So I became great and excelled more than all who were before me in Jerusalem. Also my wisdom remained with me.*

[10] *Whatever my eyes desired I did not keep from them. I did not withhold my heart from any pleasure, For my heart rejoiced in all my labor; And this was my reward from all my labor.* [11] *Then I looked on all the works that my hands had done And on the labor in which I had toiled; And indeed all was vanity and grasping for the wind. There was no profit under the sun. The End of the Wise and the Fool* [12] *Then I turned myself to consider wisdom and madness and folly; For what can the man do who succeeds the king? Only what he has already done.* [13] *Then I saw that wisdom excels folly As light excels darkness.* [14] *The wise man's eyes are in his head, But the fool walks in darkness. Yet I myself perceived That the same event happens to them all.*

[15] *So I said in my heart, "As it happens to the fool, It also happens to me, And why was I then more wise?" Then I said in my heart, "This also is vanity."* [16] *For there is no more remembrance of the wise than of the fool forever, Since all that now is will be forgotten in the days to come. And how does a wise man die? As the fool!*

[17] *Therefore I hated life because the work that was done under the sun was distressing to me, for all is vanity and grasping for the wind.* [18] *Then I hated all my labor in which I had toiled under the sun, because I must leave it to the man who will come after me.* [19] *And who knows whether he will be wise or a fool? Yet he will rule over all my labor in which I toiled and in which I have shown myself wise under the sun. This also is vanity.* [20] *Therefore I turned my heart and despaired of all the labor in which I had toiled under the sun.* [21] *For there is a man whose labor is with wisdom, knowledge, and skill; yet he must leave his heritage to a man who has not labored for it. This also is vanity and a great evil.* [22] *For what has man for all his labor, and for the striving of his heart with which he has toiled under the sun?* [23] *For all his days are sorrowful, and his work burdensome; even in the night his heart takes no rest. This also is vanity.* [24] *Nothing is better for a man than that he should eat and drink, and that his soul should enjoy good in his labor. This also, I saw, was from the hand of God.* [25] *For who can eat, or who can have enjoyment, more than I?* [26] *For God gives wisdom and knowledge and joy to a man who is good in His sight; but to the sinner He gives the work of gathering and collecting, that he may give to*

him who is good before God. This also is vanity and grasping for the wind.

After reading these passages, what are some of your thoughts and feelings about Solomon's pursuits? _____
_____
_____
_____
_____

Do you recognize any of these behaviors in yourself? _____

If you're not seeking God, there is no meaning to life. All our own pursuits,, including the desire to be thin, will not fill the emptiness only God can fill. God created you to function in His church, and until you are actively pursuing that purpose, your life will not be fulfilled.

Read **John 4:1-26** *Therefore, when the Lord knew that the Pharisees had heard that Jesus made and baptized more disciples than John [2] (though Jesus Himself did not baptize, but His disciples), [3] He left Judea and departed again to Galilee. [4] But He needed to go through Samaria.*

[5] So He came to a city of Samaria which is called Sychar, near the plot of ground that Jacob gave to his son Joseph. [6] Now Jacob's well was there. Jesus therefore, being wearied from His journey, sat thus by the well. It was about the sixth hour.

[7] A woman of Samaria came to draw water. Jesus said to her, "Give Me a drink." [8] For His disciples had gone away into the city to buy food.

[9] Then the woman of Samaria said to Him, "How is it that You, being a Jew, ask a drink from me, a Samaritan woman?" For Jews have no dealings with Samaritans.

[10] Jesus answered and said to her, "If you knew the gift of God, and who it is who says to you, "Give Me a drink,' you would have asked Him, and He would have given you living water." [11] The woman said to Him, "Sir, You have nothing to draw with, and the well is deep. Where then do You get that living water? [12] Are You greater than our father Jacob, who gave us the well, and drank from it himself, as well as his sons and his livestock?"

[13] Jesus answered and said to her, "Whoever drinks of this water will thirst again, [14] but whoever drinks of the water that I shall give him will never thirst. But the water that I shall give him will become in him a fountain of water springing up into everlasting life."

[15] The woman said to Him, "Sir, give me this water, that I may not thirst, nor come here to draw."

[16] Jesus said to her, "Go, call your husband, and come here."

[17] The woman answered and said, "I have no husband."

Jesus said to her, "You have well said, "I have no husband,' [18] for you have had five husbands, and the one whom you now have is not your husband; in that you spoke truly."
[19] The woman said to Him, "Sir, I perceive that You are a prophet. [20] Our fathers worshiped on this mountain, and you Jews say that in Jerusalem is the place where one ought to worship."

[21] Jesus said to her, "Woman, believe Me, the hour is coming when you will neither on this mountain, nor in Jerusalem, worship the Father. [22] You worship what you do not know; we know what we worship, for salvation is of the Jews. [23] But the hour is coming, and now is, when the true worshipers will worship the Father in spirit and truth; for the Father is seeking such to worship Him. [24] God is Spirit, and those who worship Him must worship in spirit and truth."

[25] The woman said to Him, "I know that Messiah is coming" (who is called Christ). "When He comes, He will tell us all things."

[26] Jesus said to her, "I who speak to you am He."

The woman at the well had been searching for someone to love her, to treat her special, and nurture her…to give her a reason and purpose for living. She had gone through many lovers in a vain attempt to fulfill that desire. She had been used and abused by men who wanted to fulfill their own desires. God says in **John 4:23** *He seeks those who will worship Him in spirit and truth.*

Read the following Scriptures:

Psalm 34:8-10 *Oh taste and see that the Lord is good; Blessed is the man who trusts in Him! [9]Oh, fear the Lord, you His saints! There is no want to those who fear Him. [10]The young lions lack and suffer hunger; But those who seek the Lord shall not lack any good thing*

Psalm. 119:103-107 *How sweet are Your words to my taste, Sweeter than honey to my mouth [104] Through Your precepts I get understanding; Therefore I hate every false way. [105] Your word is a lamp to my feet and a light to my path. [106] I have sworn and confirmed that I will keep Your righteous judgments.[107] I am afflicted very much; Revive me, O LORD, according to Your word.*

I Peter 2:3 *Therefore laying aside all malice, all deceit, hypocrisy, envy, and all evil speaking, as newborn babes, desire the pure milk of the word, that you may grow thereby, if indeed you have tasted that the Lord is gracious*

Psalm 107:9 *For He satisfies the longing soul, and fills the hungry soul with goodness.*

Proverbs 27:7 *A satisfied soul loathes the honeycomb, But to a hungry soul every bitter thing is sweet.*

Acts 14:17 *Nevertheless He did not leave Himself without witness, in that He did good, gave us rain from Heaven and fruitful seasons, filling our hearts with food and gladness."*

Write down what all these Scriptures have in common _____

_____

_____

_____

They all talk about the Bible and the relationship with Jesus being spiritual food... the only food that will satisfy the hungry soul! The only quest that satisfies is the pursuit of God. He satisfies the longing heart. If you could sit at a table and have delicious, great smelling, delectable food served to you morning and night, all day long, and do it the next day, and the next, never gaining a pound, you would still never be satisfied. The only thing on this earth that will fill that hunger is spiritual food.

John 4:31-34 *In the meantime His disciples urged Him, saying, "Rabbi, eat."*
32 But He said to them, "I have food to eat of which you do not know."
33 Therefore the disciples said to one another, "Has anyone brought Him anything to eat?"
34 Jesus said to them, "My food is to do the will of Him who sent Me, and to finish His work.

I want that to be my food. I want to finish the work God has laid out for me. That's where satisfaction is. That's the place you feel full, and not empty, doing God's work--finishing the tasks that He has given us.

John 6:47-58 *Most assuredly, I say to you, he who believes in Me has everlasting life. 48 I am the bread of life. 49 Your fathers ate the manna in the wilderness, and are dead. 50 This is the bread which comes down from Heaven, that one may eat of it and not die. 51 I am the living bread which came down from Heaven. If anyone eats of this bread, he will live forever; and the bread that I shall give is My flesh, which I shall give for the life of the world."*

52 The Jews therefore quarreled among themselves, saying, "How can this Man give us His flesh to eat?"

53 Then Jesus said to them, "Most assuredly, I say to you, unless you eat the flesh of the Son of Man and drink His blood, you have no life in you. 54 Whoever eats My flesh and drinks My blood has eternal life, and I will raise him up at the last day. 55 For My flesh is food indeed, and My blood is drink indeed. 56 He who eats My flesh and drinks My blood abides in Me, and I in him. 57 As the living Father sent Me, and I live because of the Father, so he who feeds on Me will live because of Me. 58 This is the bread which came down from Heaven--not as your fathers ate the manna, and are dead. He who eats this bread will live forever Most assuredly, I say to you, he who believes in me has everlasting life

Ecclesiastes 6:7 *All the labor of man is for his mouth, And yet the soul is not satisfied.*

What will satisfy your soul? _____
_____
_____

How *do* I satisfy my soul? It seems like the more I overeat and the more I diet, the emptier I feel. So I know food will never satisfy my emptiness, and in fact, makes by soul feel hungrier and less satisfied.

The Bible says that after Jesus had preached this sermon, a lot of the people who had been following Him left. The things He was saying were just too weird. When you first read this, it does seem bizarre, but what biological and physical things happen to you when you eat?
_____
_____
_____
_____

When you eat, you take the food into your body, and it becomes a part of you; it builds living tissue, and gives you the energy to survive. Your body uses the vitamins, minerals and proteins in food to give you fuel to burn. If you don't use all the fuel, your body stores it for when it is needed.

Reading and hearing the Word of God is equivalent to taking it into your body and using it to get you through what needs to be done. Scriptures will pop into your head right when you need them. But, just as it wouldn't help to chew the food then spit it out or eat and then lay in bed, you have to apply the food. You have to use it.

John 6:35 *Then they said to Him, "Lord, give us this bread always." [35] And Jesus said to them, "I am the bread of life. He who comes to Me shall never hunger, and he who believes in Me shall never thirst. [36] But I said to you that you have seen Me and yet do not believe. [37] All that the Father gives Me will come to Me, and the one who comes to Me I will by no means cast out. [38] For I have come down from Heaven, not to do My own will, but the will of Him who sent Me.*

Jesus says over and over that the food He eats is "doing the will of God."

It's hard; I don't have to tell you, because you know the struggle. Our hearts yearn for the things we can't have, because Satan knows exactly what he is doing. Think back on the times when you have been happy and satisfied. I know your answer; it's when you were following God's will for your life. Your heart sang and you were totally in love and gaga over the Lord. Now that is true satisfaction.

Matthew 4:4 & Deuteronomy 8:3 *"It is written, Man shall not live by bread alone, but by every word that proceeds from the mouth of God."*

God created us for Him. We all have a God-sized void that only He fits. The woman at the well, Solomon, and Michael Jackson all had one thing in common; they were all striving to fill a need for God in their life, with something other than God.

Some people try to fill the God-sized void with shopping; others try to fill it with alcohol and possessions. None of these activities satisfy. They make you want more and more. The more you eat the emptier you feel. God is the only one that can fill this emptiness; nothing else will ever satisfy. All that "stuff" will leave you wanting more. That is how some hurting people can weigh five-hundred pounds or more.

When you overload your stomach, you are seeking satisfaction contentment, comfort, all the things that God's word promises you if you seek Him with all your heart. Those who partake of Jesus, the bread of life, will never hunger.

God gives us an invitation to abundant life. He knows you through and through, He created you for a purpose, and the pursuit of that purpose is the ultimate satisfaction.

You need to figure out what the payoff for overeating is for you. What are you getting out of it? What is there about food that you desire so much? What need are you trying to fill by overloading your stomach? Spend time contemplating your answer. Ask God to help you understand why would do such a destructive thing to yourself. _____

_____

_____

_____

Is it a way to nurture yourself, because Satan makes it so difficult to go to God when we need comfort? With food there is no emotional barrier, no act of humbling ourselves, no fighting Satan. Since there is no meeting with Satan it's easier to run to the refrigerator rather than God. You can feel nurtured by the food without the emotional barrier. It's the easy way out. You don't need to humble your heart to shove food in your face but the payoff is a fake.

Read **Hosea 2:5-8** *For their mother has played the harlot; She who conceived them has behaved shamefully. For she said, "I will go after my lovers, Who give me my bread and my water, My wool and my linen, My oil and my drink."* [6] *"Therefore, behold, I will hedge up your way with thorns, And wall her in, So that she cannot find her paths.* [7] *She will chase her lovers, But not overtake them; Yes, she will seek them, but not find them. Then she will say, "I will go and return to my first husband, For then it was better for me than now."* [8] *For she did not know That I gave her grain, new wine, and oil, And multiplied her silver and gold-- Which they prepared for Baal.*

This woman was running after something she could never catch up with. She was running in wrong directions. She didn't realize her desires were already being met, if she would only see it.

The definition of nurture is: to care for feed, nourish, educate, train, foster. When we're not hungry and eat anyway, we are trying to nurture ourselves, but food won't help. Although it does bring temporary satisfaction, in the end, it brings death and destruction.

The definition of sustenance is: food nourishment a supplying with the necessities of life something that sustains or supports.

Nourishment and sustenance are all right when we are hungry. But when it's your spirit that needs nurturing and sustenance, the only way to satisfy that need is to go to God. You have to get it from the Spirit.

What do you think Spiritual food is? _____

_____

_____

_____

The Bible talks about the worship of God, being obedient, helping others in the name of Jesus, giving our will over to His, pursuing our purpose, all are spiritual food. If you're trying to feed your spirit with the thing God made to feed the flesh, you're going to reap extra flesh. Your body needs only a certain amount of calories. What goes in must come out.

It won't be this hard forever; the more you practice, the easier it becomes. God will always be there to comfort you if you feel lonely, unloved, and unattractive. Don't run away from your pain by trying to stuff it down with food. That only helps while you are chewing and then causes regrets.

Proverbs 20:17 *Bread gained by deceit is sweet to a man, But afterward his mouth will be filled with gravel.*

Instead, dedicate yourself to getting to know Jesus. Allow Him to take care of your deepest needs, and then give Him the praise and glory for it. Satan will fight you, but if you pray and apply Scripture, it not only overpowers Satan, but also nourishes your soul.

Now for the hard part. It's time to start praying that your search for happiness through losing weight and being "skinny" changes to a desire to please God.

The Bible says Satan can disguise himself in many ways. He has been a Snake, a Lion, and can even appear as an angel of light. Make certain your desire to be thin hasn't become a god you worship. Truthfully ask yourself this question… Would you still try to please God and eat only when your body is hungry, if you never shed another pound? _____

Pray that God will change your desire to be thin into a desire to be obedient. Ask him to help you accept that He loves you and only wants your best. Pray He will give you understanding that if He is holding back something you want and pray for, you will trust He is doing it to prepare you for your purpose. Because when you hit your "Goal Weight," you'll still have the desire to overeat and diet, and it's a real short trip back to the refrigerator. Ask me, I know. When I was on the other works-based Bible study, I started out at 205 pounds, went to 140, stayed there for a year, and bite by bite went right back and passed 210 pounds!

I try not to use the scale anymore, and most of the time I don't care how much I have lost or how much I weigh. Jesus has taught me to turn those thoughts over to Him, as the scale is an obstacle for me. Although, I am not saying it would be for you.

We need to be careful about trying to create a "Spiritual Formula" for weight loss. It's a process, and you shouldn't be praying to get thin, but instead to become what God wants you to be. Yes, God wants you to be thin and healthy, but when your desire to become thin supersedes your desire for God, it can become a more powerful stronghold than the addiction to food. Check your heart. Are you limiting food because you desire to be thin, or because you love Jesus with all your heart and don't want anything to come between your heart and His? If it's the desire to be thin that motivates you, think about it. Has that motivation helped with other diets you've tried?

READ: Philippians 2:3 *Let nothing be done through selfish ambition or conceit, but in lowliness of mind let each esteem others better than himself.*

Pray and ask God to reveal whether or not this is vanity or love for Him that keeps you from idolizing food and being "skinny." Write down some of your thoughts and feelings. _____

_____
_____
_____
_____
_____
_____
_____
_____
_____
_____
_____

Ezekiel 3:1 *Moreover He said to me, "Son of man, eat what you find; eat this scroll, and go, speak to the house of Israel."* [2] *So I opened my mouth, and He caused me to eat that scroll.* [3] *And He said to me, "Son of man, feed your belly, and fill your stomach with this scroll that I give you." So I ate, and it was in my mouth like honey in sweetness.*

The prophet Ezekiel eating the scroll (God's Word) is an illustration; take God's Word into our bodies. When you sit down to a delectable meal, you don't just put it in your mouth and chew and swallow. You experience it, you smell it, look at it. Taste it and feel it going down. It becomes a part of you. Your muscles use it to walk, talk, breath, and live!

Romans 14:17-18 [17] *for the kingdom of God is not eating and drinking, but righteousness and peace and joy in the Holy Spirit.* [18] *For he who serves Christ in these thingsis acceptable to God and approved by men.*
[19] *Therefore let us pursue the things which make for peace and the things by which one may edify another.*

I like how it's said in *The Message* version:

Romans 14:17-18 (The Message)
[17-18]God's kingdom isn't a matter of what you put in your stomach, for goodness' sake. It's what God does with your life as he sets it right, puts it together, and completes it with joy. Your task is to single-mindedly serve Christ. Do that and you'll kill two birds with one stone: pleasing the God above you and proving your worth to the people around you.

To be able to use God's Word, take time to let it fill your heart and mind, repeat the words to yourself think and feel them. Ask God to clarify the words to make them part of you and to teach you to experience them.

I Timothy 4:6 *If you instruct the brethren in these things, you will be a good minister of Jesus Christ, nourished in the words of faith and of the good doctrine which you have carefully followed.*

Read **Psalm 81 and Matthew 26:26-30**

In light of today's study, what was the Scripture or statement in today's lesson that most spoke to your heart? _____

_____
_____
_____

What steps of faith does God want you to take towards Him today? _____

_____
_____
_____

Rephrase the Scripture or statement into an expression of faith_____

_____
_____
_____

Memorize:

II Kings 6:17 *And Elisha prayed, and said, "LORD, I pray, open his eyes that he may see." Then the LORD opened the eyes of the young man, and he saw. And behold, the mountain was full of horses and chariots of fire all around Elisha.*

Week 6 Day 2
Who Can Be against You?

Day _____ Date _____

Romans 8:31-39 *What then shall we say to these things? If God is for us, who can be against us? [32] He who did not spare His own Son, but delivered Him up for us all, how shall He not with Him also freely give us all things? [33] Who shall bring a charge against God's elect? It is God who justifies. [34] Who is he who condemns? It is Christ who died, and furthermore is also risen, who is even at the right hand of God, who also makes intercession for us. [35] Who shall separate us from the love of Christ? Shall tribulation, or distress, or persecution, or famine, or nakedness, or peril, or sword? [36] As it is written: "For Your sake we are killed all day long; We are accounted as sheep for the slaughter.*

[37] Yet in all these things we are more than conquerors through Him who loved us. [38] For I am persuaded that neither death nor life, nor angels nor principalities nor powers, nor things present nor things to come, [39] nor height nor depth, nor any other created thing, shall be able to separate us from the love of God which is in Christ Jesus our Lord.

What then shall we say to these things? If God is for us, who can be against us? That is very powerful. Who can prevail against the mighty God? The only thing holding him back is your outstretched arm. You pushing Him away will be the furthest He will ever be from you; you are the only one who can do that. Jesus was the most precious thing God could give. If he sent his son to be crucified, why wouldn't He take care of us?

Hebrews 12:1, 2 *Therefore we also, since we are surrounded by so great a cloud of witnesses, let us lay aside every weight, and the sin which so easily ensnares us, and let us run with endurance the race that is set before us, [2] looking unto Jesus, the author and finisher of our faith, who for the joy that was set before Him endured the cross, despising the shame, and has sat down at the right hand of the throne of God.*

Jesus had a seat on the right hand of God already; the joy the Bible is talking about was He was going to be with us. Jesus' focus was not on the agony of the cross, but the joy beyond. Not the suffering, but the reward. What was the joy? Why did Jesus die such a torturous death? What was the payoff for Him? _____

_____

_____

_____

_____

He died because He loves us…because He wanted us to share His home in Heaven. His position was already established as the King of all glory. He did it only for the love of us.

You are so important to God, and He has a plan for your life. You're unique and special to God. There never has been, nor will there be, another person just like you. That's why you are so valuable to God.

READ: Matthew 7:7-12 *"Ask, and it will be given to you; seek, and you will find; knock, and it will be opened to you. ⁸ For everyone who asks receives, and he who seeks finds, and to him who knocks it will be opened. ⁹ Or what man is there among you who, if his son asks for bread, will give him a stone? ¹⁰ Or if he asks for a fish, will he give him a serpent? ¹¹ If you then, being evil, know how to give good gifts to your children, how much more will your Father who is in Heaven give good things to those who ask Him!*

God isn't out to get you, and He's not mad at you. Even the things that you thought were unpleasant are gifts when you look back on them.

Jeremiah 11-14a *¹¹ For I know the thoughts that I think toward you, says the LORD, thoughts of peace and not of evil, to give you a future and a hope. ¹² Then you will call upon Me and go and pray to Me, and I will listen to you. ¹³ And you will seek Me and find Me, when you search for Me with all your heart. ¹⁴ I will be found by you, says the LORD, and I will bring you back from your captivity.*

God says we are the apple of his eye. The apple of the eye was a Hebrew term for pupil. Look how closely you guard your eye. Anything comes near it, and your body instinctively acts to protect it. People who are being attacked will automatically put their hands up to guard their eyes, no matter how painful. When you get something in the pupil of your eye, no matter where you are or what you are doing, you have to get it out. That's how God guards us!

Zechariah 2:8 *For thus says the LORD of hosts: "He sent Me after glory, to the nations which plunder you; for he who touches you touches the apple of His eye.*

I Peter 5:7 *Casting all your care upon Him, for He cares for you.*

Psalm 118:6 *The LORD is on my side; I will not fear. What can man do to me?*

The days fashioned for me the beauty of our world each of those things we find beauty in, God fashioned for us.

Read **Romans 5:8** *But God demonstrates His own love toward us, in that while we were still sinners, Christ died for us.*

God knows what we are made of and can sympathize with our weaknesses.

Hebrews 4:15 *Seeing then that we have a great High Priest who has passed through the Heavens, Jesus the Son of God, let us hold fast our confession. ¹⁵ For we do not have a High Priest who cannot sympathize with our weaknesses, but was in all points tempted as we are, yet without sin. ¹⁶ Let us therefore come boldly to the throne of grace, that we may obtain mercy and find grace to help in time of need.*

If God's love were conditional, we would all be in trouble. We can never be good enough. We can't go two hours without sinning. Whether or not God loves you does not depend on how good you are. It's His battle; our battle is turning our will over to Him and asking for His help with what we are being tempted with. Go boldly to the throne of grace. Grace means unmerited favor, a present. Use and apply the Scriptures he has given you.

Zechariah 4:6, 7 *So he answered and said to me: "This is the word of the LORD to Zerubbabel: "Not by might nor by power, but by My Spirit, Says the LORD of hosts. 7 "Who are you, O great mountain? Before Zerubbabel you shall become a plain! And he shall bring forth the capstone With **shouts** of "**Grace, grace to it**!"*

He knows we can't do it on our own and doesn't expect us to. Look at our addiction as a great mountain we can't climb. No matter how strong you are you can't climb the mountain. It doesn't depend on how strong you are. It depends on how strong God is, and what you believe about that strength.

Matthew 17:20.21 *So Jesus said to them, "Because of your unbelief; for assuredly, I say to you, if you have faith as a mustard seed, you will say to this mountain, "Move from here to there,' and it will move; and nothing will be impossible for you. 21 However, this kind does not go out except by prayer and fasting.*

The only way I can become addicted to food again is if I believe Satan's lies over God's truth. You can pray out loud when you are being tempted, "God this is your battle and I give it to you. You say in Your word, not by *my* might not by *my* power, but by Your Spirit." This works for everything, because Satan uses so many different tactics.

I'll be going along fine with my eating and losing weight, getting closer to Jesus, when Satan will hit me with something like, "You are doing this for yourself not Jesus," or "You are prideful, God isn't going to help you with this," and he will try something different on you.

It's at that moment, that you humble yourself, acknowledge you cannot battle Satan, and you can't take care of it yourself.

Read **II Corinthians 10:3-6** *For though we walk in the flesh, we do not war according to the flesh. 4 For the weapons of our warfare are not carnal but mighty in God for pulling down strongholds, 5 casting down arguments and every high thing that exalts itself against the knowledge of God, bringing every thought into captivity to the obedience of Christ, 6 and being ready to punish all disobedience when your obedience is fulfilled.*

For every single thought or argument that exalts itself against the knowledge of God, capture it immediately before it has time to process.

"Jesus, this is your battle it says so in Your Word. It says not by might, nor by power, but by your spirit, and God, I believe what your word says, so I am going to hide in the shadow of your wings and let You fight this battle." Satan cannot stand against the simple truth of the Bible.

The Bible is your first and last line of defense. I pray right now for you the reader. I pray that God will open your eyes to this simple truth. This is God's truth. This is how Jesus fought Satan when He was being tempted by him. Satan will try to distract you from the truth, so read the following Scriptures again. Contemplate them, chew them around in your mind. Learn from Jesus how to fight Satan. These Scriptures are a wonderful teaching tool.

Read **Luke 4:1-13** *Then Jesus, being filled with the Holy Spirit, returned from the Jordan and was led by the Spirit into the wilderness, [2] being tempted for forty days by the devil. And in those days He ate nothing, and afterward, when they had ended, He was hungry. [3] And the devil said to Him, "If You are the Son of God, command this stone to become bread." [4] But Jesus answered him, saying, "It is written, "Man shall not live by bread alone, but by every word of God. [5] Then the devil, taking Him up on a high mountain, showed Him all the kingdoms of the world in a moment of time. [6] And the devil said to Him, "All this authority I will give You, and their glory; for this has been delivered to me, and I give it to whomever I wish. [7] Therefore, if You will worship before me, all will be Yours." [8] And Jesus answered and said to him, "Get behind Me, Satan!*

For it is written, "You shall worship the LORD your God, and Him only you shall serve. [9] Then he brought Him to Jerusalem, set Him on the pinnacle of the temple, and said to Him, "If You are the Son of God, throw Yourself down from here. [10] For it is written: "He shall give His angels charge over you, to keep you,' and, "In their hands they shall bear you up, Lest you dash your foot against a stone.

[12] And Jesus answered and said to him, "It has been said, "You shall not tempt the LORD your God. [13] Now when the devil had ended every temptation, he departed from Him until an opportune time.

How did Jesus resist the temptation? _____
_____
_____
_____

Did he try to argue with Satan or rationalize the sin at all? _____

No! He captured the thoughts right away by saying, "Get behind me!" He applied the Word of God; that's a great reason to memorize Scripture.

Read **II Corinthians 10:5** again, *For though we walk in the flesh, we do not war according to the flesh. [4] For the weapons of our warfare are not carnal but mighty in God for pulling down strongholds, [5] casting down arguments and every high thing that exalts itself against the knowledge of God, bringing every thought into captivity to the obedience of Christ, [6] and being ready to punish all disobedience when your obedience is fulfilled.*

Jesus captured the thoughts; he didn't mull them about in His mind. He got rid of it immediately. You do this all the time without realizing it; Satan tempts us with things all the time. It's like he is testing out the waters. Usually it passes right out of our thoughts because we won't even consider it. It doesn't process. For instance, if I were tempted to shoplift, I would push it right out of my mind instantly. I wouldn't even consider it. It would be an absurd thought to me. The battle is waged in our thoughts and it's there you need to capture them, before they go to flesh.

I had an unsaved friend who asked me, "How would you react if God, not Jesus, appeared right here (not that there is a difference but that's what he believed)?" Without hesitation, I said I would run up and give him a big hug. He couldn't believe I would do that, and I couldn't believe he wouldn't. He's afraid of God; most people who aren't saved feel that way, but think about it. We are His dear children. He sacrificed everything for you. He loves you; He is all for you.

John 3:16 *For God so loved the world that He gave His only begotten Son, that whoever believes in Him should not perish but have everlasting life. [17] For God did not send His Son into the world to condemn the world, but that the world through Him might be saved. [18] "He who believes in Him is not condemned; but he who does not believe is condemned already, because he has not believed in the name of the only begotten Son of God.*

Matthew 10:29-31 *Are not two sparrows sold for a copper coin? And not one of them falls to the ground apart from your Father's will. [30] But the very hairs of your head are all numbered. [31] Do not fear therefore; you are of more value than many sparrows.*

You have heard the expression that nothing happens to you that's not filtered through the hands of God, but the cool thing is, He doesn't allow anything through His hands that isn't good for us.

Sometimes we need to stretch and grow. It hurts while we are going through it, but it always helps us.

Romans 8:28 *And we know that **all** things work together for good to those who love God, to those who are the called according to His purpose.*

Philippians 1:6 *being confident of this very thing, that He who has begun a good work in you will complete it until the day of Jesus Christ.*

God loves you so much. He cares about every aspect of your life. My new foster kids think I am crazy when they tell me they can't find something, like socks or a shoe, and I ask them "have you prayed yet?" They just can't believe that a big God would care if they found their sock, but he does care. If I pray to find something, I'll find it almost immediately or before I need it. If I don't find it, I always figure out later that I didn't need it.

God is so cool. I have ADD, and it's getting worse with age, but I praise God that I do. It's the perfect gift! I consider ADD a gift, because I have to depend on God a lot. He helps me remember and focus. He helps me find things. I have to keep in close contact with him just to function. I love Him so much! He is so good to me.

James 1:17,18 *Do not be deceived, my beloved brethren.* [17] *Every good gift and every perfect gift is from above, and comes down from the Father of lights, with whom there is no variation or shadow of turning.* [18] *Of His own will He brought us forth by the word of truth, that we might be a kind of firstfruits of His creatures.*

Read **Psalm 139**

In light of today's study, what was the Scripture or statement in today's lesson that most spoke to your heart? _____

_____

_____

_____

What steps of faith does God want you to take towards Him today? _____

_____

_____

_____

Rephrase the Scripture or statement into an expression of faith_____

_____

_____

_____

Memorize:

II Kings 6:17 *And Elisha _____, and said, "LORD, I _____, open his eyes _____ he may see." Then the LORD opened the eyes of the _____ man, and he saw. And behold, the mountain was full of horses and _____ of fire all around Elisha.*

Week 6 Day 3
God's Truth-VS-Satan's Lies

Day _____ Date _____

In your own words write down what you think addiction means. _____
_____
_____
_____

The dictionary defines it as applying or devoting oneself habitually. The Latin root for addiction is addicene, and it means, to give assent, to assign or surrender. In ancient times, it was used to describe someone who was captured and kept in bondage or slavery.

An addiction serves us by removing us from our true feelings and provides us a form of escape. Addictions cannot be controlled by logic or reason and always involves pleasure and pain (consequence). When a person succumbs to an addiction, it brings a temporary calmness, a release, the feeling of being nurtured. While giving in to the temptation, we don't allow ourselves to think of the adverse consequences, the pain of being overweight, but we find pleasure in the act of eating itself.

Addictions are usually always destructive and unhealthy. You are not physically dependent on stuffing your stomach beyond the feeling of being satisfied; you're psychologically dependent. The battle is in your brain, not your mouth. Satan tricks you into feeling and thinking wrong; he is a liar and has us convinced that we are powerless against our addictions, and we get plenty of excuses from the medical profession to stay just the way we are.

II Corinthians 11:3 *But I fear, lest somehow, as the serpent deceived Eve by his craftiness, so your minds may be corrupted from the simplicity that is in Christ*

One of the most important concepts we need to learn is God's forgiveness. Satan is most effective in convincing us that once we have made a mistake from which we can't get back up.

You will make mistakes. If you could do it without one mistake, you wouldn't need Jesus. I'll say it again: you will make mistakes. Get back up; the next time you give into temptation, just say no! Sin hasn't the power to control you anymore. You have been set free. The only reason you think you are addicted is because Satan convinces you that you are. It's impossible for you to be in bondage if you are a Christian, because you are dead to sin and alive to Christ. You are a new creation.

This is what Jesus said about Satan:

John 8:44 *You are of your father the devil, and the desires of your father you want to do. He was a murderer from the beginning, and does not stand in the truth, because there is no truth in him. When he speaks a lie, he speaks from his own resources, for he is a liar and the father of it.*

The Lie:

Genesis 3:4-6 *Then the serpent said to the woman, "You will not surely die. [5] For God knows that in the day you eat of it your eyes will be opened, and you will be like God, knowing good and evil."*

[6] So when the woman saw that the tree was good for food, that it was pleasant to the eyes, and a tree desirable to make one wise, she took of its fruit and ate. She also gave to her husband with her, and he ate.

Satan provided Eve with an excuse to sin; he is an expert at it. He is the king of excuses, and look how good mankind is at using excuses.

Geneses 3:11-13 *And He said, "Who told you that you were naked? Have you eaten from the tree of which I commanded you that you should not eat?"*

[12] Then the man said, "The woman whom You gave to be with me, she gave me of the tree, and I ate."

[13] And the LORD God said to the woman, "What is this you have done?"

The woman said, "The serpent deceived me, and I ate."

When we choose our own path and make excuses for our behavior, we become our own little god.

The truth:

Romans 6 *What shall we say then? Shall we continue in sin that grace may abound? [2] Certainly not! How shall we who died to sin live any longer in it? [3] Or do you not know that as many of us as were baptized into Christ Jesus were baptized into His death? [4] Therefore we were buried with Him through baptism into death, that just as Christ was raised from the dead by the glory of the Father, even so we also should walk in newness of life.*

[5] For if we have been united together in the likeness of His death, certainly we also shall be in the likeness of His resurrection, [6]Knowing this, that our old man was crucified with Him, that the body of sin might be done away with, that we should no longer be slaves of sin. [7] For he who has died has been freed from sin. [8] Now if we died with Christ, we believe that we shall also live with Him, [9] knowing that Christ, having been raised from the dead, dies no more. Death no longer has dominion over Him. [10] For the death that He died, He died to sin once for all; but the life that He lives, He lives to God.

[11] *Likewise you also, reckon yourselves to be dead indeed to sin, but alive to God in Christ Jesus our Lord.*

[12] Therefore do not let sin reign in your mortal body, that you should obey it in its lusts. [13] And do not present your members as instruments of unrighteousness to sin, but present yourselves to

God as being alive from the dead, and your members as instruments of righteousness to God. [14] *For sin shall not have dominion over you, for you are not under law but under grace.*

[15] *What then? Shall we sin because we are not under law but under grace? Certainly not!* [16] *Do you not know that to whom you present yourselves slaves to obey, you are that one's slaves whom you obey, whether of sin leading to death, or of obedience leading to righteousness?* [17] *But God be thanked that though you were slaves of sin, yet you obeyed from the heart that form of doctrine to which you were delivered.* [18] *And having been set free from sin, you became slaves of righteousness.* [19] *I speak in human terms because of the weakness of your flesh. For just as you presented your members as slaves of uncleanness, and of lawlessness leading to more lawlessness, so now present your members as slaves of righteousness for holiness.*

[20] *For when you were slaves of sin, you were free in regard to righteousness.* [21] *What fruit did you have then in the things of which you are now ashamed? For the end of those things is death.* [22] *But **now** having been set free from sin, and having become slaves of God, you have your fruit to holiness, and the end, everlasting life.* [23] *For the wages of sin is death, but the gift of God is eternal life in Christ Jesus our Lord.*

What shall we say, then? Shall we continue in sin that grace may abound (**Romans 6:1**)? In the previous chapter, Paul was talking about the grace of God to forgive sins. Non-believers have said to me, "So you can get saved then go out and kill someone, and God will forgive you?" It is a valid question. Why don't we just continue in our sins? Why don't we just sit down at a table, and eat, and eat, until we die? You could show how merciful God is. How abundant His grace is.

Paul's answer to that was certainly not! That a believer should continue in sin to take advantage of the Grace of God was detestable to Paul. What kind of fruit does that produce? When we are in Christ, we not only have the promise of Heaven, but we have a better life. Our lifestyle improves, because we are not sowing seeds of sin.

When we died with Christ, you died to the world and its darkness. If you died with Christ, it logically follows that you were raised with Him, also, into the newness that is in Christ Jesus. You are not the same person as you were before you asked Jesus into your heart. You became a completely new creation in Christ. When you were baptized, and rose from the water, you identified yourself with Him. You announced you are a new creation in Him, a new life in Him, a life in the Spirit. If you are a Christian, then when you sin, you give yourself voluntarily to Satan to be his slave. It's a matter of whom you believe. Do you believe Satan's lies? He says you're addicted. Alternatively, do you believe God's truth? He says can't be addicted. You are free from addiction; it's a matter of faith.

II Corinthians 5:17 *Therefore, if anyone is in Christ, he is a new creation; old things have passed away; behold, all things have become new.*

The flesh is no longer the king. You are dead to that and free from having to submit to temptation. None of us is immune to temptation, and because we still sometimes accept Satan's lies as the truth, we can become victims of our sins again. Even after we are born into the Spirit, we can still believe we are slaves to our cravings, and what you believe about yourself is how you live or react to the temptation.

You are different from unsaved. They are slaves to sin and the addiction. If they do overcome an addiction, they just replace it with another one.

You have the power because you have been reborn into Christ. You have access to the POWER of the almighty Holy Spirit. You have the ability to quit. You are dead to sin; you just have to believe that.

If you got hit by a car and died, no matter what succulent, yummy food someone put in front of you, you would still be dead. It wouldn't matter to you; you would be dead!

Write **Romans 6:11**_____

_____

_____

_____

Romans 6:12 says *"Let not sin reign in your mortal body"*

It's a choice, whether you let sin be king in your heart. The Greek word for reckon is [9]*logizomai*. It means to determine, purpose, decide. Blueletterbible.org, says, "This word deals with reality. If I reckon (logizomai) that my bank book has $25 in it, it has $25 in it. Otherwise I am deceiving myself. This word refers more to fact than supposition or opinion."

If it weren't your choice, God wouldn't tell you in this whole chapter of Romans that it was. It's your choice to ask God to rescue you. You choose if you give it to God or become your own little god. When we make the excuse, "I am just not strong enough," and all the other excuses we make, we are flat out calling God a liar. There is no excuse. The reason you overeat is that you believe a liar more than you believe God. We don't have to obey the desires of the flesh; we *want* to obey them.

When you "let sin reign," it means you have surrendered to sin. It doesn't happen to you; you let it happen. When you are being tempted, there are only two choices: surrender to Jesus or surrender to Satan. Verses thirteen through seventeen from Romans six, take away any excuse we might think we have. You have been set free from hurting yourself. Present yourself to God. Actually tell God, "I present myself to you, do with me as you will."

Romans 6: 13-17 (The Message) *And do not present your members as instruments of unrighteousness to sin, but present yourselves to God as being alive from the dead, and your members as instruments of righteousness to God. [14] For sin shall not have dominion over you, for you are not under law but under grace. [15] What then? Shall we sin because we are not under law but under grace? Certainly not! [16] Do you not know that to whom you present yourselves slaves to obey, you are that one's slaves whom you obey, whether of sin leading to death, or of*

---

[9] http://www.blueletterbible.org, Strong's G3049 - *logizomai*

obedience leading to righteousness? ¹⁷ *But God be thanked that though you were slaves of sin, yet you obeyed from the heart that form of doctrine to which you were delivered.*

I also like how "The Message" translates it:

Romans 6

15-18 So, since we're out from under the old tyranny, does that mean we can live any old way we want? Since we're free in the freedom of God, can we do anything that comes to mind? Hardly. You know well enough from your own experience that there are some acts of so-called freedom that destroy freedom. Offer yourselves to sin, for instance, and it's your last free act. But offer yourselves to the ways of God and the freedom never quits. All your lives you've let sin tell you what to do. But thank God you've started listening to a new master, one whose commands set you free to live openly in his freedom!

19 I'm using this freedom language because it's easy to picture. You can readily recall, can't you, how at one time the more you did just what you felt like doing—not caring about others, not caring about God—the worse your life became and the less freedom you had? And how much different is it now as you live in God's freedom, your lives healed and expansive in holiness?

20-21 As long as you did what you felt like doing, ignoring God, you didn't have to bother with right thinking or right living, or right anything for that matter. But do you call that a free life? What did you get out of it? Nothing you're proud of now. Where did it get you? A dead end.

22-23 But now that you've found you don't have to listen to sin tell you what to do, and have discovered the delight of listening to God telling you, what a surprise! A whole, healed, put-together life right now, with more and more of life on the way! Work hard for sin your whole life and your pension is death. But God's gift is real life, eternal life, delivered by Jesus, our Master.

What does it take to have "a whole, healed, put-together life right now"? _____

_____

It takes faith; whom do you believe? Do you believe the Bible, God's Word, or do you believe Satan? You can have a whole, healed, put-together life right now! Right Now! You don't have to wait to be skinny; you are healed and put together right now.

Galatians 5:1 *Stand fast therefore in the liberty by which Christ has made us free, and do not be entangled again with a yoke of bondage.*

Romans 8:2 *For the law of the Spirit of life in Christ Jesus has made me free from the law of sin and death.*

John 8:36 *Therefore if the Son makes you free, you shall be free indeed.*

You are not only free from the sin, but also, free from the bondage of always thinking about your weight.

From what you have read in the Scriptures above what are some of the ways you will approach your overeating? _____

_____

_____

You can soar above the battle. Think about how an eagle flies. When they are a baby, they flap their wings furiously. It's not until they learn to lean on the wind and glide that they can soar to incredible heights.

Read **Isaiah 40:28-31** *He gives power to the weak, And to those who have no might He increases strength. [30] Even the youths shall faint and be weary, And the young men shall utterly fall, [31] But those who wait on the LORD shall renew their strength; They shall mount up with wings like eagles, They shall run and not be weary, They shall walk and not faint.*

When you are flying above the fight, you're not contemplating sin at all. You just say no. You are trusting God. You still have to resist temptation and run to God, because now, Satan tempts you with unbelief. Like we have studied before, your lack of faith limits God, and Satan tries to tempt you with that. If you believe you can run and not grow weary, you can walk and not faint. The battle is not wearing on you; you're strong through faith. Your mind is set on the goal and you are not double-minded. You have a single purpose, and that is to please God. You don't argue or whine. You simply say no. However, you need to understand, when you give into contemplating a temptation, you slide down real quick into the thick of the battle where you are worn out quickly and everything is harder. It becomes easier to fly above it by not giving in and you feel light and happy. God's way is so much easier. You feel good and right and joyful. You're always in high spirits.

Probably at least 90% of the time when you're feeling depressed without a reason, it's because you are not in God's will, and you are involved in a sin. It is so much happier to follow God.

When Jesus appeared to Paul on the road to Damascus, **Acts 9:1-5** *Then Saul, still breathing threats and murder against the disciples of the Lord, went to the high priest [2] and asked letters from him to the synagogues of Damascus, so that if he found any who were of the Way, whether men or women, he might bring them bound to Jerusalem.*

[3] As he journeyed he came near Damascus, and suddenly a light shone around him from Heaven. [4] Then he fell to the ground, and heard a voice saying to him, "Saul, Saul, why are you persecuting Me?" [5] And he said, "Who are You, Lord?" Then the Lord said, "I am Jesus, whom you are persecuting. It is hard for you to kick against the goads."

A Goad was a long wooden pole which had a sharp metal point on the end. They were used by farmers to control rebellious livestock. It kept them from kicking. The sooner they stopped rebelling and settled into their job, the sooner the pain went away. Paul was working so hard at what he thought God wanted, it was causing not only himself pain, but many of his future Christian brothers and sisters were hurt at his command. You need to give up the pain of overeating. When you do sin, it's so much harder. It's like fighting against God who is doing you good.

II Chronicles 13:12 *Now look, God Himself is with us as our head, and His priests with sounding trumpets to sound the alarm against you. O children of Israel, do not fight against the LORD God of your fathers, for you shall not prosper!"*

Satan lies to us and convinces us it's easier to give into temptation. It isn't. You may feel gratified at that moment, but the after-effects are not so peaceful. The consequences always cause stress.

Read **Matthew 11:29** *Come to Me, all you who labor and are heavy laden, and I will give you rest. ^{29} Take My yoke upon you and learn from Me, for I am gentle and lowly in heart, and you will find rest for your souls. ^{30} For My yoke is easy and My burden is light."*

Read the following statements and place a check in the correct column

The Statement	Lie/ Excuse	Truth
I'll start tomorrow.		
I will be strong!		
I can do all things through Christ.		
I just need more willpower.		
I am weak willed.		
I was born this way.		
It's God battle.		
I will hide in the shadow of God's wing.		
One little bite won't matter.		
I think I am hungry.		
This is my favorite restaurant, I'm afraid I won't be able to eat here again soon, just this one time.		
If we confess our sins, He is faithful to forgive us our sins and to cleanse us from all unrighteousness.		
I failed; I will never get over this addiction.		
I won't eat dinner, so I can finish these last few bites of lunch.		
I will use the power given to me by the almighty God to resist temptation.		
It's not that bad of a sin.		
I am not healed		
By my faith I am healed, I will go in peace and fly above my affliction		
Add your own excuses below		

The excuses you believe you have is to what you become in bondage. Go back and look at each of the statements you checked as being an excuse. You may have great excuses. In fact, the jails and underpasses are full of people who have great excuses for being in their situation. You can excuse yourself to a thousand pounds, but what good does that do you? You are in bondage to the excuses. You're holding on to them because, if you are saved you're sure not addicted. Excuses make you feel better about where you are, but they don't help you get to where you want to be. Let's face it, the more comfortable you are in your present situation, the more you won't mind staying there. Excuse may make you feel better for a while, but they hurt you. So let go of them.

W. L. Barnes, in his book "Free as a Bird," tells this story, perfectly illustrating how we become slave to our desires.

He writes, "Recently we put up a hummingbird feeder with four feeding stations. Almost immediately it became popular with the hummingbirds that live in our area. Two, three, or even four birds would feed at one time. We refilled the feeder at least once a day. Suddenly the usage decreased to almost nothing. The feeder needed filling only about once a week. The reason for the decreased usage soon became apparent. A male bird had taken over the feeder as his property. He is now the only hummingbird who uses our feeder. He feeds and then sits in a nearby tree, rising to attack any bird that approaches his feeder. Guard duty occupies his every waking hour. He is an effective guard. The only time another bird gets to use the feeder is when the self-appointed owner is momentarily gone to chase away an intruder. We soon realized that the hummingbird was teaching us a valuable lesson. By choosing to assume ownership of the feeder, he is forfeiting his freedom. He is no longer free to come and go as he wished. He is tied to the work of guarding his feeder. He is possessed by his possession. His freedom of action is as circumscribed as if he were in a cage. He is caged by a situation he has created."

When you overeat, you allow yourself to be enslaved to the behavior that you hate. If you just let go and give it to God when you pary, God will take it in His time.

Read Psalm 103

In light of today's study, what was the Scripture or statement in today's lesson that most spoke to your heart? _____

_____

_____

_____

What steps of faith does God want you to take towards Him today? _____

_____

_____

_____

Rephrase the Scripture or statement into an expression of faith_____

_____

_____

_____

Memorize:

II Kings 6:17 *And Elisha _____, and _____, "LORD, I _____, open ____eyes _____ he may see." _____ the LORD opened the eyes of the _____ man, and he _____. And _____, the _____was full of horses and _____ of fire all around Elisha.*

Week 6 Day 4
Establish Being Occupied with Weight is Idolatry

Day _____ Date _____

Remember the definition of idolatry?

Definitions:
Idol: a false God: an object of passionate, excessive devotion.
Idolize: to make an idol of, greed selfish desire beyond reason.
Idolatry: to put your trust, Love, devotion in anything other than God."

Read each of these definitions. Be honest. Do these apply to how you have felt about being thin? I know that I was passionate about being thin. You could take one look at my library of books to see how the desire to be thin had consumed me. My selfish desire to become thin was beyond reason. I put my trust, love, and devotion in the diet of the week. This desire to be thin superseded any desire I had for food.

Today's study may take a little extra time, because if you haven't already, you need to spend time contemplating the reason you want to lose weight. Do you want to please God, or please yourself? What are you hoping to accomplish by doing this Bible study? Will your weight loss give glory to God? Take a few minutes to pray about it. Seek God; wait for His answer. Write your aspirations for this study.

_____
_____
_____
_____
_____
_____

(Use more paper if you need it.)

Genesis 22:*1*-19 *Now it came to pass after these things that God tested Abraham, and said to him, "Abraham!" And he said, "Here I am."*

² Then He said, "Take now your son, your only son Isaac, whom you love, and go to the land of Moriah, and offer him there as a burnt offering on one of the mountains of which I shall tell you."

³ So Abraham rose early in the morning and saddled his donkey, and took two of his young men with him, and Isaac his son; and he split the wood for the burnt offering, and arose and went to the place of which God had told him. ⁴ Then on the third day Abraham lifted his eyes and saw the place afar off. ⁵ And Abraham said to his young men, "Stay here with the donkey; the lad and I will go yonder and worship, and we will come back to you."

⁶ So Abraham took the wood of the burnt offering and laid it on Isaac his son; and he took the fire in his hand, and a knife, and the two of them went together. [7] But Isaac spoke to Abraham his father and said, "My father!"

And he said, "Here I am, my son."

Then he said, "Look, the fire and the wood, but where is the lamb for a burnt offering?"

[8] And Abraham said, "My son, God will provide for Himself the lamb for a burnt offering." So the two of them went together.

[9] Then they came to the place of which God had told him. And Abraham built an altar there and placed the wood in order; and he bound Isaac his son and laid him on the altar, upon the wood. [10] And Abraham stretched out his hand and took the knife to slay his son.

[11] But the Angel of the LORD called to him from Heaven and said, "Abraham, Abraham!" So he said, "Here I am."

[12] And He said, "Do not lay your hand on the lad, or do anything to him; for now I know that you fear God, since you have not withheld your son, your only son, from Me."

[13] Then Abraham lifted his eyes and looked, and there behind him was a ram caught in a thicket by its horns. So Abraham went and took the ram, and offered it up for a burnt offering instead of his son. [14] And Abraham called the name of the place, The-LORD-Will-Provide; as it is said to this day, "In the Mount of the LORD it shall be provided."

[15] Then the Angel of the LORD called to Abraham a second time out of Heaven, [16] and said: "By Myself I have sworn, says the LORD, because you have done this thing, and have not withheld your son, your only son— [17] blessing I will bless you, and multiplying I will multiply your descendants as the stars of the Heaven and as the sand which is on the seashore; and your descendants shall possess the gate of their enemies. [18] In your seed all the nations of the earth shall be blessed, because you have obeyed My voice."

[19] So Abraham returned to his young men, and they rose and went together to Beersheba; and Abraham dwelt at Beersheba.

Abraham prayed for a child and heir all his adult life. He was a very old man when God finally gave him the son he desired so much. Through the hope and disappointment, God taught Abraham some very valuable lessons, the most important one being to trust Him. He was willing to give God what God asked, his most treasured gift, but instead, God provided. When you have reached the very pinnacle of what *you* can do, God will provide.

Abraham wasn't just able to obey God one day. He didn't just wake up one morning and God said, "Sacrifice your son," and he was able to do it without question. He grew to trust God through the many years that God withheld the blessing.

Do you trust God? _____

If you have ever read the struggle of David's life between the time he was anointed King over Israel by Samuel, the prophet, and the time he finally became king, you begin to understand how David learned to trust God. There were many times David could have taken the throne by killing Saul, but he had learned to trust God. He sacrificed his dreams for what he knew God had planned for him.

Saul, the king, knew God had chosen David to replace him, because Saul had shown his mistrust in God (you have read about it in the day titled, "Saul's Decision"). Saul felt threatened, jealous, and hated David. He took all his men and pursued David for years.

I Samuel 24:1-22 *Now it happened, when Saul had returned from following the Philistines, that it was told him, saying, "Take note! David is in the Wilderness of En Gedi." ² Then Saul took three thousand chosen men from all Israel, and went to seek David and his men on the Rocks of the Wild Goats. ³ So he came to the sheepfolds by the road, where there was a cave; and Saul went in to attend to his needs. (David and his men were staying in the recesses of the cave.) ⁴ Then the men of David said to him, "This is the day of which the LORD said to you, 'Behold, I will deliver your enemy into your hand, that you may do to him as it seems good to you.'" And David arose and secretly cut off a corner of Saul's robe. ⁵ Now it happened afterward that David's heart troubled him because he had cut Saul's robe.*

⁶ And he said to his men, "The LORD forbid that I should do this thing to my master, the LORD's anointed, to stretch out my hand against him, seeing he is the anointed of the LORD." ⁷ So David restrained his servants with these words, and did not allow them to rise against Saul. And Saul got up from the cave and went on his way.

⁸ David also arose afterward, went out of the cave, and called out to Saul, saying, "My lord the king!" And when Saul looked behind him, David stooped with his face to the earth, and bowed down. ⁹ And David said to Saul: "Why do you listen to the words of men who say, 'Indeed David seeks your harm'? ¹⁰ Look, this day your eyes have seen that the LORD delivered you today into my hand in the cave, and someone urged me to kill you. But my eye spared you, and I said, 'I will not stretch out my hand against my lord, for he is the LORD's anointed.' ¹¹ Moreover, my father, see! Yes, see the corner of your robe in my hand! For in that I cut off the corner of your robe, and did not kill you, know and see that there is neither evil nor rebellion in my hand, and I have not sinned against you. Yet you hunt my life to take it. ¹² Let the LORD judge between you and me, and let the LORD avenge me on you. But my hand shall not be against you.

Think about it. It took a lot of trust for David to resist killing Saul. This wasn't the last time Saul felt jealous of David. He hunted him down to try to killing him, and God would deliver Saul into David's hand and David would spare Saul, because he trusted God.

Do you trust God? _____

If God asked you to sacrifice your plans for being thin and ask you to stop dieting, would you?

_____

186

Write down your thoughts and feelings about your answer.

_____
_____
_____

Read **Romans 12: 1** *I beseech you therefore, brethren, by the mercies of God, that you present your bodies a living sacrifice, holy, acceptable to God, which is your reasonable service.*

Eventually, you must come to a point where you are ready to sacrifice your body to God, like Abraham did with Isaac. You have to come to the point where you have to sacrifice your dreams, like David did. Walking in the Spirit means dying to yourself, your hopes, your dreams, and your aspirations. Are you willing to give these up and trust God with your life?

You may say yes, but look back at the stories of Abraham and David. Look how much they were willing to trust God.

Do you trust God like that? _____

God will show you amazing things, but are you willing to trust Him? _____

Matthew 6:31-33 *"Therefore do not worry, saying, "What shall we eat?' or "What shall we drink?' or "What shall we wear?'* [32] *For after all these things the Gentiles seek. For your heavenly Father knows that you need all these things.* [33] *But seek first the kingdom of God and His righteousness, and all these things shall be added to you*

A Bible event that always confused me was Abraham and the incident with Hagar.

Genesis 16:1-6 *Now Sarai, Abram's wife, had borne him no children. And she had an Egyptian maidservant whose name was Hagar.* [2] *So Sarai said to Abram, "See now, the LORD has restrained me from bearing children. Please, go in to my maid; perhaps I shall obtain children by her." And Abram heeded the voice of Sarai.* [3] *Then Sarai, Abram's wife, took Hagar her maid, the Egyptian, and gave her to her husband Abram to be his wife, after Abram had dwelt ten years in the land of Canaan.* [4] *So he went in to Hagar, and she conceived. And when she saw that she had conceived, her mistress became despised in her eyes.*

[5] *Then Sarai said to Abram, "My wrong be upon you! I gave my maid into your embrace; and when she saw that she had conceived, I became despised in her eyes. The LORD judge between you and me."*

[6] *So Abram said to Sarai, "Indeed your maid is in your hand; do to her as you please." And when Sarai dealt harshly with her, she fled from her presence.*

I think Abram and Sarai were a lot like me. When God promises me something and I don't think He is moving fast enough, I try to help Him out a little. That's what we see here. I don't think Abraham did this because he was trying to rebel (even though it was rebellion and lack of trust in God). I think he honestly thought he was helping God out. How many times have I done that in my life? I am sure Abraham felt it was one of his biggest mistakes, and it caused him untold heartache.

The point is God knew that Abraham wasn't being obstinate; God knew Abraham had a heart for Him and loved Him.

If your spouse forgot a dinner date, while normally attentive, you would be disappointed, but it wouldn't be a huge problem in your marriage. On the other hand, if your husband or wife has been flirtatious with your best friend, uninterested in you, and forgets a dinner date, it could be the last straw on the path to divorce.

Read story of Cain and Able. It's the perfect description for a right heart.

Genius 4:1-15 *Now Adam knew Eve his wife, and she conceived and bore Cain, and said, "I have acquired a man from the LORD."* [2] *Then she bore again, this time his brother Abel. Now Abel was a keeper of sheep, but Cain was a tiller of the ground.* [3] *And in the process of time it came to pass that Cain brought an offering of the fruit of the ground to the LORD.* [4] *Abel also brought of the firstborn of his flock and of their fat. And the LORD respected Abel and his offering,* [5] *but He did not respect Cain and his offering. And Cain was very angry, and his countenance fell.*

[6] *So the LORD said to Cain, "Why are you angry? And why has your countenance fallen?* [7] *If you do well, will you not be accepted? And if you do not do well, sin lies at the door. And its desire is for you, but you should rule over it."* [8] *Now Cain talked with Abel his brother; and it came to pass, when they were in the field, that Cain rose up against Abel his brother and killed him.*

[9] *Then the LORD said to Cain, "Where is Abel your brother?"* *He said, "I do not know. Am I my brother's keeper?"*

[10] *And He said, "What have you done? The voice of your brother's blood cries out to Me from the ground.*

This is another story I was confused about. I wondered why wasn't God satisfied with Cain's sacrifice just because Able brought Him meat and Cain brought veggies. The answer to this question isn't what each one sacrificed, it's how they sacrificed. Read verse four again. Abel brought the best of his best. His heart was right; he loved God, and sacrificed the best of himself. Cain was resentful, knowing he hadn't given God his best. He blamed everyone else but himself.

Hebrews 11:4 *By faith Abel offered to God a more excellent sacrifice than Cain, through which he obtained witness that he was righteous, God testifying of his gifts; and through it he being dead still speaks.*

God will always look at our heart. He considers what motivates us.

I Samuel16:1-13 *Now the LORD said to Samuel, "How long will you mourn for Saul, seeing I have rejected him from reigning over Israel? Fill your horn with oil, and go; I am sending you to Jesse the Bethlehemite. For I have provided Myself a king among his sons."*

² And Samuel said, "How can I go? If Saul hears it, he will kill me."
But the LORD said, "Take a heifer with you, and say, "I have come to sacrifice to the LORD.'

³ Then invite Jesse to the sacrifice, and I will show you what you shall do; you shall anoint for Me the one I name to you."

⁴ So Samuel did what the LORD said, and went to Bethlehem. And the elders of the town trembled at his coming, and said, "Do you come peaceably?"

⁵ And he said, "Peaceably; I have come to sacrifice to the LORD. Sanctify yourselves, and come with me to the sacrifice." Then he consecrated Jesse and his sons, and invited them to the sacrifice.

⁶ So it was, when they came, that he looked at Eliab and said, "Surely the LORD's anointed is before Him!"

⁷ But the LORD said to Samuel, "Do not look at his appearance or at his physical stature, because I have refused him. For the LORD does not see as man sees; for man looks at the outward appearance, but the LORD looks at the heart."

⁸ So Jesse called Abinadab, and made him pass before Samuel. And he said, "Neither has the LORD chosen this one." ⁹ Then Jesse made Shammah pass by. And he said, "Neither has the LORD chosen this one." ¹⁰ Thus Jesse made seven of his sons pass before Samuel. And Samuel said to Jesse, "The LORD has not chosen these." ¹¹ And Samuel said to Jesse, "Are all the young men here?" Then he said, "There remains yet the youngest, and there he is, keeping the sheep."

And Samuel said to Jesse, "Send and bring him. For we will not sit down till he comes here." ¹² So he sent and brought him in. Now he was ruddy, with bright eyes, and good-looking. And the LORD said, "Arise, anoint him; for this is the one!" ¹³ Then Samuel took the horn of oil and anointed him in the midst of his brothers; and the Spirit of the LORD came upon David from that day forward. So Samuel arose and went to Ramah.

Can you imagine Samuel's thoughts as Jesse's sons were all paraded before him? Any one of Jesse's sons would have been a great king, especially Eliab, the oldest. By human standards, he was the best candidate. They saidm without doubt, this is God's anointed one.

God told the prophet Samuel to look at the heart. Jesse didn't even bring David with him, because he judged him an unworthy candidate. To Samuel and Jesse's surprise, God chose the least likely contender.

God looks at our hearts. He knows what motivates us. He knows our weaknesses, and He sympathizes with them.

Hebrews 4:15 *For we do not have a High Priest who cannot sympathize with our weaknesses, but was in all points tempted as we are, yet without sin.*

Offerings Accepted and Not Accepted

Leviticus 22:17-23 *And the LORD spoke to Moses, saying,* [18] *"Speak to Aaron and his sons, and to all the children of Israel, and say to them: "Whatever man of the house of Israel, or of the strangers in Israel, who offers his sacrifice for any of his vows or for any of his freewill offerings, which they offer to the LORD as a burnt offering--* [19] *you shall offer of your own free will a male without blemish from the cattle, from the sheep, or from the goats.* [20] *Whatever has a defect, you shall not offer, for it shall not be acceptable on your behalf.* [21] *And whoever offers a sacrifice of a peace offering to the LORD, to fulfill his vow, or a freewill offering from the cattle or the sheep, it must be perfect to be accepted; there shall be no defect in it.* [22] *Those that are blind or broken or maimed, or have an ulcer or eczema or scabs, you shall not offer to the LORD, nor make an offering by fire of them on the altar to the LORD.* [23] *Either a bull or a lamb that has any limb too long or too short you may offer as a freewill offering, but for a vow it shall not be accepted.*

Why do you think God didn't want the children of Israel sacrificing unhealthy or deformed animals to Him? _____

_____

_____

_____

Read **Genesis 4: 3-5** again. *And in the process of time it came to pass that Cain brought an offering of the fruit of the ground to the LORD.* [4] *Abel also brought of the firstborn of his flock and of their fat. And the LORD respected Abel and his offering,* [5] *but He did not respect Cain and his offering. And Cain was very angry, and his countenance fell.*

Why do you think God didn't respect Cain's offering? _____

_____

_____

_____

Both of the preceding Scriptures talk about halfhearted sacrifice. God would rather have you not make the sacrifice than to make a halfhearted sacrifice.

Revelation 3:15 *"I know your works, that you are neither cold nor hot. I could wish you were cold or hot.*

How would you feel if your spouse gave you a present out of the trash? There are times when I have decided to fast and later I had the opportunity to go out to eat, and I told myself "I'll fast tomorrow when the food isn't as good." Does that seem like sacrifice to you?_____

What if I got mad at God because I decided to make a sacrifice and fast for a week, and I didn't lose a pound? Do you think that is an acceptable sacrifice? _____
Why? _____
_____
_____
_____

What is the purpose of fasting? Are you fasting to lose weight? If you are, it's not called fasting; it's called dieting. Pray and ask God to give you a heart only for Him. Don't get mad if you're not losing the weight as fast as you think you should. God knows what you need to learn from this. The plateaus you experience are important learning tools. Trust God, seek Him first, and He will give you the desires of your heart.

Sin for sin, David and Saul were probably even. Its David's humble reaction to God's examination of his heart that sets him apart from Saul, whose favorite choice was to make excuses for his behavior (Sounds like me... Ouch!).

Abraham was a sinner; he lied and said his wife Sarah was his sister because he was afraid he might be killed because she was beautiful. He was going to let his wife be dishonored because he was too afraid, yet he was the same man who was going to sacrifice his beloved son because God asked him to. God knows you're not perfect. You are growing in Him, but it's those times of trial that teach you to be strong in Him.

Where is your heart? What motivates you? Pray that God will build a love in your heart for Him.

Deuteronomy 6:5 *You shall love the LORD your God with all your heart, with all your soul, and with all your strength.*

Mark 12:30 *and you shall love the LORD your God with all your heart, with all your soul, with your entire mind, and with all your strength.'*

Proverbs 27:19 *as in water face reflects face, so a man's heart reveals the man.*

Psalm 139:23,24 *Search me, O God, and know my heart; Try me, and know my anxieties; [24] And see if there is any wicked way in me, And lead me in the way everlasting.*

Psalm 111:1 *Praise the LORD! I will praise the LORD with my whole heart, in the assembly of the upright and in the congregation.*

Psalm 119:10 *With my whole heart, I have sought you; oh, let me not wander from your commandments!*

Deuteronomy 30:6 *And the LORD your God will circumcise your heart and the heart of your* *descendants, to love the LORD your God with all your heart and with all your soul, that you may live.*

Joshua 22:5 *But take careful heed to do the commandment and the law which Moses the servant of the LORD commanded you, to love the LORD your God, to walk in all His ways, to keep His commandments, to hold fast to Him, and to serve Him with all your heart and with all your soul*

In your own words, summarize what the proceeding Scriptures are saying. _____

_____

_____

_____

Contrast Mary and Martha, **Luke 10: 38-42** *Now it happened as they went that He entered a certain village; and a certain woman named Martha welcomed Him into her house. [39] And she had a sister called Mary, who also sat at Jesus' feet and heard His word. [40] But Martha was distracted with much serving, and she approached Him and said, "Lord, do You not care that my sister has left me to serve alone? Therefore tell her to help me." [41] And Jesus answered and said to her, "Martha, Martha, you are worried and troubled about many things. [42] But one thing is needed, and Mary has chosen that good part, which will not be taken away from her."*

Martha thought she was serving Jesus, but in reality, she was too worried about the stuff, too busy getting the job done, and too dependent on her own ability. Also, look at the difference between Saul and David. They both made mistakes. Look at Peter and Judas, they both denied Christ. What made one different from the other? _____

_____

_____

Which one do you see in yourself? Do you make God your first priority; do you make alone time more important than anything? Ask yourselves some of these hard questions. Your answers will probably be different each time you ask. Sometimes you will be Mary, sometimes you will be Martha, but I hope that we are Mary more than we are Martha, David more than we are Saul, and Peter more than we are Judas. Your love relationship with God is more important than any other single factor. God persues a love relationship with you. I have taken the Holy Spirit into some places I am ashamed of, and He has followed me in. We are created to have a love relationship with God, and only when we have this relationship, can we be happy and contented.

Read **Romans 8:35-39** *Who shall separate us from the love of Christ? Shall tribulation, or distress, or persecution, or famine, or nakedness, or peril, or sword? [36] As it is written:*

"For Your sake we are killed all day long; We are accounted as sheep for the slaughter."

[37] Yet in all these things we are more than conquerors through Him who loved us. [38] For I am persuaded that neither death nor life, nor angels nor principalities nor powers, nor things present nor things to come, [39] nor height nor depth, nor any other created thing, shall be able to

separate us from the love of God which is in Christ Jesus our Lord.

What does God promise about His love for you? _____

God will always love you. The question is, will you always love God, or will you harden your heart? We are not perfect, but being perfected.

Philippians 3:12-14 *Not that I have already attained, or am already perfected; but I press on, that I may lay hold of that for which Christ Jesus has also laid hold of me. [13] Brethren, I do not count myself to have apprehended; but one thing I do, forgetting those things which are behind and reaching forward to those things which are ahead, [14] I press toward the goal for the prize of the upward call of God in Christ Jesus.*

You have not only made food an idol but also dieting and wanting to be thin an Idol. You may even idolize thin people.

Deuteronomy 4: 15 *"Take careful heed to yourselves, for you saw no form when the LORD spoke to you at Horeb out of the midst of the fire, [16] lest you act corruptly and make for yourselves a carved image in the form of any figure: the likeness of male or female, [17] the likeness of any animal that is on the earth or the likeness of any winged bird that flies in the air, [18] the likeness of anything that creeps on the ground or the likeness of any fish that is in the water beneath the earth. [19] And take heed, lest you lift your eyes to Heaven, and when you see the sun, the moon, and the stars, all the host of Heaven, you feel driven to worship them and serve them, which the LORD your God has given to all the peoples under the whole Heaven as a heritage. [20] But the LORD has taken you and brought you out of the iron furnace, out of Egypt, to be His people, an inheritance, as you are this day. [21] Furthermore the LORD was angry with me for your sakes, and swore that I would not cross over the Jordan, and that I would not enter the good land which the LORD your God is giving you as an inheritance. [22] But I must die in this land, I must not cross over the Jordan; but you shall cross over and possess that good land. [23] Take heed to yourselves, lest you forget the covenant of the LORD your God which He made with you, and make for yourselves a carved image in the form of anything which the LORD your God has forbidden you. [24] For the LORD your God is a consuming fire, a jealous God.*

[25] "When you beget children and grandchildren and have grown old in the land, and act corruptly and make a carved image in the form of anything, and do evil in the sight of the LORD your God to provoke Him to anger, [26] I call Heaven and earth to witness against you this day, that you will soon utterly perish from the land which you cross over the Jordan to possess; you will not prolong your days in it, but will be utterly destroyed. [27] And the LORD will scatter you among the peoples, and you will be left few in number among the nations where the LORD will drive you. [28] And there you will serve gods, the work of men's hands, wood and stone, which neither see nor hear nor eat nor smell. [29] But from there you will seek the LORD your God, and you will find Him if you seek Him with all your heart and with all your soul. [30] When you are in distress, and all these things come upon you in the latter days, when you turn to the LORD your God and obey His voice [31] (for the LORD your God is a merciful God), He will not forsake you nor destroy you, nor forget the covenant of your fathers which He swore to them.

I have often wondered why people think it so strange that the Bible says God is jealous, like God being jealous is some type of sin. It's okay to be jealous if your spouse is cheating on you. If you are jealous without cause, that's a sin. However, if your spouse is committing adultery, that is righteous jealousy. God loves you; He is completely committed to you, and desires a committed relationship with you. Staying away from letting your mind wander to counting calories and how much you ate today will keep you from idol worship.

Food needs to become a non-issue. When you are tempted to overeat, focus, because when you make the decision to overeat, you zone out.

Read **Matthew 19:16-22**

Think and pray about what adjustments you need to make in your life to put God first.

In light of today's study, what was the Scripture or statement in today's lesson that most spoke to your heart? _____

_____

_____

_____

What steps of faith does God want you to take towards Him today? _____

_____

_____

_____

Rephrase the Scripture or statement into an expression of faith_____

_____

_____

_____

Memory Verse:

II Kings 6:17 *And Elisha _____, and _____, "_____, I _____, open _____eyes _____ he may see." _____ the _____ _____ the eyes of the _____ man, and he _____. And _____, the _____was full of _____ and _____ of fire all _____ Elisha.*

Week 6 Day 5
No More Excuses

Day _____ Date _____

After I have overeaten, I console myself with a million reasons why I did it. I did it because I didn't have a great childhood, and I am stuffing my true feelings with food. I feel lonely and depressed, and food makes me feel better. I am tired of the fight, because I am too weak. I feel sick when I don't eat. I am bored. Because I am one of nine siblings, I was trained to eat it while it was there, because someone will get to the good stuff before I do. My mom made me eat everything on my plate, so my stomach is desensitized to the feeling of fullness. I need cheering up, I never feel satisfied with just a half of candy bar, and so on and so on…

Write down some of the reasons you think you overeat _____
_____
_____
_____
_____
_____
_____
_____
_____
_____

Satan loves to supply us with excuses. That's what he does. Satan has provided excuses since Adam and Eve. They were enjoying life in paradise. They had the very best life had to offer. Then, Satan came along and presented them with a "better deal." They could have life on their own terms. It turned out to be a sham; they bought the lie completely. When confronted by God, they had plenty of excuses.

Genesis 3:11-14 *And He* (God) *said, "Who told you that you were naked? Have you eaten from the tree of which I commanded you that you should not eat?"*

Adam's excuse

[12] Then the man said, "The woman whom You gave to be with me, she gave me of the tree, and I ate."

[13] And the LORD God said to the woman, "What is this you have done?"

Eves excuse

The woman said, "The serpent deceived me, and I ate."

And so it begins. All down through the ages, we have been trying to make excuses for our mistakes. Cain made excuses for killing his brother. Sarai (later named Sarah) made excuses for trying to hurry God's plan. When Moses asked his brother, Aaron, why he made a golden calf to worship, he made excuses.

Exodus 32:21-24 *And Moses said to Aaron, "What did this people do to you that you have brought so great a sin upon them?"*

22 So Aaron said, "Do not let the anger of my lord become hot. You know the people, that they are set on evil. 23 For they said to me, 'Make us gods that shall go before us; as for this Moses, the man who brought us out of the land of Egypt, we do not know what has become of him.' 24 And I said to them, 'Whoever has any gold, let them break it off.' So they gave it to me, and I cast it into the fire, and this calf came out."

Aaron threw the gold in the fire and, "poof" a golden calf popped out, amazing! Man loves to make excuses for why He does what he does. If you ask any criminal in prison why they did what they did to get there, they will give you a ton of excuses.

Ask yourself, do any of my excuses help me? _____
Now ask yourself, how do these excuses hurt me? _____

_____

You haven't wanted to let go of your past hurts, because they have provided you with great excuses for a long time. You think you want to give your hurt over to Jesus, but deep inside you don't want to. I know that because God says if we have enough faith, we can move a mountain. He won't make us do anything we don't want to do, but as soon as you ask, His power is available to you. We just choose not to use it. We would rather hold on to our hurt, because we feel it excuses our behavior and it's easier.

Everyone has knowledge of God; his divine attributes are clearly seen in humanity and nature, from the intricate design of a human cell to the awesome strength of the pounding ocean. Nature speaks of its creator. We are without excuse.

Romans 1: 20 *For since the creation of the world His invisible attributes are clearly seen, being understood by the things that are made, even His eternal power and Godhead, so that they are without excuse.*

I so appreciate my friend Denise's views on life. She was blessed with a keen intelligence and a dry wit I love. She was telling me how she has been diagnosed with depression. She said, "I try to tell God 'look I have an excuse note and everything,' but He just says get over it." Now don't get me wrong, I know all about clinical depression. It has run in my family for generations. It took years for God to heal me, and I learned so much through that process. However, the depression and self-hate were so much worse when I was not living life the way God intended.

Even though God has healed my depression, I still love to make excuses, but when I do, I feel so unproductive and lazy. When we are out of God's will and not asking for His help when we need it, and not believing He will provide it, it leads to depression.

Some of my common excuses are: I can't do it. It is too hard for me. I don't have enough willpower. God, you made me this way.

But the truth can be found in God's word:

I Corinthians 10:13 *No temptation has overtaken you except such as is common to man; but God is faithful, who will not allow you to be tempted beyond what you are able, but with the temptation will also make the way of escape, that you may be able to bear it.*

However, you must ask God to provide the escape.

Another truth about excuses is found in **Deuteronomy 30: 11-20 The** *Choice of Life or Death*

[11] *"For this commandment which I command you today is not too mysterious for you, nor is it far off.* [12] *It is not in Heaven, that you should say, "Who will ascend into Heaven for us and bring it to us, that we may hear it and do it?'* [13] *Nor is it beyond the sea, that you should say, "Who will go over the sea for us and bring it to us, that we may hear it and do it?'* [14] ***But the word is very near you, in your mouth and in your heart, that you may do it.***

[15] *"See, I have set before you today life and good, death and evil,* [16] *in that I command you today to love the LORD your God, to walk in His ways, and to keep His commandments, His statutes, and His judgments, that you may live and multiply; and the LORD your God will bless you in the land which you go to possess.* [17] *But if your heart turns away so that you do not hear, and are drawn away, and worship other gods and serve them,* [18] *I announce to you today that you shall surely perish; you shall not prolong your days in the land which you cross over the Jordan to go in and possess.* [19] *I call Heaven and earth as witnesses today against you, that I have set before you life and death, blessing and cursing; therefore choose life, that both you and your descendants may live;* [20] *that you may love the LORD your God, that you may obey His voice, and that you may cling to Him, for He is your life and the length of your days; and that you may dwell in the land which the LORD swore to your fathers, to Abraham, Isaac, and Jacob, to give them."*

You need to speak the Word and use it to resist the excuses Satan provides. God does not accept our excuses. The following passage illustrates it:

Luke 14:15-24 *Now when one of those who sat at the table with Him heard these things, he said to Him, "Blessed is he who shall eat bread in the kingdom of God!"*

[16] *Then He said to him, "A certain man gave a great supper and invited many,* [17] *and sent his servant at supper time to say to those who were invited, "Come, for all things are now ready.'* [18] *But they all with one accord began to make excuses. The first said to him, "I have bought a piece of ground, and I must go and see it. I ask you to have me excused.'* [19] *And another said, "I have bought five yoke of oxen, and I am going to test them. I ask you to have me excused.'* [20] *Still another said, "I have married a wife, and therefore I cannot come.'*

[21] *So that servant came and reported these things to his master. Then the master of the house,*

being angry, said to his servant, "Go out quickly into the streets and lanes of the city, and bring in here the poor and the maimed and the lame and the blind.'[22] *And the servant said, "Master, it is done as you commanded, and still there is room.'*[23] *Then the master said to the servant, "Go out into the highways and hedges, and compel them to come in, that my house may be filled.*[24] *For I say to you that none of those men who were invited shall taste my supper."*

God has given us every tool we need to succeed for what He has planned in our lives.

II Peter 1:3 *His divine power has given us everything we need for life and godliness through our knowledge of him who called us by his own glory and goodness.*

We have the choice to choose life, or death.

Ephesians 4: 17-24 *This I say, therefore, and testify in the Lord, that you should no longer walk as the rest of the Gentiles walk, in the futility of their mind,*[18] *having their understanding darkened, being alienated from the life of God, because of the ignorance that is in them, because of the blindness of their heart;*[19] *who, being past feeling, have given themselves over to lewdness, to work all uncleanness with greediness.*

[20] *But you have not so learned Christ,*[21] *if indeed you have heard Him and have been taught by Him, as the truth is in Jesus:*[22] *that you put off, concerning your former conduct, the old man which grows corrupt according to the deceitful lusts,*[23] *and be renewed in the spirit of your mind,*[24] *and that you put on the new man which was created according to God, in true righteousness and holiness.*

When you asked Jesus to be Lord of your life, you become a completely new creature. You are not the same as the people walking around without Jesus. You have the same DNA structure, but now you are a temple of the Holy God. The only reason you lived as you did when you were the other creature is because you believed Satan's lies. Look back at verse twenty-two, in the above passages. *That you put off, concerning your former conduct, the old man which grows corrupt according to the **deceitful** lusts,*

Be honest with yourself, because excuses are lies we tell ourselves. I have a very obese friend who always claimed she didn't eat very much. I always felt so sad for her, because she had such a slow metabolism. Then, one day at my daughter's birthday party, I watched her eat (I was eating, too) four cupcakes, handfuls of candy and nuts, chips and dip, and then when the hotdogs were served, she said, "I am so hungry. I haven't eaten one thing all day!" I said, "What! We have been sitting here eating nonstop for an hour!" She said, "Oh yeah, but I haven't eaten breakfast or lunch yet." I think many people don't count the snacks as a meal when you probably get 90% of your calories from them.

We are a new creation, but when we listen to Satan's lies and fall, God has you covered... literally covered with the blood of Jesus. God does not get mad at you. His mercies are new every morning.

Lamentations 3: 22-24 *Through the LORD's mercies we are not consumed, because His compassions fail not.*

[23] They are new every morning; Great is Your faithfulness. [24] "The LORD is my portion," says my soul, "Therefore I hope in Him!"

When you were the old creation, you were spiritually dead. You did not have the Spirit of God, but now your Spirit is alive.

Romans 6: 4-14 *Therefore we were buried with Him through baptism into death, that just as Christ was raised from the dead by the glory of the Father, even so we also should walk in newness of life.*

[5] For if we have been united together in the likeness of His death, certainly we also shall be in the likeness of His resurrection, [6] knowing this, that our old man was crucified with Him, that the body of sin might be done away with, that we should no longer be slaves of sin. [7] For he who has died has been freed from sin. [8] Now if we died with Christ, we believe that we shall also live with Him, [9] knowing that Christ, having been raised from the dead, dies no more. Death no longer has dominion over Him. [10] For the death that He died, He died to sin once for all; but the life that He lives, He lives to God. [11] Likewise you also, reckon yourselves to be dead indeed to sin, but alive to God in Christ Jesus our Lord.

[12] Therefore do not let sin reign in your mortal body, that you should obey it in its lusts. [13] And do not present your members as instruments of unrighteousness to sin, but present yourselves to God as being alive from the dead, and your members as instruments of righteousness to God. [14] For sin shall not have dominion over you, for you are not under law but under grace.

The definition of the word present is, 1: To give or bring into the presence of someone especially of superior rank or status. 2: To make a gift to   3: To give or bestow to aim, point, or direct (as a weapon) so as to face something or in a particular direction.

There are only two choices here. You give yourself to God and make a gift of your will to Him, and point your weapon at Satan or … you give yourself to Satan and make a gift of your will to him, and point your weapon at God. I hate it when I hear of someone professing to be a Born-again Christian, and they live their life in such a way that only God can repair the damage they have inflicted (I have probably been that person once or twice myself). When you present yourself to God or Satan, you are a weapon. People are watching you. Make sure you aim yourself in the right direction.

II Corinthians 5:17-21 *Therefore, if anyone is in Christ, he is a new creation; old things have passed away; behold, all things have become new. [18] Now all things are of God, who has reconciled us to Himself through Jesus Christ, and has given us the ministry of reconciliation, [19] that is, that God was in Christ reconciling the world to Himself, not imputing their trespasses to*

them, and has committed to us the word of reconciliation.
[20] Now then, we are ambassadors for Christ, as though God were pleading through us: we implore you on Christ's behalf, be reconciled to God. [21] For He made Him who knew no sin to be sin for us, that we might become the righteousness of God in Him.

Ephesians 4:22-24, says, *that you put off, concerning your former conduct, the old man which grows corrupt according to the deceitful lusts, [23] and be renewed in the spirit of your mind, [24] and that you put on the new man which was created according to God, in true righteousness and holiness.*

The text tells us that our old man grows corrupt. So if you are not saved, you get worse as you grow older, but if you're saved, you are renewing your mind and getting better. However, your mind can't be transformed if you are using excuses for your behavior instead of confessing your sin to God.

Satan can't make you do anything; you're not helpless. There is a natural law. The food can't fly into your mouth. There has to be a human will that controls the act, and unless someone is force-feeding you, it's your human action… your will. There are many promises in God's Word that we refuse to lay hold of, and a lot of the time the real reason we don't lay hold of the promise is because it provides us with so many great excuses.

You can use a tool God gave me. It is so simple, but helps so much. We read before that when you present yourself to God or Satan, there are only two choices. When you want to overeat, ask yourself a question. The question has to have a yes or no answer. Ask, "Do I want to be fat?" Tthere is no other answer than yes or no. No excuses. No, "I'll do it later." No, "I am too weak." No, "but it looks too good, and I may not get the chance again!" The answer has to be "Yes" or "No." You can change the question. The question can be, "Do I want to live to see my children walk down the aisle?" Or "Do I want to live to play with my grandchildren?" Yes, or No? You can use this same tool for other areas with which you struggle. Like, when you go shopping for things you don't need and can't afford, "Do I like being in debt?" Yes, or No? You are trading things that mean so very much for a chip or even lobster, or whatever. Even if you never eat lobster again, it is not that important!

Read what the Bible says about excuses.

Matthew 5:37 *But let your 'Yes' be 'Yes,' and your 'No,' 'No.' For whatever is more than these is from the evil one.*

Read **Psalm 42**

In light of today's study, what was the Scripture or statement in today's lesson that most spoke to your heart? _____

_____

_____

_____

What steps of faith does God want you to take towards Him today? _____

_____

_____

_____

Rephrase the Scripture or statement into an expression of faith_____

_____

_____

_____

Memory verse:

II Kings 6:17 _____

_____

_____

_____

Dear Reader, If you have been touched by FLOWERS OVER THE WALL, please refer this book to your pastor, church, family and friends. You may also log on to www.amazon.com and give your review. This will help Amazon recommend FLOWERS OVER THE WALL to other readers in the Amazon community. A five-star review would be greatly appreciated! You can also give FLOWERS OVER THE WALL as a gift, or please consider sharing your thoughts about this book on a website or blog.

Please visit our website at http://www.flowersoverthewall.com/
Email me at: killigrim@flowersoverthewall.com/
Twitter me at: http://twitter.com/#!/DietBibleStudy

Thank you and God bless you!

Other Books by Kelli Grim

Flowers Over the Wall Two, Busting through the Wall.

Custom Cake Decorating on the Cheap

Made in the USA
Lexington, KY
19 August 2011